Praise for *90 Second*

'Joan's approach is simple, practical and effective. It represents a significant breakthrough on the path to success. If you want unwavering confidence to pursue your goals and dreams, then this will guide you to it.'

— Jack Canfield, co-author of the *Chicken Soup for the Soul* series and *The Success Principles*

'Every once in a while, you meet someone capable of turning conventional wisdom on its head. Dr Joan Rosenberg is both a brilliant clinician and compassionate presence. Her book inspires and invites people to be authentic, to become their best and most fully expressed selves. It's a game changer for anyone ready to take their life, relationship and career to the next level.'

— Ron Howard, film director, producer and actor

'Joan Rosenberg is an excellent teacher with a deep understanding of the interdisciplinary field of interpersonal neurobiology. She combines a wonderful sense of humour with clear, concise explanations for the process of psychotherapy and human development.'

— Dr Daniel Siegel, executive director, Mindsight Institute, author of *Mindsight, Brainstorm* and *The Developing Mind*

'*90 Seconds to a Life You Love* is a must-read. Imagine what would happen in your life if you had unwavering self-esteem and greater emotional strength. This book is the roadmap, and Dr Joan is the perfect guide.'

— Brendon Burchard, author of *The Motivation Manifesto, The Charge,* and *The Millionaire Messenger*

90 Seconds to a Life You Love

90 Seconds to a Life You Love

How to Turn Difficult Feelings into Rock-Solid Confidence

JOAN I. ROSENBERG, PhD

yellow
kite

First published in Great Britain in 2019 by Yellow Kite
An imprint of Hodder & Stoughton
An Hachette UK company

1

First published in the United States of America in 2019 by Little, Brown Spark,
an imprint of Little, Brown and Company,
a division of Hachette Book Group, Inc.

A CIP catalogue record for this title is available from the British Library

Trade Paperback ISBN 978 1 473 68700 4
eBook ISBN 978 1 473 68702 8

Typeset in New Baskerville

Printed and bound in Great Britain by CPI Group (UK) Ltd, Croydon CR0 4YY

Hodder & Stoughton policy is to use papers that are natural, renewable and recyclable products and made from wood grown in sustainable forests. The logging and manufacturing processes are expected to conform to the environmental regulations of the country of origin.

Yellow Kite
Hodder & Stoughton Ltd
Carmelite House
50 Victoria Embankment
London EC4Y 0DZ

www.yellowkitebooks.co.uk

www.hodder.co.uk

Contents

90
Seconds
to a Life
You Love

Foreword

I've been in the personal development industry for 47 years, hosting or teaching alongside my friends—luminaries such as Wayne Dyer, Les Brown, Bob Proctor, Marianne Williamson, Deepak Chopra, Gay Hendricks, and more. I am a mentor to many recognizable thought leaders in the personal development field. I have also served at the request of the Dalai Lama for a peace initiative on three separate occasions, collaborated with Dr. Martin Luther King Jr.'s children on Season for Nonviolence initiatives, and spoken at the United Nations three times.

Joan and I share degrees in Counseling Psychology, me with my master's, Joan with her doctorate, and while we share more than a 40-year history in personal development, Joan delved deeply into it from a psychology standpoint while my focus was dialed-in to understanding the spiritual side of success.

I distinctly remember my hour-long conversation on the lawn of The Old Manse, the home of Ralph Waldo Emerson, where I first had the opportunity for an extended conversation with Joan, in September 2013. Joan caught my attention for a variety of reasons; though soft-spoken and a bit reserved on first meeting, her warmth, quick wit, and insightful comments quickly stood out. At that time, I was leading a personal development training as part of the Concord Experience, a program intended to deepen one's understanding of Transcendentalism, the American contribution to the world's body of theological knowledge.

During our conversation, Joan pulled out a one-page diagram representing 25 years of her life's work and shared her perspective on personal growth and well-being—which included what it takes to develop unwavering self-confidence. In all my years of study, I had never seen such a brilliant yet simple approach to REAL transformation.

This book, *90 Seconds to a Life You Love,* is the embodiment of that one-page document. I understood right away that she had outlined a very important process for others to follow.

I find the simplicity of the concept so inviting and so practical—the idea that you can move from one side of an unpleasant emotion to the other side in roughly 90 seconds, if you just allow yourself to really experience it. And, it definitely works.

The technique Dr. Rosenberg lays out (which she calls "The Rosenberg Reset") really does build on the foundation of this small window of time, 90 seconds, and your ability to tolerate eight different unpleasant feelings.

What's so fascinating is how Joan takes this simple concept and applies it to countless common emotional challenges that most of us face. Not only does handling these eight feelings help lead to emotional strength, confidence, and resilience, it can help diminish anxiety and end harsh self-criticism, making it easier for you to speak up and end your fear of failure. In my experience, all of us can benefit from some help in these areas. And that's only the start!

To that end, given Joan's unique perspective on many areas of personal growth, I've invited her to speak to my audiences and train them on multiple occasions—and her 90-seconds approach is something I often refer to in my own trainings.

You'll have a chance to read more about the science behind the 90-seconds approach, unpleasant feelings, and learn from Joan's insights, gleaned from her decades of work in this field. She really outlines how such a simple method can help you move through difficult emotions into a healthier way of thinking and acting. Joan's strategies intersect well with my work in helping people change their results so they can live a life they love. And Joan's work integrates equally well with many familiar psychotherapy approaches.

And now I'm prompted to ask: Why has no one encouraged this before? Why is such a logical, digestible, and absolutely *doable* technique not the centerpiece of every confidence-building course, counselor training, and psychotherapy practice in America?

The methods outlined in this book not only make sense academically, but in example after example that Dr. Rosenberg points to in order to illustrate and illuminate her methods, we see stories of how this system works in real life. What you are about to encounter in the following pages is not just theoretical mumbo jumbo or "feel-good thinking" rooted in little more than optimism; *90 Seconds to a Life You Love* is a guided tour through unpleasant feelings and damaging thought patterns into real, meaningful, and lasting confidence, resilience, and change for the better.

What you hold in your hand is perhaps one of the MOST important books you will ever own. Read it once with curiosity and then the second time as a manual for learning how you too can have a life you truly love, one 90 seconds at a time. Then, share this book with all those you truly care about.

I believe you will join me in forever being grateful for Dr. Joan Rosenberg's unique contribution to bettering all of our lives.

Mary Morrissey
Founder, Life Mastery Institute

Introduction

If you think back on your childhood or adolescence, you can likely recall a handful of boys and girls who were the last to be picked for activities by their peers. They were often a little withdrawn, and instead of participating, they spent their time away from the rest of their classmates. Maybe you were one of them. These so-called "wallflowers" seemed to be waiting for someone to notice them, start a conversation, or invite them to join in.

That was me. As a young child, I was self-conscious and exquisitely shy. I started kindergarten at four, and that early beginning left me the youngest and smallest in my class, which became a real liability over time. Feeling embarrassed and vulnerable was a constant. Inside, I felt raw and exposed. I distinctly remember my elementary school teachers having to ask my peers to be friends with me. On top of my feelings of vulnerability and my difficulties fitting in (and likely because of them), I became the target of unceasing teasing and bullying throughout my childhood and adolescence.

Why couldn't I join in and have a good time like the other kids? I desperately wanted what I thought they had: happiness, confidence, and a sense of belonging. It wasn't until much later that I realized I was under the innocent but false impression that I simply needed to be around them to have all those things, too. But confidence isn't contagious. I couldn't magically develop an inner contentedness or find enjoyment in life just by being in their presence.

There was no dramatic or obvious reason I couldn't have what the other children had. I came from a stable and loving family; although we certainly had our ups and downs like any family, there were no addictions, mental disorders, or abuse. I never resorted to using drugs or alcohol, controlling my food consumption, binge eating, cutting myself, or injuring myself in any way. As I got older, I didn't lose myself in shopping, gambling, or any other kind of compulsive behavior.

Just because I wasn't using those ways of coping, however, didn't mean that I wasn't hurting. I recognize now that the emotional pain I believed no one understood, noticed, or heard was there, in part, because I wasn't fully experiencing it inside myself or expressing it to others.

At 19 years old, I started to recognize how I could change, a realization that was largely influenced by two life events. One involved a comment made in passing: I was told I was boring. The unkind comment, made offhandedly by a peer counselor at the end of a summer camp hayride, left me reeling. It felt like someone had stuck a fork in my gut and spun it around. Just like that, my world shifted. Her cavalier and off-the-cuff critique prompted me to reflect deeply on how I saw myself, how I imagined others saw me, and what it meant for my future. As painful as her remark was, some aspect of it hit me as true. In fact, I wasn't sure which caused more pain in those moments: her words or my recognition of the truth.

I wanted to understand what was at the root of her comment and change accordingly so that others saw me as an interesting and desirable person. I wasn't thinking that I needed to change so I could fit in with this particular group, or any other for that matter. Instead, I wanted to understand what makes people likeable and attractive, in an emotional sense, to others. I felt driven to uncover why her comment was so painful, especially since it made me see myself in a new light.

The second event, at age 21, involved the death of a close friend. After his passing, I was aware of *knowing* I was sad, and I knew it was appropriate to feel sad. Yet in those moments I couldn't actually *feel* my own sadness. My awareness of this gap acted as another catalyst in my life, demanding I take notice and find answers.

Every one of us has our own version of that gut-punch that challenges, or even demands, we change direction and wake up to who we are supposed to be. For me, those punches, and others, were the painful moments behind my desire to become a psychologist and to understand what truly helps us develop confidence, emotional strength, and self-esteem. I now know that anyone can create a life they love because even though my early life was the very picture of doubt and disempowerment, my adult life has been the opposite.

Maybe you feel like you don't belong or fit in. Perhaps you feel different, closed off from relationships, or anxious about the goals and dreams you think you'll never reach. You look at others who seem to radiate confidence and wonder why you can't have that, too.

You don't have to be stuck. There is a way to build and maintain lasting confidence, and it starts with the intention to change. With consistent focus, you can experience rapid progress as you transform your life into one you love.

The Rosenberg Reset™

As counterintuitive as it may sound, the key to cultivating confidence and creating a life you love lies in the ability to handle unpleasant emotions. Confidence develops when you have the deep sense that you can handle the emotional outcome of whatever you pursue. If you can experience and move through eight unpleasant feelings, you can pursue anything you want in life.

> *Confidence develops when you have the deep sense that you can handle the emotional outcome of whatever you pursue.*

How do you move through these feelings? By following one simple formula: *one choice, eight feelings, 90 seconds.*

The Rosenberg Reset[1], as one of my colleagues affectionately termed my method, is composed of just three steps, each occurring almost simultaneously:

First, you make one choice to be present—to be aware of and in touch with as much of your moment-to-moment experience as possible. When you make this choice, you open yourself up to encountering your whole range of feelings, from pleasant to unpleasant.

Second, since unpleasant feelings are generally harder to face, you acknowledge your willingness to deal with or tolerate the following eight common unpleasant feelings:

- sadness
- shame
- helplessness
- anger
- embarrassment
- disappointment
- frustration
- vulnerability

Third, you bear and move through, or, for some, endure, those unpleasant feelings by riding one or more 90-second waves of bodily sensations; physical sensations, such as warm cheeks, a pounding heart, or a pit in the stomach, are how the body communicates our feelings to us. Riding out the physical sensations and the emotions they represent is an essential part of the Rosenberg Reset.

Disconnect or distract from these experiences and you'll go through life feeling unfulfilled, knowing deep down that something is missing. Connect to your moment-to-moment experience by riding the waves of one or more of eight uncomfortable feelings, for up to 90 seconds each, and you connect to the vitality of life. Master this reset process, and you are headed into a life that feels fully lived and expressed—a life of your own design.

The Reset resolves a broad array of common complaints. You can put an end to worry, anxiety, fear of failure, and feeling judged by others. The negative self-talk that belittles you with harsh self-criticism can be silenced almost immediately. Letting go of that old emotional baggage will seem simpler and will free you to take risks, trust others, and let yourself be open and vulnerable. You will begin to welcome change. And as long as you continue to use the Reset, unwavering confidence and emotional strength will become your new normal.

The Book

As you read, I want you to be aware that the difficult feelings I've chosen to include were distilled from the common, practical, everyday use of the words we employ as we go about our daily lives. My list is drawn from more than four decades of clinical work—day in and day out with clients and graduate supervisees. Over this time I found certain words were too vague (e.g., "pain," "hurt," "stressed," "under pressure"); for instance, therapy conversations about being "hurt" failed to provide genuine relief. Yet, when someone would use a more specific word to describe what they were feeling (e.g., disappointed), there was often an "aha" moment—a click of knowing as if something had just lined up inside them. Clarity and a sense of calm would invariably follow.

I do use feelings and emotions interchangeably. No doubt, we could engage in long conversations about the complexities and science behind these two words. And you may have other ideas about what you would include as difficult or unpleasant feelings. Mostly, I just want you to understand that the 90 Seconds approach and the specific feelings I discuss are included because they best represent our everyday experiences and use of those words.

With the exception of trauma, the 90-second range I discuss here holds true across *most* circumstances; in fact, it's often less than 90 seconds. You may be thinking, "No, way—feelings last so much longer than that." I explain later in the book why feelings seem to linger on and on. You can also let the idea of this 90-second range serve as a metaphor for the brief time it takes to move toward your difficult feelings. As others have told me they've said to themselves: "I can handle 90 seconds." You can handle 90 seconds, too, right? Then you have just what it takes to lead a confident, resilient, and authentic life.

90 Seconds to a Life You Love is a strategic and practical "how-to" guide for building the emotional strength, confidence, and resilience that will help you deal with your most difficult emotions. As much as this is an emotional practice, it's also a philosophy for living. To show how that can happen, you'll read stories of people who reinvented their lives by giving themselves permission to be who they really are.

The Reset promotes rapid insight and accelerates sustained personal transformation. It enables you to confront what is holding you back by embracing your emotions, and, in doing so, lets you set yourself free to create and live the life you want. It's a tested and proven process, drawn from more than four decades of clinical practice and my personal experiences supervising and teaching psychologists-in-training at the University of Southern California; the University of California, Los Angeles; and now at the Pepperdine University Graduate School of Education and Psychology. *90 Seconds to a Life You Love* offers a provocative approach to change, transformation, and personal growth.

Now it's up to you. Your ability to develop core emotional strength, achieve confidence, and build a fully authentic life is literally in your hands.

It only takes 90 seconds to change your life. *What are you waiting for?*

PART I

Skills Building

CHAPTER 1

Living a Life by Design

More. Did you ever want to be more or have more in your life? Even if you've accomplished all you've dreamed of or desired, perhaps you've noticed that there's a part of you that keeps nudging you toward whatever is next. As I've made my way through life, I, too, have always desired more. I didn't want to have more *things* in a physical sense; instead, my aim was to become a better person: more knowledgeable, more thoughtful, more generous, and more loving. Despite my professional successes, I never fully understood why I continued to desire more until I met Mary Morrissey, a premier personal development expert, cherished mentor, and dear friend. Mary was the first to introduce me to the idea that, as human beings, we are always seeking a freer, fuller, more expanded version of ourselves and that life is always seeking its fuller expression through us.[1]

Take some time here and really think about how this might manifest itself in your life. Consider the following questions: How do *you* want to live *your* life? If you were living a life you truly loved, what would it look like?[2] How would it be different than it is now? What would your health look like? What would your relationships be like—romantic, familial, and otherwise? With whom would you be hanging out? Would you travel or pursue hobbies you love? What would you be doing with your time?[3] Since I know it's tempting to breeze by these questions, I'd like to encourage you to grab a journal or notebook so that you can jot down some initial ideas.

Journal 1: How Do You Want to Live Your Life?

Take time to write out answers to the questions above.

When I ask clients these questions, I get responses that range from impassioned, detailed descriptions about a great imagined future to quizzical looks that convey countless doubts about the ability to achieve any of their dreams. Yet most people share a few important responses:

1. They desire to be fully engaged in something that feels meaningful and purposeful.
2. They want to experience their impact on the people and situations in their lives.
3. They consistently want to feel more confident and empowered, and less affected by life's daily challenges.

No matter how many times people have been advised to be more confident or have higher self-esteem, rarely are they told how to achieve these goals. Rest assured, it can be done. In fact, you can definitely learn how to be confident and resilient.

The challenge is that most people believe that life is doing something *to* them, so they live by constantly reacting to life's dilemmas. If you perceive life as a set of difficult problems, criticizing and complaining can become coping strategies you use to deal with what you perceive as the harshness of such a life.

People often don't realize that they have a hand in *creating* the life they want. Once you start setting clear intentions and taking inspired action to meet specific goals, then you begin to develop a sense that you have a say in how life unfolds for you. In fact, many people find their purpose in life by actively pursuing their goals or dreams. When you experience purpose and meaning in what you are doing, it often feels like you are the conduit through which life is fulfilling itself instead of a mere victim of life's hardships. Personal development trainers often describe these two very different approaches — reactionary versus creative — as, respectively, living "life by default" and "life by design."

This book was written to help you live life by *your* design. You have a hand in creating a life you love — one that enables you to be confident, emotionally strong, enthusiastic, purpose-driven, and resilient. The process involves embracing all of life: all of the good, fun, enjoyable, happy experiences, *and* all of the crummy, messy, unexpected, and unpleasant ones, too.

The Gift of Unpleasant Feelings

Most of us want to avoid unpleasant thoughts and feelings either because they are so darn uncomfortable or because they elicit some measure of pain. This avoidance, what some psychologists call *"experiential avoidance,"*[4] occurs through distracting yourself. By moving away from difficult feelings, you actually cut yourself off from emotional information that could help protect or enhance your life. Consistently distracting from or avoiding what is unpleasant and uncomfortable is, unfortunately, often the start of a slow trek to increased anxiety, bodily pain, vulnerability, and disempowerment. If you continue to distract or stay disconnected from the truth of your own life experiences over long periods of time, you may experience feelings of emptiness, numbness, and *soulful depression*™ — a result of being disconnected from yourself. Eventually, this can transform into something worse: intense feelings of isolation, alienation, or hopelessness.

But it doesn't need to move in that direction at all. Just as there's a path to soulful depression[5], there's a path to confidence, emotional strength, and resilience—three qualities that have a direct impact on your ability to lead a meaningful life.

How, then, *do* you develop into an emotionally stronger and more capable person? As paradoxical as it seems, the answer is tied to your capacity to tolerate pain—or your capacity to handle unpleasant feelings. The more you are able to face the pain you experience, the more capable you become. The essential keys to developing confidence, feeling emotionally strong, and being resilient involve an openness to change, a positive attitude toward pain, a willingness to learn from any experience, and a capacity to experience and express unpleasant feelings.

> *The more you are able to face the pain you experience, the more capable you become.*

When you're able to effectively handle unpleasant emotions, you're likely to feel more centered, confident, capable, and calm in the moment. Your consistent ability to deal with difficult feelings translates into relief from anxiety, harsh self-criticism, and negative self-talk. As you continue the practice of experiencing these unpleasant feelings, you increase your capacity to engage in courageous conversations, which often results in mending and deepening relationships. If you stay well connected to your moment-to-moment experience, not only will you move your life more fully into who you want to be and do more of what you love, you'll start to develop a greater sense of purpose and meaning in your life.

Why wouldn't you want to embrace your unpleasant feelings if it results in living the life you've always wanted?

Building the Framework

Early in my career, I worked as a psychologist in the student counseling center at the University of California, Los Angeles. I was initially hired because of my skills and experience counseling women who struggled with a variety of eating problems like anorexia, bulimia, and compulsive overeating. Without exception, their attention was always on food, weight, or appearance.

Liz was a prime example. At 20 years old, she carried an extra 30 pounds on her five-foot, four-inch frame. Liz told me that emotional eating, or what some call compulsive overeating, defined her.

"Whenever I'm upset, lonely, or bored, I eat. Sometimes it's because of a low grade on a paper or exam, sometimes it's because I'm procrastinating, and sometimes it happens when I'm upset with one of my friends and don't feel like I can say anything to her. Other times I don't even know what it's about."

When I talked with Liz about her eating habits, she said that she ate until she felt sick and then tried to stuff down even more food. She hated carrying the extra weight and finally acknowledged that consuming all that food wasn't solving anything. It never took away what was really bothering her. Instead, she would feel even more upset about her eating and the extra pounds, and she would still have to face the other problems that remained long after she binged. This understanding fully clicked into place the day after she'd eaten a large pizza because she was angry and wanted to "get back at" her mom; it dawned on her that her mother wouldn't feel any of the effects of eating the pizza—only Liz would. And she was still angry. Nothing went away, and nothing changed.

From my work with Liz and countless others, it quickly became apparent that the problem for which they came to therapy was a clear signal of something deeper and harder for them to experience. There were consistent patterns to the students' thoughts, feelings, and behaviors. For students with eating-related struggles, their overfocus on food, weight, and appearance kept their attention on the wrong issue. Rather than an eating disorder, they had what I describe as an *emotional management disorder.*

Invariably, there were two layers of problems. Despite the fact that eating-related behaviors were significant—and sometimes even life threatening—they served as the cover and distracter for the true sources of these behaviors. By the end of the first session with each of these students, it was apparent that the real problem they faced was an inability to comfortably manage their everyday emotional reactions and experiences. They had difficulty tolerating their thoughts, feelings, needs, and perceptions. Their particular focus on food, weight, and appearance kept them totally distracted from painful thoughts, feelings, or needs that were harder to bear. They had been focusing their efforts on "controlling" the wrong thing.

Journal 2: Where Is Your Focus?

Perhaps you put your attention on issues or concerns that shift the focus away from what is really bothering you. Instead, you find ways to distract yourself from your real concerns.

What do you do to cover up what is really going on for you? Where do you put your attention that has less meaning for you? Think about activities, conversations, people, events, or situations you intentionally avoid. Consider distractions like emotional eating, excessive exercise, or "shopping therapy" as signals that other issues may be present. What concerns really need to be addressed?

Grab your notebook or journal again and take a moment to write down your answers to these questions.

Emotional Strength and Weakness

Over my four decades of counseling, I came to recognize a pattern among many of my clients that involved common-yet-destructive misconceptions about emotional strength and emotional weakness. I found that individuals with the lowest levels of self-confidence generally held tightly to the beliefs or behaviors described below.

Track yourself here, too. If you notice similarities, highlight the belief or put a check by it.

Low-confidence individuals:

◆ disdain uncomfortable and unpleasant feelings
◆ doubt or question most things they say or do
◆ are hesitant to take risks
◆ often feel anxious
◆ tend to worry about being a burden to others
◆ worry about what others think of them
◆ believe they have to do everything independently
◆ hate asking for help
◆ make other people's needs and feelings more important than their own
◆ are not emotionally expressive to keep from feeling vulnerable
◆ don't want to show any signs of vulnerability because they might be perceived as weak
◆ diminish their hard work and accomplishments
◆ hide their successes or devalue appropriate recognition of success and achievements
◆ refuse compliments

I came to realize these beliefs and behaviors all lead to problems with emotional management. They can be found underneath many concerns, including anxiety, depression, eating disorders, and drug and alcohol misuse or abuse.

What also captured my attention were the long-held yet damaging views of what it means to be emotionally strong or weak. What have you been taught about emotional strength and weakness? Do any of the following statements sound familiar to you?

- Tearfulness and crying make you look weak.
- Tough it out.
- Buck up.
- Get over it.
- Will it away.
- Snap out of it.
- Do it yourself.
- Don't be such a baby.
- Don't show your soft side.
- You're not feeling that way.
- That's not like you.
- You create your own success.
- Don't even think of asking for help.
- Tender emotions are a sign of weakness.
- Pull yourself up by your own bootstraps.
- You want help? You have a hand at the end of each arm.

While potentially helpful in the short-term, these clichés sustain views of emotional strength that are generally hurtful in the long-term to the individuals who abide by them. I have an entirely different view of what it takes to be emotionally strong. Let's start with my redefinition of the essential elements of emotional strength.

Emotional Strength Redefined

Emotional strength means feeling capable and being resourceful. Feeling capable of facing life's challenges emerges out of your experience of effectively handling the eight unpleasant feelings. It's entirely internal—you deal with your own emotional experience on your own emotional terms. Your sense of being resourceful has an external element to it that involves relying on others and includes acknowledging needs and limitations, asking for help, and graciously receiving the support offered. Thus, believing you are capable and resourceful means you possess the emotional resources to go after the dreams and goals you have set for yourself and the courage to ask for help when needed.

Although it may seem obvious, many people maintain a faulty perception of emotional strength; they believe being emotionally strong means controlling, shutting down, or shutting out thoughts, feelings, needs, and perceptions—in other words, *dismissing what you know.* When you distract yourself by shutting out what you experience, you can no longer use the emotional reactions that evolved to protect you or help you connect with others.

Shutting down in this way actually leaves you feeling weaker and more exposed. This "emotional weakness"—or, rather, *vulnerability*—is experienced even more intensely when you avoid, suppress, or disconnect or distract from your everyday, in-the-moment reactions to life. Such disconnection is *"trying not to know what you know"* and is directly related to avoiding the difficult feelings instead of making the one choice to stay present to your moment-to-moment experiences.

By contrast, when someone stays aware of and attuned to their experience (*"know what you know"*), they consistently feel more empowered and more willing to take risks in all areas of their life. Likewise, when they stay well connected to their friends and family, let others really know them, and are willing to lean on those who offer their help and support, individuals become more centered and calmer; that sense of inner peace is another outgrowth of emotional strength. Both feeling capable and being resourceful are necessary in order to develop true emotional strength, confidence, and a sense of well-being.

Feeling Capable—Relying on Yourself

As I started to weave together my observations from all the clients and stories I encountered over the years, a distinct pattern emerged and I came to what may seem like an obvious understanding: people have an unbelievably difficult time dealing with unpleasant feelings. And the more I addressed the issue (over several tens of thousands of hours), the more elements of the pattern came into focus. First, I recognized that the same unpleasant feelings kept resurfacing (sadness, shame, helplessness, anger, embarrassment, disappointment, frustration, and vulnerability). Second, by keeping these feelings out of their awareness or avoiding the feelings altogether, my clients complained of not feeling fully themselves, not feeling comfortable in their own skin, not feeling centered, not feeling emotionally strong, and not feeling whole. Third, several common psychological challenges could be traced back to their difficulty experiencing these feelings, including anxiety, lack of authenticity, distractions, difficulty speaking up, soulful depression, fear of failure or reluctance to take risks, low confidence, and harsh self-criticism. Fourth, most people I counseled hated asking for help and were concerned about being a burden if they actually asked. And, fifth, when clients would shift their focus and welcome or embrace unpleasant feelings by using the Rosenberg Reset, *all of those challenges* would reverse course.

As soon as you increase your awareness and acceptance of the full range of your feelings—pleasant and unpleasant—

your experience of yourself starts to change. Once you are able to tolerate unpleasant feelings, everything else changes, too. There is an almost immediate experience of growth, movement, and momentum. People feel stronger and more empowered; they become willing to speak up and have difficult conversations, take risks that once felt too difficult or frightening, and actively pursue dreams that previously felt out of reach.

I am certain that a person will not achieve that deep inner knowing—that unwavering belief in their capacity to deal with problems or go after what they want in life—until they can experience and move through these eight difficult feelings. *This* is the centerpiece upon which the whole 90 Seconds approach is built, and it is what initially gives the first boosts in confidence and enables an individual to feel capable in the world. Everything else emerges from it.

Why is this so important? Because when you worry about or refuse to take risks, no matter what they are, you are actually less afraid of the risk itself than of the unpleasant feelings that might result if things don't turn out the way you want. *Your sense of feeling capable in the world, then, is directly tied to your ability to experience and move through the eight difficult feelings.*

As you heighten your self-awareness, you will likely find you develop a greater capacity to tolerate, face, know, bear, feel, embrace, and express as much of your moment-to-moment experience as possible. Typically, the greater your self-awareness and willingness to stay present to your experience, the more capable you become in negotiating all aspects of life.

> *When you worry about or refuse to take risks, no matter what they are, you are actually less afraid of the risk itself than of the unpleasant feelings that might result if things don't turn out the way you want.*

Being Resourceful—Relying on Others and Asking for Help

Being resourceful is the second defining element of emotional strength. It involves being comfortable with your need for both independence and dependence, as well as your feelings associated with both. Particularly important in being resourceful is having the ability to depend on others. When you are open to and willing to rely on others, it becomes much easier for you to:

a) acknowledge your needs and limitations,
b) ask for help, and
c) openly and warmly receive what is given (support, love, time, energy, etc.).

We are inherently social beings. Yet most people who have grown up in individualistic cultures like the United States are often raised with the belief that relying on others and asking for help is a burden. Despite this view, there is ultimately very little that any of us do on our own, even if that is hard to acknowledge. You need both—independence *and* dependence—not one or the other. Our need to be alone and to pursue our individual goals must balance with our need to be with others, and when necessary, to request help.

Being resourceful involves embracing the dependent side of your nature; it takes feeling vulnerable, courageous, and comfortable enough within yourself to recognize when you need help. When you are able to do that, you are more apt to openly and genuinely acknowledge your specific needs and limitations. This acknowledgment enables you to take the next, most essential move—that of asking for help. This means that *asking for help is an integral aspect of emotional strength.*

Asking opens the door to the last step: receiving graciously. It is appropriate to absorb what is good and to feel grateful for the appreciation and support of others. When others extend their assistance, wisdom, availability, time, talents, or enthusiasm to you, unquestionably, they are giving of themselves. Gracious receipt of their generosity not only meets whatever needs you may have, it also honors them. When you allow yourself to receive, and thus honor, you have reached that harmonious balance between independence and dependence.

Depending on others, experiencing needs and limitations, and asking for help are all part of being emotionally strong and of the human experience at large. Asking for help is not a sign of weakness; it's a sign of humanness.

> *Asking for help is not a sign of weakness; it's a sign of humanness.*

It may seem counterintuitive to think that allowing yourself to feel unpleasant feelings will make you emotionally stronger. You may prefer to believe that if you don't feel or think about emotional distress and actively push it away or shut down that you will be—or appear to be—emotionally strong. But that's not how it works. Handling your feelings in this manner just makes situations worse. The more you tamp down those unpleasant feelings, the worse you will feel. Often the way out of pain is through the pain. That's what happened with Christa, one of my patients.

In her therapy sessions, Christa spent considerable time talking about her relationships with her friends, especially after a major conflict with Ellie, with whom she was especially close. The incident led Christa to entirely rethink her relationship with Ellie and the others in their social group.

"Even though I'm in college on financial aid," Christa told me, "I often pay for meals, social events, and trips for my friends. I'm always the 'go-to' person if someone needs a ride, so I end up ditching my classes or exams to help out. I always make my place available if someone needs a place to crash for a night, but it always ends up being longer. On several occasions, some friends have stayed for up to several weeks at a time."

When I asked her how all this made her feel, she slowly and reluctantly began to get in touch with feelings of disappointment, sadness, and anger about the way her friends were treating her. Given the sheer number of times this happened, and the extreme manner in which it occurred, I asked Christa whether she had ever recognized how her friends had been treating her while it was taking place. She was aware they had taken advantage of her goodwill though she thought some of these behaviors were part of friendship; mostly she found it difficult to deal straightforwardly with the instances as they occurred.

She replied, "I was aware of some of the stuff that was happening, but if I had feelings about it, I would try to reason or think them away."

My focus was to help Christa think *about* her experiences instead of thinking them *away*. Over time, as Christa's sadness and anger surfaced, she could experience the full intensity of these feelings and use both to help her set limits and boundaries with her friends. Others who had exhibited such blatant disregard for her feelings could no longer take advantage of her goodwill.

Had Christa been consciously aware of the truth of her own feelings of anger, disappointment, and sadness, and allowed herself to experience them as the situations occurred, it is very likely she would have stopped allowing these people to take advantage of her much earlier. Had she talked with them about what she'd noticed, voiced her concerns, set limits with them, or stopped seeing them altogether, she could have protected herself from being used. These growth-promoting acts of protection are also acts of loving oneself.

As Christa discovered, if you want to possess the emotional presence and capacity to build a closer relationship with yourself and deeper connections with others, you can. Before Christa set those boundaries, she was living a life by default. Reasoning or thinking away what she knew to be true for her had led to others taking advantage of her and left her believing life was just happening to her. But, over time, through introspection and collaboration, Christa and I were able to help her discard the habits that were holding her back and move her into a life of her own creation.

So how, exactly, did Christa create a life she loved? By making the choice to be in touch with her moment-to-moment experiences, being open to fully experiencing her unpleasant feelings, and learning to take them as they came. Practicing these skills helped Christa become confident in her capabilities, open to embracing change, and certain that she could handle whatever came at her. And as she cultivated these three attitudes, she developed the capacity to create the life she had always desired.

Given her newfound strength and self-assurance, Christa realized she could pursue whatever she wanted and handle it if it didn't work out. She stopped communicating with her old social group and developed new friends who were more responsive to and supportive of her. She completed her bachelor's degree, aced a professional exam in her discipline, and landed a position at a respectable business firm. As her confidence grew, she decided she wanted to be a bit of an entrepreneur and used her artistic skills to open a part-time business, which is now being recognized by others in her field. She is excited about what she has accomplished and remains open to how her life continues to unfold.

Are you ready to get started?

CHAPTER 2

The Rosenberg Reset

Naomi, a 27-year-old woman, came to see me at my practice several years ago. She expressed an array of concerns over the course of our initial conversation. She had grown up and was still living with parents who drank and fought a lot. She had recently experienced a sexual assault and was increasingly anxious, sad, fearful, and couldn't stop crying. As we talked, I learned that she was drinking and smoking pot; she would binge large quantities of food and then purge; and she would pull her hair out a little bit at a time. And when the pain got to be unbearable, she would bang her head against the wall or go into uncontrollable rages, yelling at her parents, sister, or friends. She would put herself down, call herself names, and berate herself for what had happened and for the direction her life was going. Needless to say, she was extremely overwhelmed and didn't know where to turn or how to ease her pain.

At the end of our initial meeting, I remember telling Naomi that despite the number of different problems she described and the challenging nature of them, I thought she really had only *one* problem. She looked at me stunned and speechless, yet curious. With the exception of the sexual assault, I told her that I thought the other problems she described were coping strategies. The real problem was that she was using all those separate strategies because she couldn't tolerate the emotional pain she was experiencing related to aspects of her childhood, adulthood, and recent sexual assault. She was trying to distract from and "forget" about all her hurts.

Our focus over the next three plus years was to help her more comfortably and effectively tolerate the emotional pain associated with so many of her life experiences and understand the impact they had on her. If we could zero in on this issue, then she wouldn't need all those other destructive, distracting strategies. If Naomi could allow herself to feel, identify, and name her natural emotions, she could, in effect, begin to more fully address the core problems rather than the symptoms. She was up for the task and seemed a good candidate for learning and using the Rosenberg Reset.

While Naomi unquestionably endured many difficult life-long challenges, her experience is not at all unique. In fact, it's more common than we would like to believe, even with so much information available about how to raise healthy children into healthy adults.

Many people have not learned to cope with life's challenges in healthy ways—quite the contrary. The world is filled with countless distractions and ways to easily avoid difficult emotions. As young children grow up, we hope they learn to tolerate and manage the naturally difficult feelings inherent in life. Yet many learn to avoid their unpleasant feelings instead, using such distractions as junk food, electronics, and alcohol to hide from these feelings. And these distractions can turn into more serious problems themselves.

Journal 3: Handling Emotional Pain

Naomi struggled with emotional pain. How well do *you* experience and move through unpleasant feelings? What were you told growing up about dealing with feelings? How were you taught to handle emotional pain? Take some time to jot down your thoughts.

The Rosenberg Reset Formula

While working at the UCLA student counseling center 25 years ago, I drew a diagram that became my blueprint for counseling clients. I can look back now and recognize that this drawing marked the beginning of the Rosenberg Reset. Essentially, the diagram captured two pathways: the first is one of avoidance, and the second is one of awareness. Naomi, as we saw earlier, was traveling the path of avoidance. The healthier option, however, is to choose the path of awareness.

Even in my earliest years of counseling clients, it was easy to see how pervasively negative thinking contributed to the problems these clients faced; it took a real toll on their emotional and physical health and compromised any sense of well-being. Yet I found these individuals had an even harder time dealing with, and would thus avoid, unpleasant ("bad" or "negative") feelings.

Negative thinking, or what some call negative talk, has been described by many as your inner voice; it includes conscious thoughts or attitudes and/or unconscious assumptions and beliefs. It is an internal dialogue or conversation you have with yourself—about you, others, the future, or the world—that is self-deprecating or anticipates poor or unwanted outcomes. Harsh self-criticism is negative thinking that is singularly focused on harsh judgments or attacks on *one's self*. Negative feelings are unpleasant or difficult feelings.

It is too easy and tempting to fall into the trap of defeatist thinking and harsh self-criticism. In fact, some people rely on this way of engaging with their feelings because they believe this is how they take responsibility for their own failures or shortcomings. Thus, negative thinking becomes the process by which people tend to deal with negative feelings. I believe avoiding these difficult feelings is more damaging and, in chapter 6, you will learn the role harsh self-criticism plays in this avoidance. What is far more beneficial for your health and well-being, however, is to start by dealing with *emotion*. And while overwhelming and uncomfortable emotions are at the base of the most frequent primary complaints I see in my practice, most of us have never been taught how to handle these unpleasant feelings.

What I was observing, and the frequency with which I saw it, made me realize that this was an issue that demanded an answer. *What made it so hard to experience unpleasant feelings?* I wrestled with this question for several years. It wasn't until neuroscientific discoveries were disseminated more broadly that I was able to identify concepts that not only unlocked this mystery but also helped me more fully understand how successfully managing difficult feelings relates to confidence, resilience, and authenticity. Understanding how people experience feelings and the approximate length of time they last helped me develop the Rosenberg Reset, a strategy that enables people to more fully lean into unpleasant emotions.

The Rosenberg Reset is based on a simple formula: *one choice, eight feelings, 90 seconds.*

Here's how I think about it: If you can make the *one choice* to stay aware of and in touch with as much of your moment-to-moment experience as possible, and you are willing to experience and move through *one or more 90-second waves* of *one or more of eight unpleasant feelings,* then you can pursue whatever you want in life.

First, you make the decision to allow yourself to fully feel your feelings, thoughts, and bodily sensations. It is about choosing awareness, not avoidance, as the way you approach your life.

> *Choose awareness, not avoidance, as your approach to life.*

Second, in any given situation, you experience and move through whichever of the eight unpleasant feelings that have surfaced: *sadness, shame, helplessness, anger, embarrassment, disappointment, frustration,* and *vulnerability.* I've had a front-row seat to emotional pain for more than four decades and what I've found is that avoiding difficult feelings gets in the way of confidence, happiness, authenticity, and success; these eight feelings are at the center of it all.

Third, you experience and move through these unpleasant feelings by riding one or more 90-second waves of bodily sensations. These bodily sensations help you access and begin to understand what you are feeling emotionally; feelings are generally known at a physical level before you are consciously aware of them. As much as it can seem at times that difficult feelings just linger and won't go away, the truth is that feelings are temporary.

Emotions provide vital information. Your body and brain are communicating this information so you can take action, most often to protect yourself or engage with others. But these bursts of information are temporary in nature. Physiologically, our bodies cannot maintain arousal states for very long. Making your way through feelings—especially uncomfortable ones—mainly involves tolerating the bodily sensations until the body re-regulates. The body prefers to be at homeostasis, its typical state, and will try to get back to baseline as soon as possible.

The One Choice:
Connect to Your Moment-to-Moment Experience

Based on my clinical observations, many people believe that it's the big choices that make us happy over the course of our life—the partner or spouse we have, the job we accepted or turned down, the party we did or didn't attend, the college we went to, or any number of other big decisions. From my perspective, these major decisions influence opportunities but not overall happiness, inner peace, or well-being. Instead, it's the attitudes we choose to hold and how we approach everyday experiences, events, and situations that have much greater sway over both our day-to-day and lifelong happiness than the small number of big choices we make.

The moment-to-moment decisions you make impact your well-being more. Did you speak up when you heard your coworker's sarcastic tone? How did you talk to your spouse or child when you were under a hard deadline for work? How did those experiences follow you for the rest of your day or week? Consider, also, the little moments when you either denied your feelings or paid attention to them. Did you listen, for instance, to your gut reaction when you were spoken to in a manner you didn't like or during an awkward first date? Perhaps you were aware of feeling disappointed by a conversation with a friend even though you were reluctant to say anything to them.

It turns out that all those little reactions and the decisions that follow—whether to pay attention, or not—count a lot. The key, then, is to make the one choice to stay in the present moment by remaining aware of and in touch with as much of your moment-to-moment experience as possible. This includes paying special attention to your thoughts, feelings, and bodily sensations. When you are able to notice and respond to the eight unpleasant feelings with ease, you'll experience a greater sense of inner peace and emotional freedom.

Check in with yourself here from a compassionate and mindful place. Notice your experience in the present moment, absent judgment. When you start to feel any one of the eight feelings, what do you do? Do you withdraw or shut down? Do you escape by staying distracted in obvious ways, for instance, through alcohol, drugs, food, social media, or shopping? Or do you distract yourself in less obvious ways, for example, by tightening your muscles or clenching your fists in an effort to make the feelings stop or go away?

Or do you stay present by noticing what you are feeling,

thinking, or sensing? While staying present is the choice I recommend to all of my clients in service of developing confidence and building a life of their own design, it's ultimately your decision to make.

This first step of the Reset is designed to help you stay aware of and connected to your experience ("knowing what you know") as opposed to distracting from and avoiding your experience ("trying not to know what you know"). Knowing what you know requires self-awareness and self-attunement, which leads to greater emotional strength and confidence.

Increase Self-Attunement

Interoception or *interoceptive awareness* describes your capacity to be aware of, perceive, or know the internal state of your body. Think of interoception as knowing your internal world or "inside self." Interoceptive awareness helps you know when you feel hungry or thirsty, have a temperature, are nauseated, or have a pain in your body. This type of awareness, sometimes called our sixth sense, also connects you to the emotions linked with your body sensations.[1] It helps you notice, for example, sadness when you feel heaviness in your chest, embarrassment when you feel heat in your face, or anxiety when you feel butterflies in your stomach. All of these are "inside self" experiences.[2]

Interoceptive awareness, then, involves being aware of and open to the subtle moment-to-moment shifts you may experience inside your own body. It includes all of "the little cues and signals from your muscles to your heart to your intestines to your skin...or what amounts to the overall feeling inside yourself."[3]

Awareness of your moment-to-moment experiences brings many benefits. It enables you to notice your thoughts, feelings, needs, perceptions, bodily sensations, desires, memories, beliefs, intentions, and more—all leading to a deeper understanding of yourself. If you've never really thought about what is important to you or if you don't have strong opinions about many things, know that this awareness can help you more easily access your likes, interests, passions, and creativity. Being well attuned and connected to yourself also allows you to be much more attuned to, connected with, and empathetic to others, thus enabling you over time to create and sustain deeper and more fulfilling relationships.

This ability to be aware of and sensitive to your inside experience is also known as self-attunement. This idea links closely with what Dr. Jon Kabat-Zinn and others have called "mindfulness" or mindful awareness.[4] Think of mindfulness as awareness of the present moment without judgment or reactivity, regardless of what is happening inside and/or outside of you.[5] You can develop this ability to focus your attention through countless practices, including meditation, mindfulness practices, martial arts, yoga, and more.

Proponents of mindfulness,[6] Dialectical Behavior Therapy (DBT)[7], and Acceptance and Commitment Therapy (ACT)[8] talk extensively about awareness and acceptance of one's experience without judgment. Though developed fully independently of all three, my Reset approach is consistent with their work and the work of professionals in each of these domains. If you are familiar with these approaches or engage in mindfulness practices, you are likely to notice similarities; they integrate well with the Reset formula.

Your Brain as Body/Your Body as Brain

Dr. Dan Siegel offers an insightful and expanded definition of the brain. Rather than being confined to the gray matter in our skull, as we tend to think of it, the brain, he suggests, is the entire central nervous system, including the spine and nerves that run the length of the body.[9] Our bodies contain vast amounts of information—far more than most of us realize— and the brain and body constantly feed information back and forth from the heart, intestines, bones, and muscles; interestingly, as he notes, what you casually describe as "heartfelt," "a gut feeling," or your "gut instinct" are grounded in science.[10] Personally, I like to think of us as a brain on two feet. If you have ever seen television commercials with the image of the M&M chocolate candies with limbs and sneakers, that's sort of what I mean.

Let's take this one step further. There are "top-down" and "bottom-up" mental processes related to how the brain functions.[11] To simplify this a bit, "top-down" processes use your background knowledge, information, experiences, mood, prior learning, and expectations to influence what you perceive. Top-down mental processes, then, involve accessing memories (or thinking about any given memory, life event, or situation) and then experiencing the sensations or feelings that go along with those memories. For instance, think of a man or woman you feel attracted to and notice the sensations that follow; your thoughts about a given memory or situation seemingly evoke the feelings associated with your experience of it.

"Bottom-up" processes involve sensory perceptions or bodily sensations followed by conscious awareness and thinking; you start with no preconceived notion of what you are encountering. This type of mental processing refers to processing sensory information like sounds, sights, or physical sensations once the sensory information is in your conscious awareness.[12] For instance, you understand balance only after you have successfully learned to ride a bicycle, or weightlessness after jumping on a trampoline. Or maybe you recognize bottom-up processing through something more common: perhaps you had runny mascara, smeared lipstick, or spinach caught in your front teeth as you were meeting people you wanted to impress, or realized your pant zipper was down during an important presentation. In these situations, it's likely your face and neck got flushed and red, you felt hot, and then, almost simultaneously, you recognized that you felt embarrassed. With bottom-up processing, you become aware of visceral, physical responses and then, micro-moments after they occur, you become aware of the emotions.

Knowing what specific emotions you experience seems to be a bottom-up process, as neuroscience discoveries suggest bodily sensations travel faster than our thoughts can form. What is so fascinating is that we tend to identify what we feel emotionally based on the sensations we feel in our physical body first. Think for a second about how we generally talk about feelings. We never talk about "feelings coming down"; we always describe feelings as "coming up." It seems a little surprising that something we experience in our body helps us know what we feel emotionally.

If you make an effort to shut down or suppress your bodily sensations, you affect what is processed. Thus, when you try to disconnect or distract from the physical sensations in your body, it becomes much more difficult to know what you are feeling on an emotional level. Generally speaking, then, you will tend to know your feelings through these bodily sensations first, before you can describe them with words (e.g., sad, angry, frustrated). As neuroscience continues to explore the brain-body connection, the interplay between the two becomes increasingly apparent.[13]

Intensity and Overwhelm: The "Felt" Experience of Feelings

Renowned brain researcher Dr. Joseph LeDoux says we have little direct control over our emotional reactions.[14] LeDoux's research suggests you can't control *that* you feel or *what* you feel, meaning simply that you are not in charge of the surges of energy or bodily sensations or feelings that you naturally experience in reaction to everyday life events. You can't really control your emotions—that is, you can't shut them down entirely and not feel them at all. Rather than exerting control, however, you can *monitor, modulate,* or *modify* the energy and sensory input you receive once it is in your conscious awareness.[15]

Monitoring means noticing or staying aware of what is happening within you; with such awareness you can modulate or modify your responses to the energy and information you are taking in.[16] For instance, let's say you notice bodily sensations that precede and signal a possible panic attack; because you have monitored this pattern so well, you are able to modify an old reaction of getting scared and instead engage in deep, slow breathing to avert the panic attack.

Because of the intensity and overwhelming nature of unpleasant feelings, many of my clients have expressed a desire to be a bit more like *Star Trek*'s Dr. Spock, moving through life in a robotic and unfeeling manner. While this can certainly seem appealing when we think of what it would allow us to avoid, we must remember that Dr. Spock's emotional flatlining meant he avoided both the lows *and* the highs. He didn't experience pain, but joy wasn't accessible, either.

Turning toward the pain, rather than away from it, allows you to connect with, and therefore address, your emotions instead of allowing them to fester unresolved. And if you are someone who has actively and intentionally shut out, shut down, disconnected from, or distracted from unpleasant feelings, then it is common to perceive feelings as overwhelming or flooding when they break through the wall you've built to protect yourself, or when you first open yourself to fully experiencing them again.

Any first attempts to allow yourself to reconnect with these emotions and sensations will likely feel intense simply because this is new and (initially) unfamiliar to you. If there are a lot of thoughts, feelings, and memories that you have shut down over the years, once you start to welcome your emotions, you may feel flooded by the unprocessed memories and feelings that surface. Over time, the flooding sensation abates.

Metaphorically, it seems that all that "emotional stuff" senses an open door. Without knowing the next time that door will be open, it's as if all the pent-up (unpleasant) feelings look back and forth at one another and simultaneously yell "RUSH!" so they can all make it out before the open door slams shut again. Just imagine waiting in line for the doors to open at a popular electronics store on Black Friday, and you'll get the idea.

Neuroscience helps further explain why feelings—especially the unpleasant ones—often seem so hard to bear. Dr. Antonio Damasio, a renowned neuroscientist, suggests that each distinct feeling you are able to identify and feel has its own unique neural firing pattern that also includes a "felt" experience within your body. He describes these distinct physical sensations as somatic markers—that is, bodily feelings or a bodily indicator that helps us to know what we are feeling and assists in our decision-making processes.[17]

One group of researchers used an online self-reporting method to have 701 respondents from West European and East Asian countries indicate where they felt certain emotions in their bodies.[18] While their results will not tell you how and where *you* experience certain feelings, because physical sensations linked with each emotion are different from person to person, they offer a picture of a cross-cultural and near-universal connection between bodily sensations and emotion. For instance, anger was generally experienced mid-torso up into the head and throughout the arms, into the hands; sadness was centered in the chest at the heart level and also up through the throat, into the face and eyes. Love was located throughout the body from the head to upper thighs, and happiness radiated across the whole body.

One way to help you "read" your emotional reactions better is to enhance your ability to be aware of, acknowledge, and experience, rather than deny, your bodily sensations. Check out the exercise below to discover this connection in your own body.

Awareness Exercise:
The How-What-Where of Feelings

1. Carefully read through the Awareness Exercise steps below.
2. Find a comfortable position. Slowly take a deep breath in for five counts, and then exhale for five counts. Do this two more times.
3. Close your eyes. Bring to mind a time when you felt sad, and notice *how* (the intensity, for instance), *what* you feel (the sensation itself), and *where* in your body you're feeling this feeling. Write down what you experienced.
4. Slowly repeat this process with the following emotions, noticing how, what, and where you're feeling these feelings in each instance. Take a deep clearing breath in and exhalation out before going on to the next feeling. Bring to mind a time you felt:
    ◆ angry
    ◆ disappointed
    ◆ content
    ◆ deeply satisfied
    ◆ joyful
    ◆ excited and happy about achieving something important to you

---

* Companion worksheets, guided exercises, and more resources can be found at www.DrJoanRosenberg.com/resources90/

During the course of the Awareness Exercise, maybe you found that it was hard to access bodily sensations tied to any of the feelings, or that all your feelings were experienced in the same location in the same way. Perhaps you noticed each particular feeling had different bodily sensations linked to it. Maybe you experienced a few feelings the same way (for example, sadness and disappointment), while the rest were more distinctly felt.

Some examples: Sasha may know she is getting angry when she feels heat at the back of her neck, whereas Connie may experience her anger as heat and tingling in her arms. Mark may find that both sadness and disappointment land right in the middle of his upper chest near his heart, but that sadness is just a heavy feeling and disappointment comes with a sinking quality to the heaviness. Lisa experiences warmth lifting and spreading through her upper body when she feels content and deeply satisfied; Mason describes a circle of lightness around his heart for joy.

Generally, most people describe unpleasant feelings as tighter, heavier, more distinct, or more constricted, and pleasant feelings as more relaxed, calmer, warmer, lighter, whole body, or more expansive. There is no right or wrong answer. How you experience a feeling is *unique to you,* and this exploration exercise is simply a way to increase awareness of how you experience these feelings within your own body.

Acknowledge Eight Unpleasant Feelings

Awareness is the necessary first step for using the Rosenberg Reset and takes us to the (nearly) simultaneous next step: experiencing and moving through eight unpleasant feelings.

You must be open and willing to face, tolerate, bear, and even embrace difficult or painful feelings. Here's the list of those unpleasant, yet very familiar, feelings that I have observed people struggling with and avoiding the most:

- sadness
- shame
- helplessness
- anger
- embarrassment
- disappointment
- frustration
- vulnerability

We'll go into this in more detail in the next chapter, but avoidance of these feelings initiates a downward spiral to low confidence and poor self-esteem. Such avoidance is also a primary cause of worry, anxiety, fear of failure, fear of risk-taking, lack of persistence and perseverance, worry about what others think of you, fear of speaking up, harsh self-criticism, negative self-talk, fear of vulnerability and trust, and a range of other emotional and mental health difficulties, including drug and alcohol problems. Manage these eight unpleasant feelings well and you can resolve many of the problems listed above.

The bodily sensations that help you know what you're feeling emotionally are at the core of what makes it so hard to experience and move through or handle feelings. It is the discomfort of these bodily sensations from which most people want to disconnect or distract.

It's not that you don't really want to feel what you feel emotionally; instead, you want to separate yourself from the uncomfortable bodily sensations that let you know what you are feeling. This is where the real problem lies. Learning to identify and become mindful of these bodily sensations is crucial to effectively using the Rosenberg Reset.

Experiencing and Moving Through Feelings

Dr. Jill Bolte Taylor, a neuroscientist and author of *My Stroke of Insight,* suggests that when an emotion, such as anger, is triggered, chemicals released by your brain surge through your body and activate bodily sensations. Then, within roughly 90 seconds, they're flushed out of your bloodstream.[19] You might experience these feelings as a "wave" that begins with this biochemical rush and ends with the flush. This chemical rush or wave brings about uncomfortable physical sensations, such as blushing, heat in your arms, or heaviness in your chest, as mentioned earlier. This is the key and worthy of repeating: *What we feel emotionally is often experienced first in the body as a physical sensation.* Simply put, unpleasant emotions don't physically feel good in our bodies.

Remember, the brain is engaged in the exchange of information from constant input and output to the rest of the body and back. As Dr. Candace Pert, research scientist and author of *Molecules of Emotion* has written: "…emotions are the informational content that is exchanged via the psychosomatic network, with the many systems, organs, and cells participating in the process."[20] Consequently, you can consider feelings one source of information that exists for your protection and growth. Your ability to face the circumstances, challenges, obstacles, traumas, tragedies, losses, and even successes that you experience in life essentially comes down to how well you comfortably experience and move through emotions, including—especially—these eight unpleasant feelings.

What do I mean, then, by moving through your emotions? I mean being aware of your feelings and fully experiencing them by tolerating the waves of feelings or the intensity of the bodily sensations tied to the biochemical rush and flush. As you become better at tolerating feelings, you can use them more effectively for decision-making and responding to others. When you can experience and move through these eight difficult feelings, you are on your way to emotional strength and confidence. The next time your feelings emerge, pay attention. Take a moment, breathe, and really notice what is taking place inside of you on a physiological level.

Ansel started using this technique five hours after he heard me speak about the Rosenberg Reset at a conference. He had always had trouble starting conversations with people he admired and wanted to get to know. The typical situation began with a desire to introduce himself, then turned to fear due to his negative self-talk ("I'm not as accomplished as that person"), and then to feelings of vulnerability and embarrassment that he would allow to prevent him from approaching the person he had wanted to meet. He wouldn't reach out; instead, he would simply walk away feeling disappointed for missing another opportunity. He'd make matters worse by berating himself for being "such a loser," thus validating his belief that he wasn't "as good" as the other person.

The day he learned the Reset, he decided to use it to meet people he admired, understanding now that the bodily sensations of embarrassment and vulnerability were getting in his way. Ansel soon found his feelings were brief and tolerable, and the upshot was that he had great conversations with the individuals he approached. In a few instances, he was able to arrange follow-up meetings about possible business ventures. Based on these successful encounters, he realized he could engage people in other settings in a similar manner. He left the conference feeling excited, happy, and more confident, knowing he now had the emotional skills to initiate contact and converse easily with people he admired. He recognized how hard he had made it for himself for so long.

Jim attended the same conference. He sought me out a year later to tell me that using the Reset helped him land a contract worth several hundred thousand dollars. He described himself as an aggressive businessman and said he was competing with another consultant for business. Both men were presenting in front of the panel doing the hiring, but the other consultant presented first and left no time for Jim to describe his strategy and plans. Jim became increasingly furious as more and more of his time was eaten away. He told me that usually, in this type of circumstance, he would lose control, become rageful and explosive, and often create an ugly scene. This time, however, he paused, sat with his anger, and though he was visibly distressed, he remained composed throughout the experience and after. While he sat there, feeling the intensity of his anger rise and fall, he realized he could be more considerate in how he expressed his extreme dismay about the situation. The business liaison who had brought him in to pitch his ideas was so impressed with how Jim handled himself that Jim was awarded a separate contract well beyond the initial contract.

90 Seconds: The Solution

So how do you deal with painful feelings? Let's go back a moment to what neuroscientist and author Dr. Jill Bolte Taylor described when an emotion gets triggered. She suggested that once a feeling is evoked, "the chemical released by [your] brain surges through [your] body"[21] and activates bodily sensations (the neural firing pattern) that are unique to you. Again, think of this rush of chemicals as a wave. As these chemicals are completely flushed out of your bloodstream, and the physiological feelings subside, it feels as if the wave has passed.

From the point of an initial trigger, Dr. Bolte Taylor described that each surge or wave of emotion has a biochemical lifespan of roughly 90 seconds. Depending on the intensity and one's subjective experience of the feeling[22], its lifespan could be considerably shorter (as brief as a few seconds)[23]; yet the rush isn't going to last *any longer than 90 seconds.*

One of my clients put the 90-seconds concept into such great perspective: It's less time than half a song! You may have to experience one or more waves of any given feeling or feelings, but any feeling, no matter how overwhelming it might be in the moment, is temporary.

Lingering Feelings

When I explain the Reset, the question that always arises is, "My feelings seem to last *so much longer* than 90 seconds. What's up with that, Dr. Rosenberg?" Increased cortisol,[24] the stress hormone, can cause that effect, yet rumination appears to play a major role.[25]

If you continue to feel the feeling (e.g., sadness, anger, disappointment) for more than 90 seconds, it is generally because you continue to think about the triggering situation or memory over and over, often in an effort to resolve or make sense of it. Each time you think about the situation, you trigger roughly the same biochemical waves, meaning you experience approximately the same bodily sensations tied to the emotion, memory, or situation.

It is your memory of the emotion — not the emotion itself — that lasts minutes, hours, days, years, perhaps even decades past the initial event. It is your remembering that elicits a physiological experience or bodily sensations similar to the ones you initially felt. In other words, the emotions may be *re-membered* (felt in your body) each time you recall the memory. Thankfully, you have the choice of what to think about — and thus feel. Once you are conscious of this process, you can change it.

If, for instance, you feel disappointed about a friend canceling a lunch date at the last minute, within about 90 seconds of the initial trigger, the chemical component of the disappointment will have released from your bloodstream and your natural biological response is over. If you remain disappointed for any length of time after this automatic or biological response, as Dr. Bolte Taylor notes, it is because you "have chosen to let that circuit continue to run."[26] The more you can acknowledge, feel, and move through your feelings in the moments they are present, the less you will have the sense they are lingering. If you are able to understand what triggered you and the impact the situation had upon you, the less you will replay those same reactions. You have choice here.

At times, feelings seem to linger because of the choices you make to ruminate — to repeat a memory or an experience (or to run the same circuitry over and over), especially in an effort to resolve it. Often people revisit memories over and over again in an attempt to make sense of the situation.

A second possibility involves avoiding or trying not to think about something that you are already thinking about. The more you attempt to suppress, distract, or disconnect, the longer it takes to move through painful or unpleasant memories and resolve their accompanying feelings. Despite our best efforts to prevent awareness of our feelings, we still remain affected by them.[27] Some psychologists call this "thought suppression." Psychologist Daniel Wegner, along with his colleagues and other researchers, found across multiple studies that trying to suppress thoughts seems a virtual impossibility.[28]

Try it for yourself. You'll need to set a timer. Just keep track by writing a check mark each time you think of the thought you are supposed to suppress. Follow the same instructions Wegner provided to the study participants assigned to the initial suppression group: "In the next five minutes, please verbalize your thoughts as you did before, with one exception. This time, try not to think of a white bear. Every time you say 'white bear' or have 'white bear' come to mind, though, please ring the bell [make a check mark] on the table [a writing pad] before you."[29]

What did you notice for yourself?

Consider how many times you or someone you know has said: "I'm not going to think about _____" — as if avoiding the issue will simply make it go away. The reason there is no relief is that you have to think about the thought or feeling you *don't want* to experience *first*, in order not to experience it! What's more, there is a rebound effect, meaning that the more you try to suppress the thought, the more it creates a preoccupation with the very thoughts or feelings you are trying to shut out. As a consequence, the unwanted thought intrudes—it comes into your awareness more frequently than if you'd never attempted to suppress it in the first place.[30] That's why thought suppression can never work.

Thought suppression helps us understand why the more you push feelings away, the more intensely they seem to be felt and the longer they seem to stay. If, for example, you continue to feel lingering anger, disappointment, or sadness, then you have to take a close look at the thoughts that restimulate the neural circuitry connected to the painful experience. Again, you may linger in the pain because you keep replaying the same thoughts. Rather, take the time you need to acknowledge your feelings and understand what triggered you, the impact the situation had upon you, and what you need to resolve the situation. Some of these thoughts may be tied to difficult events in your life history; in chapter 8, I will provide you with a framework for resolving long-standing hurt and pain.

I've also found that feelings seem to linger when you shift your awareness away from the feeling itself (e.g., embarrassment or disappointment) and, instead, continuously engage in harsh self-criticism. The harsh self-criticism keeps generating unpleasant feelings underneath, so as long as you engage in that practice, the feelings will appear to persist.

Intense emotional experiences involving feelings such as fear, profound grief, terror, or rage may also linger.[31] Though the 90-seconds approach may be helpful for relieving post-traumatic stress responses in some cases, it is not intended for these kinds of experiences. These mental health challenges are complex disorders and may require more intensive and structured interventions to achieve long-term resolution.

Journal 4: Lingering Feelings

Do you experience lingering feelings? What might keep them lingering for you? What memories are your feelings attached to? What seems unresolved?

Ride Feelings as if They Are Ocean Waves

If you've ever watched ocean waves as they land on the beach, you've probably seen some that appear tumultuous and crashing while others are a gentle roll. And if you've ever walked along the shoreline you'll notice that no matter how the wave washes up on the beach, it seems to linger and hang for a few moments just before it ebbs back into the ocean. No matter how waves come in, they always subside.

That's how feelings, experienced first as bodily sensations or surges of energy in our body, seem to move as well. Feelings rise up within us just as ocean waves rise up on the shoreline. They can leave us feeling flooded or overwhelmed, or they can offer only a hint of emotion, like a slight flush from embarrassment. And feelings linger, too—for what might subjectively seem like minutes—yet, like ocean waves, they *always subside.* The most effective strategy, then, for experiencing and moving through difficult feelings is simply to "ride the waves" of emotion until they inevitably subside—in most cases sooner rather than later. Think of it as surfing, sailing, boogie-boarding, or body-surfing: just hang tight and ride the wave.

The key to "riding the waves" and bearing especially unpleasant or uncomfortable feelings is to tolerate the bodily sensations that accompany those feelings. Generally speaking, the intense physical response will pass in moments. The feelings will similarly subside. Again, we are only talking about an upper limit of roughly 90 seconds for any given wave. Notice it happen, feel it, and then watch as it dissipates.

Simply continuing to breathe normally as opposed to holding your breath can help you ride the wave and move through these feelings and physical sensations. In the next chapter I'll delve more fully into tolerating feelings. Briefly, you'll want to both simultaneously experience the bodily sensations linked with the emotion you feel and also learn how to be a curious observer, noticing and thinking about what you are feeling. That way you can decide, as Dr. Bolte Taylor put it, whether you want to keep running the same circuitry, or not.

I am frequently asked, "Is it only one wave?" No. If you repeatedly think about the memory, then you fire off the same approximate feelings tied to that memory. The best way to move through one or more feelings is to give in to the waves as you experience them. Surf them any way you need to. Let them run their 90-second course. Benefits are immediate. In the moment, you'll likely feel some relief and calm. Anxiety is reduced. Insights often follow that might include becoming aware of what triggered you, connecting to an older memory and gaining clarity about a past experience or past behavior pattern, identifying more clearly what you are feeling in a given situation, making a decision, or deciding to take action based on what you're feeling.

Consistent practice usually results in no longer being hooked by old life patterns or stories, mostly because you no longer need to avoid what you know. Instead you are aware, clear, and "know" the truth of your own experience.

The ability to successfully surrender to the emotion and ride the wave is precisely how Debbie, a 30-year-old client, was able to identify and alter one of her destructive life patterns. By doing so, she developed the resilience to be truer to herself. She had historically used sarcasm as a way of relating to others. She came into my office one evening and described a fight she had had with her boyfriend of five months. As she tried to address an emotionally charged topic with him, he got quieter and quieter and eventually shut down, stopping all conversation completely.

You can imagine how infuriating this was to Debbie, and her response was to escalate—particularly through sarcasm—pushing and cajoling him to talk. It didn't work; she was only met with more silence. Feeling that much more infuriated, she then picked up her things and left his apartment with nothing resolved, experiencing anger, sadness, and frustration related to the fight. As she drove away, she thought about how to handle the pain and had fleeting thoughts of drinking and cutting, two maladaptive emotional coping strategies she had relied on when she first came to see me.

Still feeling the intensity of her anger about the fight, and with tears streaming down her face, her thoughts shifted. Because she was committed to using more effective coping strategies, she took some deep breaths and reminded herself to ride the waves of anger and sadness running through her body. By the time she reached her home, the emotional intensity had abated, allowing her to have greater clarity about the real cause of the fight and how she had behaved. Had she been able to handle the intensity of her anger, disappointment, and sadness more effectively in the first place, she may not have resorted to escalating the fight by being sarcastic and hurtful, nor would she have left her boyfriend's home. Despite those challenges, once she physically left the situation, she was able to incorporate deep breathing and the practice of riding the wave to further calm herself down. That's when her insights came. As she reflected on her tearfulness, she realized she had shifted to anger and sarcasm in order to avoid being sad and disappointed. She also acknowledged she would escalate her anger when she felt helpless to influence situations—a behavior she also resorted to with her father. With heightened awareness, she could commit to making a different decision the next time she felt inclined to be hurtfully sarcastic. By making her way through several of these experiences, over time, Debbie learned to default to the Reset instead of to sarcasm, greatly improving her sense of well-being and her relationships.

Parental Influence on Feelings

Challenges in facing difficult feelings generally start in childhood. (To a lesser degree, they can begin with very painful events experienced in adulthood.) There is an extensive body of research on how infants and children bond with parents or caretakers that describes the importance of relationships on a child's developing brain. How a child is raised, what he or she is taught, and even what was experienced in utero have significant influence on that person's capacity to manage or modulate his or her own feelings well, and this carries right on through into adulthood.

Simply put, we generally develop an emotional range that can encompass that of our parents/caretakers. Dr. Dan Siegel believes that how a parent has made sense of his or her own childhood pain has much to do with how that individual responds when parenting his or her own children.[32] In the best of circumstances, you grew up with a parent who joined thoughtful reasoning with emotional warmth and well-modulated feelings. However, if your parents did not make sense of or work through their own pain, then it likely came splashing out on you and your siblings in a messy sort of way. It could have shown up as chaos, rageful episodes, the silent treatment, withdrawal, or total shutdown.

What's the effect? If you grew up with a parent who withdrew love, affection, and attention when you expressed feelings, you might have learned to shut down your own feelings. Or, you may have witnessed or directly experienced the misuse of anger or been the target of extreme rage. It's common to push away your own feelings of anger and helplessness when you have been unable to control the danger you faced with a parent's unpredictable angry outbursts or rageful behavior.

Any one of these experiences can affect how much you allow yourself to feel. Growing up with a raging parent often results in children who either never want to let themselves feel angry or use rage themselves. Maybe you have similar outbursts. Or maybe you just learned to shut down.

Dealing with your feelings also might feel scary or uncomfortable depending on how your parents or caretakers reacted or responded to you, including what they told you about yourself (e.g., "crying makes you weak," "you'll never amount to anything").

The physical climate of your home life plays a part here, too. Your adult self is influenced by whether you grew up in impoverished conditions, in comfort, or with unlimited wealth. Likewise, how you experience and express feelings is impacted by what you were exposed to as a child. People who grow up in impoverished, chaotic, and hostile conditions tend to focus on survival and all the stresses and strains associated with not having enough; the unpredictability of chaos and hostility often result emotionally in states of confusion and fear. The potential effects carry forward into adulthood at multiple levels (physical, neurological, psychological, etc.). If your parents modeled impulsive, inconsistent, harsh, or even seemingly desperate behavior rather than considerate, reliable and supportive actions, you may struggle with recognizing appropriate responses to stressful situations, or even considering what kinds of long-term consequences your choices may have to your quality of life. This is in contrast to those who were raised with a sense of stability, consistency, warmth, responsiveness, and opportunity as their baseline during childhood.

Any of these circumstances, at least initially, might have contributed to how much you allow yourself to be aware of and in touch with what you experience on a day-to-day basis and how safe or dangerous it might feel for you to experience anything at all, pleasant or unpleasant. Yet it's essential that you learn how to tolerate and experience unpleasant or painful feelings since those are the ones that trip people up the most. If you don't manage them well they become relationship killers and dream destroyers, collapsing your drive to pursue goals and adventures and sapping your ability to be resilient in the face of change. Using the Reset can help you change maladaptive patterns learned early in life.

Underneath everything I talk about here is the awareness that nature (genetics and innate temperament) and nurture (life experiences) are always at play. I fully recognize that difficult, painful, tragic, and traumatic experiences and events unequivocally affect how we function during our earliest years and as we age. My intent is not to talk about these each time, yet I recognize and acknowledge their influence on any one person's development and capacity to handle unpleasant feelings. I am also aware that if we have the capacity to think, then we have the capacity to change—and in this regard, I hope that the past can help explain problems, though not excuse them.

The commitment to awareness rather than avoidance as your immediate response to emotions makes all the difference. This is the "one choice" I ask you to make. The more often you make it, the more natural it will become until your mind almost automatically chooses to respond by experiencing the emotions rather than trying to push them aside or reacting before they've run their course. Using the Reset can be a choice you make *every day*. The desire to stay connected to your moment-to-moment experience by being aware of and experiencing 90-second waves of any of the eight unpleasant feelings will, over time, build confidence, resilience, and authenticity. It all comes down to your willingness to experience the biochemical surges of emotion and tolerate the unpleasant or uncomfortable bodily sensations that let you know what you are feeling emotionally.

CHAPTER 3

Understanding the Eight Unpleasant Feelings

Feelings are available to us for the threefold purpose of protection, connection, and creativity. When you feel safe and secure, both alone and with others, your mental, emotional, and physical resources are not required for protection or basic survival needs. At these times, your feelings are available for connection and creativity, often in the form of relationships, risk-taking, and novel or meaningful pursuits.

It seems most people experience pleasant feelings with relative ease but find one or more painful feelings unpleasant, uncomfortable, or difficult to bear. In fact, there may be some who find it extremely difficult to tolerate the whole range of unpleasant feelings that humans are capable of experiencing. Yet, when difficult feelings are not dealt with, they can intensify. They can seem to linger longer than we think they should, and avoiding them may muffle or dull the intensity of our pleasant emotional states.

People often wonder why the experience of unpleasant emotions is so strong and why there are so many painful and unpleasant emotions. The answer is that at the most basic level, these difficult feelings can protect us and help us survive in the world.

Think about it from an evolutionary standpoint. Those who were more able to identify threats were also more likely to sur-vive and have children.

As author and researcher Rick Hanson suggests, we have a negativity bias for the sake of survival: paying attention to pain-ful and potentially dangerous stimuli is vital to our ability to stay alive and pass along our genes. We learn more from the nega-tive so we tend to put more focus there.[1] Negative emotions pro-vide information necessary for perceiving threats, reacting to the environment, and surviving. For instance, anxiety height-ens our alertness for danger; disgust potentially prevents us from ingesting poisonous or tainted food; fear helps keep us alive. Thus, our survival is far more dependent on our aware-ness of our negative emotions than our experience of pleasant ones.

We absolutely need to be able to access and make use of these difficult emotions; as unpleasant as these feelings are, they are necessary. Going forward, I'd like to challenge you to no longer label feelings as "negative" or "bad" since they serve an important protective function. Instead, I urge you to term them "unpleasant," "uncomfortable," "unsettling," or "diffi-cult," which more accurately describes what you are physically feeling. If you experiment with using these different words, you might notice that changing what you call these emotions can change how you experience them. For the purposes of this book, we'll focus only on your capacity to deal with the eight difficult feelings I've listed previously: *sadness, shame, help-lessness, anger, embarrassment, disappointment, frustration,* and *vulnerability.*

So why these eight feelings? I've identified these particular feelings because they are the feelings that most commonly occur when things don't turn out the way you want. During more than 30 years as a practicing psychologist, I observed that my clients' avoidance of these feelings acted as the greatest obstacle to confidence and authenticity and the greatest contributor to challenges like anxiety, harsh self-criticism, and worrying about what others think.

Essentially, these eight feelings are what most people withdraw or run away from. They become the barriers to success in almost every aspect of life, including finances, health, career, and relationships. In fact, we back off from pursuing what's important to us mostly because we find it hard to move through the unpleasant feelings that might result.

And why is moving through unpleasant feelings so important? As I've mentioned, it's important because our belief and trust in feeling capable in life — or feeling emotionally strong — is directly tied to our ability to experience and move through difficult feelings. As soon as you increase your awareness and acceptance of the full range of your feelings — pleasant and unpleasant — your sense of yourself starts to change. Develop your capacity to deal with these feelings, and you will find growing confidence and the freedom to be more fully yourself in every aspect of your life that is important to you. You will gain new insights that will help you recognize what you truly value and desire rather than what you gravitate toward out of comfort or a tendency to play it safe. As you strengthen your ability to face and tolerate the surge of unpleasant emotions internally, you will also feel more capable of facing difficult external challenges. Once you believe you have the resiliency to ride the 90-second waves of unpleasant feelings and emerge unscathed on the other side, you will begin to see yourself as more capable and more in charge of your own choices. You'll start to feel more comfortable in your own skin as you experience progress toward a life you have intentionally designed.

Why do we avoid these feelings?

- We're afraid that they will start and never stop.
- We're afraid that they will be too intense and overwhelm us.

- ◆ We're afraid that they will make us feel out of control.
- ◆ We're afraid we will verbally or physically spiral out of control.

The Eight Difficult Feelings

Let's take a look at the purpose and physiological experience of these emotions. As I discuss each one, it is important to remember that everyone experiences feelings in their bodies differently. To some, for instance, sadness comes with an ache in their heart or tension in the shoulders; to others it is experienced with gut-wrenching sobs or a hollowing out in the pit of the stomach. When considering these feelings, take time to identify how you experience these emotions in your body. This would be a great time to do the Awareness Exercise: The How-What-Where of Feelings found in Chapter 2, page 44, if you didn't do it earlier.

Sadness

Sadness can be especially painful because it often brings up unhappy memories from the past, which can feel overwhelming. We associate it with situations caused by circumstances or people over whom we believe we have little impact or control,[2] and also with grief, loss, and an overpowering or heartrending ache.

When people are sad, they frequently describe themselves as depressed. Sadness is temporary and the result of a specific moment or experience.[3] Depression is a persistent sad mood and an inability to experience positive emotions.[4] Although an experience or trigger may initiate a depressive episode, it is not the sole factor in maintaining the depression.

With sadness comes increased activation of our limbic system,[5] which is composed of areas of the brain associated with memory and learning; as a result, we are predisposed to attend to more negative stimuli. When the amygdala—the main area of the brain responsible for emotional responses—is excited, we are inclined to respond more fearfully. We also have a tendency to bring up more memories from the past, with sad memories, in particular, being more salient.[6] Stimulating this brain region also activates our innate tendencies to approach what is safe or pleasurable and avoid what is dangerous.[7] Sadness can inspire us to reach out to others and convey to them we are in pain and need comfort. Further, it helps us approach those who are most likely to provide comfort and help us through difficult moments. Yet, if we learn that others are unsafe, we tend to avoid them, isolating ourselves with the sadness.

Shame

Shame is often associated with the belief that one is inadequate, defective, flawed, damaged, or bad.[8] It is likewise linked with high levels of harsh self-criticism, which further exacerbates feelings of shame. These two become intertwined in a vicious cycle where shame leads to self-criticism and self-criticism leads to shame. Consequently, it is easy to understand why many people try to avoid feelings of shame.

As with sadness and depression, there is a parallel distinction between general shame, which serves a social function, and core shame, which is tied to the experience of feeling unlovable and so innately flawed that one cannot make up for this defect.[9]

General shame often results from perceived social rejection or feeling as though one's self-esteem or social status has been threatened.[10] As with any perceived threat to self, the body reacts with a fear response: cortisol is dumped into the body[11] to prepare it to act in order to protect itself.

The most common response to shame is to be submissive. This submissiveness and acknowledgment of wrongdoing tends to reduce aggression from others.[12] Expressing shame invites more positive social behavior from both parties. The submissive person engages in prosocial behavior to make up for his or her actions, and the aggrieved person or one hearing shame expressed tends to behave by being more cooperative and forgiving. Despite negative connotations about shame, when people express shame via submissiveness, it encourages people to treat one another well and facilitates close bonds that keep people together.[13]

Core shame is often seen in people who experienced significant criticism, physical abuse, or verbal abuse as children; it results from chronic and detrimental exposure to these encounters without appropriate reconnection or healing.[14] The cortisol and fear response associated with general shame is persistently tolerated at a great cost to the person's physical and emotional health.[15] This enduring shame state also results in withdrawal, decrease in self-esteem, greater social anxiety, and vulnerability to depression.[16] In my psychotherapy practice, I've observed such shame, including from sexual abuse or sexual assault, lead to chronic withdrawal from others.

Helplessness

Helplessness is frequently tied to feeling small, powerless, and vulnerable and is often elicited when you are unable to have an impact or influence on an individual, event, or situation. It's a sense of being on edge, waiting for whatever is coming, which can result in anxiety. Helplessness may be felt in situations where you have less control, no control, or where you feel out of control.

A lack of control makes it impossible to avoid difficult or

painful situations.[17] As with shame, helplessness activates fear responses and arousal in the body so one can prepare to deal with these unavoidable situations.[18] Feeling helpless can motivate change.[19] And dealing with stressors, even those beyond one's control, provides the opportunity to develop self-esteem, problem-solving skills, and a sense of self-efficacy.[20]

However, when people are exposed to prolonged periods of feeling helpless—for instance, when they are abused or neglected—this state becomes more lasting and damaging. Animals and humans can experience "learned helplessness," which is similar to a depressive state; they have become so accustomed to facing inescapable pain that they no longer have motivation to act or make changes.[21] Similar to core shame, learned helplessness is an enduring state and may require more in-depth attention; as such, it is not a focus of this book.

Anger

Anger serves two primary functions. It is a protective response, and it facilitates social communication. You need to have it available as a way to respond to distress, harm, or pain. It is often elicited when you believe you have been wronged in a certain situation and where you also see yourself as morally right in that same situation.[22] Despite the overwhelming view of anger as a negative emotion, it can also elicit protective, prosocial responses (e.g., acting on behalf of those less advantaged, reacting to unfairness to someone else, or helping when someone is being victimized).[23]

Anger reflects your emotional investment in something important to you; properly expressed, it lets others know that they hurt you and that they should not engage in similar behaviors again. Likewise, if you did something to hurt them, anger is the emotion that expresses that pain.[24] I see many clients who have never expressed anger to those who are aggrieving them, and without that information, their partners, friends, peers, and others may continue to engage in injurious behavior.

Anger can be uncomfortable as it is associated with increased blood pressure, heart rate, and blood flow to the face (flushing)[25]— body reactions we often associate with fear or panic. Because it's unsettling, people tend to avoid it. Unfortunately, avoidance is ineffective and can even be damaging. It is imperative that anger be expressed in an appropriate, helpful, and respectful way, and this varies by culture.

When anger intensifies (either as a result of being avoided, because someone feels helpless or the anger is hooked to prior painful memories) it often gets vented in a rageful or aggressive manner, moving from demeaning words to violent acts. By and large, countries such as the United States, United Kingdom, Australia, and France have deemed such acts unlawful even though these behaviors still widely occur. Yet there are many places across the globe where cultural and social norms continue to support aggression, including child maltreatment (e.g., Peru, Nigeria, Turkey, Sudan), intimate partner violence (India, China, Pakistan, Jordan), or sexual violence (Pakistan, South Africa). Around the world, community violence continues, in the form of intolerance, stereotyping, and discrimination of selected groups, and violence persists as a way to resolve conflict.[26]

Anger never has to be explosive, wounding, or destructive, something that many people struggle to understand because of their own experiences with anger. The great irony is that harboring your feelings and avoiding anger can lead to catastrophic explosions later. Emotions will not be ignored forever. Even certain kinds of thoughts can contribute to these angry eruptions; they could be thoughts like: "I'll just keep quiet, it's better not to

> *Anger never has to be explosive, wounding, or destructive.*

say something that will hurt someone else"; "Saying I'm angry won't matter, it never has any impact anyway"; or "They only listen to me and take me seriously if I yell." Even yelling, an often-damaging way of expressing feelings, tends to lead to more anger rather than to the release that people expect.[27]

In the best of circumstances, you'd be able to convey your anger by simply saying you are angry. Achieving this is possible especially if your aim is to be well intentioned and your efforts are directed at promoting a family, social, or work environment that feels safe to those in it. Yet people often escalate how they express anger by getting louder, meaner, more intense, more sarcastic, more unpredictable, or more physical when they don't "feel" like they are being heard, understood, or taken seriously; or when they feel helpless, believe they have no influence or impact, think they have no options, or poorly manage their own emotional states.[28]

Misuse of anger and the inappropriate expression of it is a decision that the person escalating it makes. However, this way of expressing anger should be separated from the emotion itself, which is not inherently hurtful or "bad."

David is an excellent example of someone who learned how to express his anger more constructively and changed his aggressive manner with his girlfriend, Carrie, once he made a firm decision to do so. They came to see me for couples therapy. David was physically abused as a child and had witnessed his mother suffering domestic violence at the hands of his father, so he was familiar with the misuse and poor expression of anger. David would escalate arguments with his girlfriend quickly, saying cruel things and imposing himself in physically threatening ways near her, though he never laid a hand on her. Carrie would withdraw from David and refuse to talk as a result of his behavior, something that often led to more escalation because he felt shut out and believed he had no way to reconnect with her; they were caught in a vicious cycle. I asked David if he ever behaved this way at work. He said that he didn't, and gave as reasons for his good conduct potential embarrassment, workplace standards, fear of getting fired, and the desire to be a good role model in his new supervisory position. Just to be sure that David and I were on the same page, I confirmed with David that he was making a decision to express his anger more constructively at work for the reasons he noted. Then I talked with him about the double standard and different set of rules he held for his personal relationship—for someone he loved and was considering marrying. If he could behave without aggression and escalating behaviors at work, then he surely had the same measure of control at home. I challenged him to make the same decision for his relationship as he did with colleagues and suggested he could start that night. He took up the challenge and throughout the course of seeing David and Carrie, I learned he never again engaged in an aggressive manner with his girlfriend. He could feel his anger building yet he consistently made the decision to alter his old patterns with Carrie.

Modulating Your Anger

If you struggle with how your anger gets expressed, there are many steps you can take to modulate it more effectively. They include:

- Acknowledging that how you manage your anger is a problem.
- Deciding and committing to kind and well-intentioned behavior that does not escalate, demean, threaten, or physically hurt others.
- Noticing how, what, and where anger is experienced in your body.
- Noticing your patterns of expression before you erupt.

- ◆ Knowing your patterns and observing your bodily cues of anger so you can choose how to express yourself more constructively.
- ◆ Taking five to ten deep, slow breaths to slow yourself down if you feel angry.
- ◆ Holding your hands clasped together behind your back till you calm down.
- ◆ Engaging in self-talk that encourages you to be well-intentioned and stay calm.
- ◆ Riding the waves of anger until they have subsided before you utter a word.
- ◆ Speaking without raising your voice and without intensity or a sarcastic tone.

---

* *Companion worksheets, guided exercises, and more resources can be found at www.DrJoanRosenberg.com/resources90/*

Embarrassment

Embarrassment is an acknowledgment to ourselves and to others that we made a mistake or did something that went differently from how we had hoped. One might experience physical discomfort, including increased heart rate, muscle tension, blushing, and a rise in temperature; when people feel embarrassed, they typically decrease eye contact, experience speech disturbances, smile, and move their bodies more.[29] The physical and social discomfort that comes with embarrassment is often hard for people to tolerate. Yet, socially, it actually makes us more likeable; people tend to be more forgiving when we can acknowledge errors via embarrassment.[30]

Others also tend to be more compassionate when we convey that we feel bad about what we did, which allows for healing and reconnection. By acknowledging mistakes, embarrassment can help us grow by motivating us to change. Yet, if we refuse to see that something isn't working, we remain stuck in maladaptive patterns of thinking, acting, and relating to others.

Disappointment

Disappointment is experienced when we are faced with unmet needs, desires, and expectations. We hope, expect, or anticipate something positive yet we are met with an unwanted and unfavorable outcome.[31] Disappointment highlights our helplessness and lack of control over certain situations.[32]

People struggle with disappointment partly because it generally catches them off guard.[33] While we frequently understand this feeling is a potential outcome, it repeatedly gets dismissed or played down as people pursue their hopes and dreams. This unanticipated outcome leads to uncertainty, a state often associated with unforeseen situations. Uncertainty is more fear-provoking than even the worst familiar environments. In other words, whenever we are met with something surprising or unexpected, a sense of uncertainty sets in.

Disappointment helps people gain the support they need by inspiring empathy in others. Within relationships, expressing disappointment helps communicate that someone may need to change their behavior.[34] Disappointment can be motivational; people who have experienced disappointment may be motivated to persist and work harder so they are able to accomplish what they had hoped to achieve.[35]

Disappointment is often contrasted with regret. Regret comes from believing you made a bad decision when you dislike your obtained outcome relative to your desired one.[36] By contrast, with disappointment, you would have still made the same choice; it's just that you wanted a better outcome.

Let me offer one more distinction. Disappointment is the

feeling; "disappointed in," as in "I am disappointed in myself for doing poorly on the exam," is a judgment. (This is true for shame relative to "I'm ashamed of myself.") In both cases, use the former when you are talking about feelings, not the latter.

Frustration

Physiologically, frustration is associated with high levels of arousal or activation of the acute stress response (the fight-or-flight system).[37] The fight-or-flight reflex enables us to respond quickly to perceived life-threatening situations by either fighting off the threat or fleeing to safety. High levels of frustration can be detected through increased heart rate, respiration, and muscle activity in the face.[38] It serves the function of directing and sustaining attention, usually toward outside stressors or challenges.[39] Frustration can also be motivational; it challenges individuals to be more adaptive so that they can address and reduce a threat or stressor.[40]

On a practical level, I think of frustration as a combination of anger and disappointment. Often, people with the greatest difficulties experiencing frustration are those who were brought up with parents who protected them from sadness or disappointment or other difficult feelings. Individuals who only experienced immediate gratification of needs, wants, and desires (via lax parenting) or for whom accomplishments and successes (in school, for instance) came easily often struggle with the reality of frustration.

When things come easy early in life, you tend to have fewer experiences of frustration. Consequently, as you age, these experiences feel more difficult to navigate because you didn't learn how to deal with the feelings before. Regardless, it is important to learn in adulthood.

I often watch people give up and withdraw or else quickly

turn toward anger or throw a tantrum when they don't handle frustration well. Psychology calls this "low frustration tolerance." The goal, of course, is to develop the capacity to tolerate frustration so that you can pursue what you desire with greater ease.

Vulnerability

Vulnerability is the most unique of the eight feelings, in part because of its interplay with the other feelings. I define vulnerability as "an openness and willingness to be hurt or to learn." Not only am I proposing two kinds of vulnerability—one that is innate and has to do with protection and survival, and another that we choose to lean into—I am also suggesting that there is a dual nature to vulnerability: it can be considered your greatest emotional strength and can also be associated with emotional weakness.

Non-Conscious Vulnerability

This kind of vulnerability is best explained by the idea of neuroception, named by Dr. Stephen Porges, a renowned psychologist, neuroscientist, and researcher. Neuroception is our subconscious ability to detect safety, danger, and life-threatening situations.[41] It is hardwired into us as an innate, biological protective response; I call it "non-conscious vulnerability." It's tied to the notion that, at some level, we are all vulnerable, all of the time. We can all be hurt. We *all* experience this. We are not in control of it. Vulnerability is never not present.

This type of non-conscious vulnerability is made palpable as we experience life circumstances that change on a dime. The real-life events and encounters that evoke our stress response or alert us that we could be hurt intensify and magnify feelings of vulnerability. Anytime you witness or experience sudden, unexpected tragic or traumatic events—no matter whether you are exposed to them in real life or merely on-screen—your awareness of your own vulnerability becomes heightened.

However, in the absence of such threats, that awareness is generally not something we consciously think about on an hourly or even a daily basis. Yet, knowledge or images of people suffering or dying in other locations often evoke responses of empathy and vulnerability, especially if circumstances in our own lives parallel what we observe (e.g., we enjoy attending big musical events and we know lives have been lost or forever altered because of the shooting in Las Vegas). Consequently, if we are a witness from afar to natural disasters (earthquakes, floods, mudslides, fires, tornadoes, hurricanes, etc.) or man-made ones (gun violence, rape, war, etc.) we aren't necessarily physically more vulnerable in those moments. Instead, what changes for us is *the degree to which we are aware that we are vulnerable.*

Conscious Vulnerability

Then there is the vulnerability we choose to lean into. When we get serious about taking a personal, professional, or social risk, we open ourselves up to being hurt (laughed at, ridiculed, teased, or embarrassed). Think about public speaking, engaging in athletic competition, acting, singing, playing a musical instrument, or sharing a piece of writing or art. Even acting in front of friends in the social game charades can elicit feelings of vulnerability. Embarrassment and helplessness are the feelings most often identified with vulnerability.

On an even more personal level, allowing yourself to share important elements of your personal history requires conscious vulnerability. Expressing disappointment, sadness, anger, or even sentiments of caring and love are all ways to experiment with being consciously and deliberately vulnerable.

I believe that *we are at our greatest emotional strength when we*

> *We are at our greatest emotional strength when we **choose** to be vulnerable.*

make the choice to be vulnerable. When you know that the most likely unwanted outcome of being vulnerable (assuming that the outcome is not success) is that you will experience one or more of the other seven difficult feelings, and you know you can handle these feelings, you are more likely to choose *more* activities or pursuits that elicit vulnerable feelings. It is easier to keep taking risks to pursue what you want.

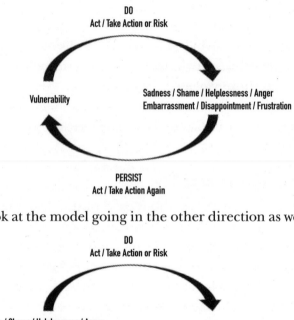

We can look at the model going in the other direction as well.

When you believe you can comfortably experience and move through the above feelings, you are more likely to be vulnerable and take risks to pursue what you want.

Conscious vulnerability, then, is *choosing to be vulnerable.* Choosing vulnerability means you can tolerate the other seven feelings. That is what it takes. Why? Because *these are the feelings that most commonly result when things don't turn out the way you want.* And if you can handle the other seven feelings, then you can handle being vulnerable, whether at a conscious or nonconscious level. It doesn't really matter where you start; it just matters that you start. Lean into the feelings from either direction. They both lead to the same outcome: feeling capable and being resourceful.

Vulnerability and Emotional Weakness

Let me return to the connection vulnerability has to both emotional strength and weakness. As noted above, you are at your greatest emotional strength when you consciously choose to "put yourself out there"—to take risks to pursue what is meaningful to you.

Yet, if you think about or refer to yourself as emotionally weak, it is typically because you are feeling vulnerable in the other direction—in this case, vulnerability is tied to the awareness you could be hurt, because you are not willing to risk facing an unwanted emotional outcome. As a quick reminder, I suggested in chapter 1 that any attitude or behavior that leaves you disconnecting from, distracting from, or suppressing your emotional experiences renders you vulnerable (emotionally weaker). When you behave in this manner, you don't have access to the thoughts, feelings, needs, perceptions, or other streams of information that can help protect you. As a result, you're more likely to *be hurt* because you have fewer emotional resources to respond to difficult situations and events in an authentic and beneficial way.

For example, a woman consistently ignores and plays down the disappointment and anger she feels toward a partner who is insulting her. A couple of situations may result. Over time she may have difficulty accessing these feelings, or, if she can access them—because she is consciously shutting them down—her anger is not available to help her protect herself. In either case, she is likely to feel less capable and more vulnerable (weaker).

Emotional Awareness Grid™

The Emotional Awareness Grid™ is intended to help you become more fully aware of how you respond to your feelings. The eight unpleasant feelings are listed down the left side, and across the top from left to right are categories listing possible responses to your feelings. Place a ✓ or X underneath the descriptor that most accurately describes how you experience your feelings.

Most people have a challenging time with one or more of the feelings listed below—only rarely do I meet someone who experiences all of these feelings with relative ease (though that, of course, is the goal). Some people actually have difficulty experiencing the full range of feelings listed in the grid. If that is you, don't worry; we will work together to achieve such ease.

How comfortably or effectively do you manage—not suppress nor distract from—these feelings? This first step is all about awareness. Go ahead and fill out the grid.

	Over-whelmed by	Act as if it doesn't exist	Ignore	Avoid	Acknowl-edge	Tolerate	Accept	Embrace and learn from
	1	2	3	4	5	6	7	8
SADNESS								
SHAME								
HELPLESSNESS								
ANGER								
EMBARRASSMENT								
DISAPPOINTMENT								
FRUSTRATION								
VULNERABILITY								

Companion worksheets, guided exercises, and more resources can be found at www.DrJoanRosenberg.com/resources90/

Emotional Experience Grid™

Now take note of how you make use of your feelings along a different continuum—from distracting or dismissing your feelings on one end to expressing them on the other. Check (✓) whether you: **distract/dismiss/suppress** or are **preoccupied by** the feeling; are **aware of** the feeling (i.e., sense you are sad and might cry); allow yourself to **experience** it fully within your body (i.e., become tearful and cry); and finally, whether you comfortably and appropriately **express** the feeling to the people affecting you.

	DISTRACT/DISMISS/ SUPPRESS/PREOCCUPIED	AWARE OF (bodily sensations)	FULLY EXPERIENCE	VERBALLY EXPRESS
SADNESS				
SHAME				
HELPLESSNESS				
ANGER				
EMBARRASSMENT				
DISAPPOINTMENT				
FRUSTRATION				
VULNERABILITY				

Difficulties with regulating your emotions contribute to challenges experiencing and expressing feelings. Using your responses to the grids above, notice the feeling or feelings you find difficult to experience and express. What are the challenges you face with these particular feelings? Do you know what makes it hard for you? Write down your observations.

> *You are braver than you believe, stronger than you seem, and smarter than you think.*
> —*A.A. Milne*

Emotion Regulation

Now that you have a better idea about how you experience your difficult feelings and which ones may be harder for you to manage, let's explore what to "do" with your feelings when you feel them. This involves acknowledging, accepting, and trusting your thoughts, feelings, needs, sensations, and perceptions.[42] Once these elements of your emotional experience are in your awareness, you can evaluate, make sense of, and use this information to make decisions, express yourself, and/or take action.[43]

When difficult feelings are present, some people move quickly to disconnect from, distract from, or shut down the felt experience. Recently, I talked with two women in their forties who wouldn't allow themselves to cry, and frankly, hadn't cried in decades. One shut down her sadness and tearfulness for so long that she suffered from intense headaches and jaw pain. The other woman couldn't fully experience her emotional life; she would talk about what she thought, never about what she felt. Once these women developed an understanding of the Reset, each allowed tearfulness to be present; they immediately experienced a quiet calm following the wave of emotion. With continued practice, they also both reported a shift in closeness in their relationships, since their partners now had more access to their inner lives.

For more than 25 years, I've lectured in graduate courses about this idea of distraction away from emotion. One semester, within weeks of my lecture on this topic and the ensuing class discussion, one of my graduate students, Ariel, described how she had been handling her own feelings by distracting and disconnecting, especially from the bodily sensations associated with her feelings.

Ariel started by describing her pattern of watching television: She would change TV channels anytime she began to see anything that stimulated any uncomfortable feelings within her. It didn't matter whether she saw suspense scenes that elicited anxiety, shows that depicted anger or violence, news that evoked empathy, or sad and evocative commercials—anything that elicited feelings (and, consequently, stimulated bodily sensations) led her to change the channel.

The goal was for her to be able to handle her emotional experiences in what Dr. Dan Siegel describes as the "window of tolerance."[44] This is the zone within which you are able to handle and make sense of your varying emotional (and physical) reactions to life events and situations without allowing them to disrupt your ability to function effectively.[45]

Ariel's newfound awareness of her own efforts to avoid feelings led to a significant change in how she experienced and processed feelings—first by just noticing her pattern, and second by ignoring her urges to change the channel when she felt emotional stirrings. She learned to ride the waves.

Ariel was highly motivated to change her behavior. She slowly became aware of what feeling was being evoked and noticed how, what, and where she felt it physically in her body. Next, she stayed with the experience so that she could increase her ability to tolerate that feeling in the future. Over time, she realized she had avoided uncomfortable feelings while watching TV in order to escape reminders of past painful life events but could now look at them simply as memories, focusing instead on what she could learn from those situations. Later, she began expressing to others what was on her mind. She stopped using her habit of distancing herself from her emotions, which had kept her stuck for so long.

As Ariel used the Reset to confront her own emotional discomfort, she began to expand her window of tolerance by increasing her ability to modulate uncomfortable thoughts, feelings, and bodily sensations. As this zone expanded, she found that her emotional responses to previously triggering situations, such as television programs, began to feel less threatening.

Ariel's story is interesting because it involves something as seemingly simple and mundane as watching television. Yet even in this everyday act, she was purposely—albeit subconsciously—resisting even the opportunity or possibility of feeling something she feared would create discomfort. Until our class discussion, she had merely regarded herself as a chronic channel-surfer; it never occurred to her that her habitual channel-changing was really a coping mechanism to avoid unpleasant emotions.

Expand Your Window of Tolerance:
The Scary Movie Factor

Ariel had been too triggered, stirred up, and activated—or in neuroscientific terms, *hyperaroused*—and was therefore unable to handle all the images, thoughts, feelings, memories, and bodily sensations television evoked to function well and maintain her sense of self.[46] She experienced these extreme emotional-flooding reactions in situations that were nonthreatening, and they left her feeling off-balance emotionally.

A person can also experience the other extreme, that of feeling *hypoaroused* or completely numb. Rather than being reactive and explosive, as with hyperarousal, the hypoarousal response is to shut down and still oneself. With hypoarousal, a person might experience an absence of bodily sensations, little emotional reactivity, emotional numbing, or a sense of deadness or emptiness.[47]

Extreme reactions in either direction—especially if these are the "go-to" responses in situations that don't call for such reactions—become maladaptive over time. It's apparent that in both cases—both hyper and hypoarousal—people feel overwhelmed or flooded by feelings; the strategies for handling the flood of feelings, however, are different. One strategy is to be reactive and explode; the other is to shut down and withdraw. Perhaps you can think of people who fit either description. Consider, too, which type of response seems to fit you better.

Many factors influence a widening or narrowing of your window of tolerance on a daily or even hourly basis. For instance, feeling calm, centered, content, refreshed, and energized can help widen your window of tolerance; on the other hand, physical fatigue or feeling emotionally spent may narrow your window of tolerance.[48] Being with people you love and feel supported by can widen your window of tolerance; being with people you don't know or don't like can narrow the window. Holding an attitude of curiosity can widen the window; being judgmental narrows it.

To put one aspect of the window of tolerance in perspective, think about whether you like or dislike going to scary movies. People who enjoy scary movies often say they enjoy them in part because of the rush of adrenaline or other bodily sensations that they elicit. People who hate scary movies hate them primarily for the same reason: They hate the bodily sensations that are triggered by the threat of violence, anxious anticipation, assaults, or surprise. In this example, there is no "better" or "worse" reaction. Individuals who hate scary movies have a narrower window of tolerance and those enjoying these movies have a greater tolerance of the bodily sensations evoked by the content they are watching.

The window of tolerance helps us begin to understand why there are so many individual differences in how we experience feelings. Along with the window of tolerance, factors that impact how we perceive emotion, such as intensity, sensitivity, and recovery processes, are particularly relevant here.[49] For instance, we may experience each of the eight feelings at differing levels of *intensity*, the wide-ranging degree to which we are stimulated by feelings and how much or how little we experience a feeling once we are aware of it. Once you react to a stimulus, the intensity with which you register any given feeling will depend on the amount of neurotransmitter released and the number of neurons firing in the brain at that time.[50] When we feel "flooded," neurobiologically speaking, we are.

Many of us are comfortable dealing with certain unpleasant feelings but not others. By way of example, let's say I'm comfortable enough with sadness, anger, and embarrassment that I don't explode or shut down. Any measure of disappointment, however, leads to a feeling that I am unraveling or falling apart. Disappointment feels too intense and too hard to tolerate in the same way I do other unpleasant emotions.

The same holds true of *sensitivity*—which is the smallest amount of stimulation needed to kick our "appraisal systems" into gear.[51] Appraisal is an aspect of brain function that alerts us to pay immediate and close attention to what's happening in the moment. You'll notice a pattern: Some people respond almost instantaneously, needing little stimulation or provocation; others, however, may seem like they are impervious to anything happening around them.[52] The latter group might not even notice something is upsetting. Some people are so hypoaroused that they are completely numb to external cues. For instance, on a scale of 1 (low) to 10 (high), I notice embarrassment when it is at a 3, and because you don't embarrass easily, you notice it at a 7.

The window of tolerance, intensity, and sensitivity help us understand how people experience varied emotional states within themselves and the different ways each of us responds to feelings. Let's say we are dealing with the same situation: a close friend of ours failed to show up at your birthday party *again*. I react by feeling sad and you respond by feeling angry. Perhaps it takes a great stimulus to elicit an angry reaction from me and it takes a greater stimulus to provoke a reaction of sadness from you. One emotion may come more naturally than another depending on the individual.

And when it comes to "getting over" our reactions, I may

move out of it more quickly and easily than you do. That's what is described as the *recovery process*—the ease and speed with which you are able to soothe and calm yourself once you've gone beyond the boundaries of your windows of tolerance.[53] Deep breathing, meditation, reengaging your ability to reason or reflect on your thoughts and feelings, talking with a supportive friend, journaling, or taking a walk are all activities that can help regulate emotions, decrease the intensity of your reaction, and facilitate recovery.[54]

I've observed intensity, sensitivity, and recovery differences in how clients and others experience the eight difficult feelings. How you feel sad is different from how I perceive it. How I experience and express my anger is different from how you experience and express it. How quickly I recover from various feelings is different from how quickly you recover. And on and on. Differences in experience are deeply individual. These differences make sense given that genetics, temperament, life history, and trauma influence a narrowing or widening of the window of tolerance, intensity, sensitivity, and recovery with regard to how you process particular feelings (e.g., disappointment, anger) and how they affect your interaction with others.[55]

Highly Sensitive Individuals

I'm around a lot of individuals who describe themselves as highly sensitive people or empaths. These individuals feel with great intensity and sensitivity and will often say they not only feel their feelings but also "absorb" the feelings of others. Consequently, they often feel flooded with and by emotion. If you are highly sensitive you may need to develop other strategies for working with emotion. If this sounds like you, you may find Elaine Aron's book *The Highly Sensitive Person* really helpful.[56] Check it out.

Labeling Feelings

Research helps explain why accurately naming or labeling feelings is so important; when we put feelings into words, we actually change our neural responses to the emotions themselves. Dr. Matthew Lieberman, a UCLA psychologist, suggests that affect labeling or labeling feelings has the effect of shifting the emotional state to a thinking state. In his studies, he found that once feelings were labeled, a shift was observed in the brain with less activity found in the amygdala (the fight/flight center) and other limbic regions and more found in the right ventrolateral prefrontal cortex (the thinking part of the brain).[57]

While Lieberman called affect labeling an "incidental emotion regulation strategy" (his subjects incorrectly predicted the effects), intentionally thinking about or reflecting on unpleasant emotions can be an effective way of handling and modulating your emotional experience.[58] Naming or labeling feelings can have multiple effects, including calming or slowing you down, centering you, decreasing the experience of being flooded with feeling, decreasing impulsivity, and increasing a sense of control. It's very effective; these same benefits are observed whether you do it through speaking or writing.[59]

If you have avoided feelings for a long time, you may initially start out noticing that you feel either "good" or "bad," with less ability to distinguish specific feeling states; over time you may move to more general descriptions such as "hurt" or "upset." As you become more skillful at identifying and describing your feelings, you can change your experience entirely. The result will leave you feeling more empowered, emotionally stronger, more confident, and more at peace.

Across all of my work and also in my personal life, I know that when a feeling is expressed or reflected back more accurately, a greater sense of calm follows. In this case, then, it means going beyond just saying you are hurt or upset, as these descriptions may be too general and vague and fail to fully capture what you are really feeling. In order to develop your own language for difficult emotions, start by using the eight difficult feelings as a reference point.

I'll often hear clients say they were "freaked out." More often than not, they mean they were sad and started crying. Yet, some might use this phrase to mean they were angry or frustrated. You can see how "freaked out" is vague and simultaneously much more extreme than saying you are sad, angry, or frustrated. Labeling feelings accurately can make a difference in how intensely you experience them.

The eight unpleasant emotions I have identified—sadness, shame, helplessness, anger, embarrassment, disappointment, frustration, and vulnerability—are our most common, everyday, uncomfortable reactions. They are central to the decisions we make, the relationships we are in or want to develop, and the goals or dreams we want to pursue, yet we go to great lengths to avoid experiencing them.

A wide range of common emotional problems or challenges can be distilled down to difficulty experiencing and managing these eight unpleasant feelings. Certainly, you are a far more complex person than this, but if you have difficulty tolerating these unpleasant emotional states, then it is possible you are struggling in one or more areas of your life, such as in relationships, with addictions, or in taking risks to pursue your interests, goals, or dreams. You may not be struggling with all eight unpleasant feelings at once—in fact that is highly unlikely. At any given time you are probably just facing a few, or even just one.

Yet if you can experience and move through the eight unpleasant feelings you'll feel more centered, calm, confident, and resilient. The experience precedes the confidence, not the other way around. You can't feel capable, nor confident, until you have a sense that you can handle the feelings associated with things not working out the way you wanted. Being able to fully experience and handle the range of these eight unpleasant emotions is the first step to confidence, resilience, and authenticity, and a first step to loving yourself. Loving yourself is also part of living a life you love!

PART II

Avoiding Pitfalls

CHAPTER 4

Identifying and Overcoming Distractions

The ways you keep yourself from being well attuned and connected to yourself—in essence, how you sabotage or undermine your emotional strength—is the main focus of this chapter. When you make the choice to disconnect or distract from your feelings, you opt for the fleeting relief that comes from distancing yourself from an uncomfortable situation or experience. Unfortunately, over time, those momentary conscious and unconscious decisions may extract a high price. When you distract by consistently avoiding your truth—what you think, feel, sense, observe, or know—you open the door to an array of challenges.

Distraction can be identified via such behaviors as denying, discounting, doubting, questioning, and any type of compulsive or addictive behavior (alcohol or drug use, overeating, and compulsive shopping are some of the most obvious ones) or any other thinking pattern or behavior that allows you to check out. The degree to which you stay distracted and the length of time you've been doing it (months, years) influences the types of challenges you may face, which may include genuine body aches and complaints, anxiety, feeling emotionally numb, or becoming soulfully depressed. The key is to identify the distractions in which you tend to engage so you can make the choice to stay connected to your moment-to-moment experience.

When you make that choice, you become aware of and intentional about knowing what you know. Instead of ignoring or tamping down unpleasant thoughts and feelings, you acknowledge their presence. You face and then feel them. Awareness of and connection to your experience are the first building blocks of emotional strength, the very antithesis of disconnection. This level of awareness opens the space for you to make decisions, express yourself, and take action—all factors that lead to increased confidence.

This ability to be aware of and sensitive to your inside experience is known as self-attunement. Specifically, it involves taking in and making sense of information at three basic levels: cognitive (thoughts, attitudes, beliefs, interpretations, memories, intentions, values, and meaning), emotional (emotion and affect or how that emotion is expressed), and sensorimotor (physical and sensory responses, bodily sensations, and movement).[1] The information and knowledge this attunement brings is at the base of emotional strength.

Our feelings exist for a reason. When we deny them expression, we deny their purpose. We must allow ourselves to experience our honest emotions in order to develop the strength to deal with life's challenges. Emotional strength, as I've suggested, requires being fully present and aware of your moment-to-moment experience and knowing what you know. When you see yourself as able to comfortably manage difficult feelings, you will begin to feel more capable than ever.

Losing Control

People distract or shut down when they are focused on having control or being "in control." One might feel exposed, threatened, or in a state of upheaval or chaos if any of the eight unpleasant emotions were allowed to run their course. Even though we have just seen that this is erroneous, and that emotions exist for our protection, we often find it safer to operate under a false notion of control. How many people have you heard describe themselves as "control freaks"? Or say that they hate "losing control"? Perhaps you feel this way, too.

The word "control" implies that something is being imposed from the outside or is occurring outside the self. You may have noticed that certain people will try to control situations or events (e.g., the way a day gets planned out, the order of vacation activities, how closets and drawers are arranged, how things are organized on desktops and flat surfaces, etc.). Or you may find them trying to control others' reactions, decisions, or emotions (e.g., manipulating people's emotions for a desired outcome, trying to cultivate a particular image or reputation, etc.).

The trouble is that people think this issue of control has to do with managing all those external situations, for example, by the way they are perceived or how they conduct themselves in highly emotional circumstances. But the real focus needs to be on their internal life—where all the messy, "out-of-control" feelings are. When the "inside life" seems unmanageable, it feels comfortable to try to enforce a measure of control on external, "outside life" matters instead.

Consequently, I find people are often confused about the notion of control; they think they can control (that is, *prevent* or *stop*) their feelings. You do have some control over *what* and *how* you think (your actual thoughts and patterns of thinking), and over your behavior, but you do not have control over what you experience. What you are really trying to control in these situations are the natural, spontaneous, in-the-moment reactions to everyday life events or situations.

Remember, thoughts, feelings, needs, and perceptions can be managed once they enter your conscious awareness, not

> The fear of losing control actually means *the fear of feeling something you don't really want to feel.*

prevented. In this context, the fear of losing control actually means *the fear of feeling something you don't really want to feel*—most often, the eight difficult feelings.

So, when people talk about control, the issue is usually difficulty experiencing their internal emotional life. They don't want to experience it, would like to prevent or stop it altogether, or want to be able to dictate the terms by which they engage with it. And, often, being out of control or losing control translates to losing "comfort" (e.g., feeling sad, disappointed, or angry); the eight unpleasant emotions move you away from comfort and into an emotional state that feels painful or uncomfortable. Loss of comfort or loss of control can also mean feeling more vulnerable.

When we become conscious and aware of our emotional states, then we have the capacity to monitor, modulate, or modify our feelings and emotions—but not until those moments of awareness. With this awareness, you can choose how you respond to and interpret your experience, as well as decide what actions to take. But you need to work with your experience,[2] not shut it out, shut it down, disconnect from it, or distract from it.

The aim, then, is to help you be in touch with as much of your emotional experience as you can bear. Ideally, you will be able to freely, fluidly, and spontaneously access the emotional information made available through your experiencing and knowing self. You want to be able to modulate your feelings well and be able respond to situations and events in an adaptive and flexible manner.

Disconnection and Distraction

Leah and Cotter, a professional couple in their early 40s, both work in white-collar professions: she works in the entertainment industry and he is a business consultant. They have been married for just over 12 years. They have two children, Jason, who is 10, and Chloe, 7. Their marriage became troubled for a variety of reasons: an intrusive mother-in-law, work demands that included travel and time away from family, strained finances, and a tendency to withdraw from each other rather than communicate clearly. Leah became angry when Cotter was preoccupied with his phone, which was constantly buzzing with social media posts, news alerts, texts from friends, and updates from his fantasy football leagues. Cotter was upset with Leah's spending habits; she binge-shopped online when upset. And he also became concerned with her drinking, given how easily she downed multiple glasses of wine each night. Clearly, they both found ways to check out from themselves and their marriage. Helping Leah and Cotter reestablish a good connection started with showing them how, through all these distractions, they were essentially walking away from rather than moving toward each other. Over time, each made agreements to cease use of their respective distractions, to learn what purpose they had been serving, and to lean into the difficult feelings and conversations that were often the sources of the distraction. Then they could work on the more challenging issues that kept them apart in the first place.

Despite the fact that emotional awareness and connection to your moment-to-moment experience are the most important goals, many people like Leah and Cotter have developed habitual patterns of relating to their emotional experiences in such a way that there is a disconnect between their experiencing self and their knowing self.

Obviously there are countless ways for you to try not to know what you know—in essence, coping strategies to separate you from the unpleasantness of your own experience. Some may seem closely related or even repetitive, but each is designed to address the issue of distraction and disconnection from a slightly different angle; you may not see yourself in one, but you may very well recognize yourself in others.

Journal 5: List Possible Distracters

Before moving into the exercise below, consider what you may use to distract from difficult feelings. Take a few moments to list these distracters—you'll have a chance to see how they match up with the ones I've identified. Perhaps you'll describe some that I haven't. If you're not sure, simply use this list as your reference point.

Identifying Distractions Exercise

In the list below, put a check mark (✓) next to any common distraction techniques you recognize in yourself. If you want to take it one step further, see if you can notice what you are trying to move away from. More often than not, we are trying to move away from one or more of the eight difficult feelings or an unpleasant thought or observation. Take the time to write down what's really going on for you.

☐ *Are there activities you use to disconnect or distract from, suppress, or shut down any one or more of the eight feelings?*
   Working, sleeping, and exercise are common distracters. Which ones, if any, do you use?

☐ *Do you use technology, screens, gaming, or devices to distract yourself?*

One can get easily distracted and lost in gaming, surfing the web, and checking handheld devices to distance oneself from feelings and emotional conflict. Do you get lost in any of these?

☐ *Do you use any type of addictive or compulsive behavior to shut out or disconnect from emotional pain?*

Examples include compulsive or emotional eating or overeating; starving yourself; exercising excessively; abusing alcohol, street drugs, or prescription medications or steroids; compulsive shopping; or hoarding. List what behaviors you tend to participate in.

☐ *Are you overly focused on your body or bodily complaints to distract from unpleasant feelings?*

It's often much easier and more acceptable to focus on your body or express bodily complaints than it is to deal with what is unpleasant emotionally. Sometimes you can use your bodily concerns in a metaphorical manner to help identify what is happening emotionally. For instance, with shoulder pain, what are you "shouldering" or carrying around that might be excessive? With skin irritations, what might be "getting under your skin" or irritating you that hasn't been acknowledged or expressed? Do you ever complain about bodily concerns when emotional ones are really the focus?

☐ *Do you use commonly known defense mechanisms to move away from painful feelings?*

It's common for someone to engage in frequent use of such defenses as denial, humor, intellectualization, rationalization, or displacement. Do you resort to one or more of these? Which one(s)?

☐ *Do you transmute feelings?*

In this case, you take the feelings that are hardest for you to bear and express them as other feelings. Though it may seem like a generalization, men often struggle with the "softer" feelings of sadness, disappointment, or vulnerability, expressing them instead as anger, frustration, pressure, stress, irritability, or rage. Women often struggle with the "harder" feelings of anger or frustration, and express them instead as hurt, disappointment, sadness, or tearfulness. What feelings, if any, do you transmute?

☐ *Do you rely on a default feeling?*

Is there one feeling that you either have difficulty experiencing or use to express all your unpleasant feelings, no matter what they are for you? This might mean that your reaction to most situations comes out one way—like feeling sad, for instance—even though it is quite likely you are experiencing other feelings. For some people, all reactions show up as anger, even though there are other feelings present besides just anger. When a person consistently allows only one feeling to be expressed, there is a good chance that he or she is having trouble experiencing and expressing the other difficult feelings, especially those at the opposite end of the continuum. Do you rely on a default feeling? Which one?

☐ *Do you allow feelings to be experienced only as anxiety rather than anger, sadness, disappointment, or other unpleasant feelings?*

Do you feel anxious? If you are really honest with yourself, you might realize that your anxiety is actually masking other unpleasant feelings. We'll discuss this further in the next chapter, but, in my experience, I've found that it can seem easier to feel anxious than to feel some other unpleasant feeling (like disappointment or anger), especially when that uncomfortable feeling is directed at someone else and needs to be expressed, potentially resulting in even greater discomfort. To be able to experience the genuine feeling that is present at the time you experience it is truly liberating. If you feel anxious a lot, is it possible you may be masking other unpleasant feelings? If so, which of the eight do you mask?

☐ *Do you question or doubt most things you experience? Do you then get into an endless loop of questioning your questions?*
This approach likely leaves you feeling emotionally paralyzed and inhibits you from expressing yourself or from taking action to accomplish goals. Constant questioning and doubt is paralyzing, toxic, and distracts from feeling vulnerable. Make a list of some recent questioning loops in which you were entangled or major doubts that still plague you. Choose one of your doubts, then write about the feelings that seem to be driving it.

☐ *Do you use reasoning as a way to distract from feeling?*
Similar to questioning and doubting, making up explanations for and stories about why something is happening often moves you away from your genuine reaction to what's going on. Do you engage in reasoning, rationalizing, or creating a backstory for something rather than accepting it? If so, how does reasoning or creating a backstory help you?

☐ *Do you feel confused or indecisive?*
Being indecisive or claiming confusion are ways to keep from making a decision, especially if making that

decision might lead you to believe you made the wrong one or to feel disappointed or embarrassed that the results of your decision didn't live up to your expectations. Confusion and indecision are distracters. List any decisions you have been putting off because you feel confused or indecisive.

□ *Do you feel "stuck"?*

When you start to think about initiating a project or even if you've already begun, do you feel stuck? There can be a tendency to pause when you fear being disappointed about the outcome—and then ultimately feel disappointment *because* you stopped. Or you might feel stuck because you set expectations extraordinarily high. The way out of stagnation is to take action. Start something. Commit to it and don't stop. Just keep going. Creating momentum invites more momentum. What project would you like to complete or what goal would you like to achieve? What actions will you take to create momentum?

□ *Do you have feelings about having feelings?*

Do you start to feel sad and then get angry that you are sad? Or do you feel angry, but consider anger unacceptable, and then you feel disappointed that you're angry? Or feel embarrassed that you're disappointed? Having feelings about having feelings acts as a distracter from your initial reaction and most authentic feeling experience. It serves as a second layer covering your real feelings, and that second layer creates more emotional distress and emotional problems. There are countless variations on this theme. Does this ever ring true for you?

☐ *Do you take any of the unpleasant feelings and make them more extreme than they really are?*

For instance, Janell experienced multiple disappointments close together; as we talked, she went from describing these upsets as "disappointing" to "hopeless." She could handle each respective disappointment on its own, but the timing of all of them together felt overwhelming and that's when she shifted to hopelessness. Ted turned his disappointment into bitterness and resentment until it kept people from wanting to hang out with him because of his negativity. Perhaps you experience sadness and instead describe it in a more extreme way. The challenge with experiencing feelings as more extreme than they really are is that the natural and healthy feelings you experience then become toxic. A feeling like sadness can easily turn into an amplified, more damaging equivalent, like bitterness or resentment. Our extreme responses to certain emotions can create internally generated stress. This strategy is paralyzing, debilitating, and leads to inaction or withdrawal. Have you ever found yourself exaggerating unpleasant emotions so they become more extreme? What was the result?

☐ *Do you engage in a lot of negative self-evaluation, negative self-talk, or harsh self-criticism, thereby turning your feelings into a mean or hateful judgment about yourself?*

Many people are skilled at this form of distraction, whereby you change an unpleasant feeling into a thought or belief. Common examples include turning a feeling of helplessness into beliefs that you are inadequate, undeserving, or worthless; or believing embarrassment is a reflection of your inherent inadequacy. How might you be converting feelings into self-destructive judgments?

☐ *Do you compare yourself to others?*

Comparing yourself to others is a variation on harsh self-criticism. It dismisses your own experience because you are placing your focus on others instead. The only positive reason to compare yourself to others is for aspirational purposes—in order to see yourself as able to accomplish what others have done. Otherwise, it's a way to distract from feeling vulnerable, disappointed, sad, or frustrated. With whom are you currently comparing yourself? Do you do it for aspirational reasons or as a form of distracting?

☐ *Are you focused on being perfect in all areas of your life, including how you behave in front of and speak with others?*

If your focus is on being perfect, this can keep you from living in the imperfect (but very real) present and from being spontaneous and authentic. It's an effort to control your responses so others will see you in a favorable light. Do you use perfectionism as a way to distance yourself from your own vulnerability or from any of the other unpleasant emotions? What feelings might you be covering up with your perfectionism?

☐ *Do you focus on one issue to distract or move away from your real concern or feelings?*

I often hear women consistently return to fears that their respective boyfriends will leave them for other women they find more interesting. This concern often becomes a focus when, in truth, they feel vulnerable or are preoccupied with distressing feelings or other concerns that are actually unrelated to the fears they express. Is there a nagging fear that seems to creep up every time you find yourself facing unpleasant emotions—even if that fear is totally unrelated to your present experience?

☐ *Do you pay too much attention to irrelevant details in order to distract from feeling?*

Rather than focus on one particular issue, you might do the opposite and get caught up in paying excessive attention to unimportant details in any given situation as a way to distract from what is really important in your life. This kind of nit-picking can be paralyzing because it allows you to analyze but never actually act. Is this a distraction-trap that you fall into at times?

☐ *Do you use a focus on the past or future to distance yourself from your emotional experience right now?*

Some people constantly run events over and over in their minds so they are *living in the past;* others use anticipation and *living in the future* as a means of distracting from present experience, and still others use *planning and organization* as a way to manage emotional discomfort. Tracie conjured up countless possible disappointing scenarios as a way to anticipate and attempt to have mastery over any disappointed feeling she might experience in the future; the result was heightened anxiety without the openness to and therefore acceptance of vulnerability. Do you ever try to re-live or pre-live events as a way of avoiding the present reality of them? What do you think you might really be avoiding?

☐ *Do you use a "geographic solution," where you literally pick up and either temporarily or permanently leave an area to physically move away from the source of your pain?*

Some people leave the room during an argument to separate themselves from feelings they don't want to feel. Others go to the extreme of traveling out of town to avoid parties or social engagements that are likely to be uncomfortable, or else permanently move to a different city, state, or country as a way to distance themselves from the source of their pain. But it doesn't matter where you go; your emotional challenges stay with you. Can you think of any situation where you have literally created physical distance between you and the source of the emotions you were trying to avoid? What might have changed if you had allowed yourself to feel and then move through those emotions, rather than trying to run from them?

☐ *Do you say or act like you don't care about an event, situation, person, or opportunity?*

"I don't care" is a common reaction to unpleasant circumstances—except saying it and repeating it doesn't change things if, underneath it all, you really do care. It would be more accurate to say, "I don't *want* to care." The emotions are still there. What are the feelings you are trying to get away from?

☐ *Do you project aspects of your own experience that you don't like onto others?*

This strategy is about projecting onto others what you don't like about yourself. For example, if you tend to feel embarrassed about your appearance or socially awkward, you may judge others on their appearance or comment on their social awkwardness. In fact, these are your thoughts about yourself and they represent an attempt to feel less vulnerable. Do you find yourself projecting as a means of disconnecting from your own emotional experiences? Are you aware of this at the time you are doing it, or do you only realize it after the fact (or maybe not until this very moment when it was pointed out)?

☐ *Do you engage in mind-reading?*

Mind-reading involves making assumptions about what others are thinking or saying about you. It often occurs to keep feelings of embarrassment or vulnerability at bay. Do you worry about what others think about you? What do you imagine they are saying?

☐ *Do you tell lies or omit information from conversations because the truth feels too hard or embarrassing to tell?*

Check yourself here. How much do you cover up by lying or omitting information because you're likely to experience a lot of emotional discomfort if you tell the truth? What difficult feelings are you distancing yourself from?

☐ *Do you keep your attention and energy focused on meeting others' needs in an effort to not focus on yourself?*

It is often difficult to acknowledge our own feelings, needs, and limitations. Seeing others as having more problems, more extreme problems, or greater needs allows you to stay focused on meeting *their* needs. The problem is that by doing this, you minimize your own needs, and dismiss and avoid your real feelings and concerns. Have you ever used someone else's situation as an excuse to not face your own feelings and needs?

☐ *Do you use self-sacrifice, an exaggerated sense of responsibility, or martyrdom as ways to distract yourself?*

Consider this strategy a slight variation on the one mentioned immediately above. You are diminishing your genuine needs, feelings, and concerns because it seems easier to think you're a burden to others, or victimized, than to feel the physical discomfort of unpleasant emotions. Does this sound like you?

☐ *Do you blame, criticize, gossip, or complain to get away from your own experience?*

Blaming, criticizing, gossiping about others, and complaining are strategies that keep the focus off of you and on other people and situations. These behaviors make it easier to not be responsible for your true feelings, which might include one or more of the eight difficult feelings—especially those of sadness, anger, disappointment, embarrassment, and vulnerability. They also enable you to distract from your own experience and from taking responsibility in any given situation. Do you ever catch yourself engaging in blaming or gossiping because it allows you to deflect from your own emotions?

☐ *Are you pessimistic, cynical, or sarcastic?*

Pessimism and cynicism are attitudes that result from past experiences that left you feeling sad, helpless, angry, or disappointed. Maintaining a pessimistic and cynical attitude or being sarcastic are *ways for you to deal with disappointment before it occurs.* You hold those attitudes *now* by living with the expectation that things will just turn out poorly for you in the future. It's a way for you to distract from the sadness, helplessness, anger, and disappointment you are struggling to overcome. How often do you resort to pessimism, cynicism, or sarcasm because they feel easy or comfortable, even though you know they can be destructive?

☐ *Do you obsess over injustice as a way to distract?*

Staying wrapped up in thoughts about why life isn't fair and why you have to go through certain difficult experiences keeps you from experiencing the sadness, anger, disappointment, helplessness, and frustration that is underneath those thoughts. What might change for you if you actually gave "full voice" to the emotions that are begging to be felt, and rode these 90-second waves? How might experiencing those emotions fully change your perspective on a given situation?

☐ *Do you use aggressiveness, hostility, threats, or violence to keep painful feelings away?*

Aggressiveness, hostility, threats, and violence are the more extreme versions of blaming and criticizing. The effect is the same—these distract you from your own feelings and experience and from taking responsibility for a given situation. By what aggressive verbal or physical means have you ever tried to keep deeper unpleasant feelings at bay?

☐ *Is chaos a way of life for you?*

Staying engaged in too many activities, being overly dialed-in to other people's problems, and always paying attention to what's "going wrong" or what you have to fix are all ways that keep you from noticing or being present to your own experience. Does the desire to feel needed come from a desire to dismiss or drown out your own emotional demands?

☐ *Do you rush through everything you do?*

Moving from one activity or experience to the next is a way to bypass your emotional reactions to the experience itself. Busyness is an easy distraction; you simply give yourself too much to do and leave yourself with no time to feel feelings—plus, you have the added bonus of tremendous productivity. But you also run the very real risk of physical and emotional burnout stemming from almost manic "doing." Imagine how much calmer you would feel if you allowed yourself to take more time with each activity; you might notice the impact, meaning, and value it has for you, and you might leave room to feel your feelings. Periods of rest or quiet might help you access what is really going on. What's percolating that merits your attention?

☐ *Do you procrastinate so you don't have to deal with unpleasant feelings associated with the task, project, or conversation you need to complete?*

This behavior is common and familiar to most of us. Which feelings are linked to procrastination for you?

☐ *Do you use silence or withdrawal as strategies to disconnect?*

You might use silence or withdrawal to quiet or still your own emotional reactions (e.g., shut out sadness, anger, or disappointment), with the effect of disconnecting from yourself and, likewise, potentially disconnecting from important people in your life. In some ways, this is the ultimate avoidance—but it doesn't mean the feelings have gone away at all. It simply means you aren't acknowledging them. How might you be able to "unsilence" your feelings in order to allow you to move through them?

The list above highlights a number of different strategies—both conscious and intentional and also not so conscious—all in service to the effort of "trying not to know what you know," avoiding being fully present, and keeping unpleasant feelings, thoughts, and understandings out of your awareness. As I said to a client recently, the whole purpose of this book is to "give you back to you." One aspect of doing so is to help you identify all the types of distractions you might use that keep you away from your essence.

Let's make these distractions a thing of the past for you. Instead, let's have you welcome and accept all of you, including all the things that get tucked away, buffered, and falsely protected by distractions. Clear these distractions and you have a pathway back to you—and a pathway back to loving yourself.

I hope you found the exercise illuminating, and I hope you took the time to journal about the patterns that you found most relevant. If any of these distractions resonated with you, please know you are not alone. The fact that there are such a wide variety of ways to emotionally distract or distance yourself illustrates how common and pervasive these behaviors are. The important thing, though, is how you use this new awareness to develop yourself.

Diminishing Distractions Exercise

1. Using the list of distracters, identify all the different ways you keep yourself from knowing your experience (that is, your thoughts, feelings, needs, perceptions, sensations, memories, and beliefs). Write down the ones you use.

2. For one week, notice how you experience and respond to life situations, good or bad. In your journal, describe the observations you are making. Do you tend to move toward feelings or away from them?

3. After those seven days, identify the deflecting or disconnecting behavior that is easiest to change. For the next 14 days, notice when you use or are inclined to use that deflecting response. Track your progress in your journal. In what situations does your distraction surface? Is there a theme to what you are doing? In an effort to re-pattern a new response, stop yourself from using the distraction and instead, ask yourself: "What do I actually think, feel, need, or perceive right now?"

4. Once you are aware of what you might be avoiding, see if there is a new response you can make. For example, I taught about these distractions several years ago during a graduate school course, and the conversation was centered on caffeine consumption as the distraction. This was making some students really uncomfortable when, in the intensity of the moment, one of the students reached for her Coca-Cola can—and then noticed what she was doing. She laughed, and then went on to reflect about why she felt so uncomfortable in the first place (which had to do with the role caffeine played in her life). The new response or "correction," in this case, was getting at the root of the issue and acknowledging it so it could be addressed. What is your new response?

5. Once you've completed 14 days of identifying and consciously moving away from the deflection you've selected, choose the next deflection on your list, notice what happens for 14 days, and repeat for each kind of distraction strategy you use.

Companion worksheets, guided exercises, and more resources can be found at www.DrJoanRosenberg.com/resources90/

CHAPTER 5

Releasing Anxiety

What if you could get a handle on the worry and anxiety you experience on a day-to-day basis so you felt it only occasionally? How would that change your life?

Worry and anxiety are commonly felt by most of us, yet to quite varying degrees. While we tend to use these words as if they are interchangeable, there are differences to note. Worry is considered a verbal thought activity that is negative in nature and primarily focused on anticipating negative events in the future.[1] The purpose of worry is to cope with the anticipated threat, yet worry is linked to avoidance, specifically, with thoughts directed at:

- preventing or avoiding bad or negative events from happening;
- helping someone prepare for the worst if the feared event is unavoidable;
- preventing emotional processing, thus maintaining anxious thinking;
- reinforcing a superstitious thinking style—worriers think that worry is effective because a concerning event did not occur; and/or
- distracting from emotionally charged topics.[2]

Worries tend to have an intrusive quality, with the focus of the worry seeming excessive, unrealistic, uncontrollable, and chronic; when these worries become excessive or intrusive, they are problematic. In fact, chronic worry is a central feature of generalized anxiety disorder, and the effect of worrying seems to both create and maintain the physiological indicators of anxiety.[3]

Anxiety, or anxious apprehension, on the other hand, is described as more encompassing than worry and includes bodily sensations (e.g., heart palpitations), cognitive elements (fear), and behavioral elements (avoidance and escape).[4] Dr. David Barlow, a psychologist and preeminent scholar on anxiety disorders, defines anxiety as a "negative mood state that is accompanied by bodily symptoms such as increased muscle tension, a sense of unease, and apprehension about the future."[5]

These bodily symptoms are:[6]

◆ restlessness: feeling agitated, jittery, keyed up, or on edge
◆ becoming easily fatigued
◆ difficulty concentrating or mind going blank
◆ irritability
◆ muscle tension, aches, or soreness
◆ disturbed sleep: trouble either falling asleep or staying asleep, or restless sleep
◆ sweating
◆ stomach distress in the form of pain, nausea, or butterflies

---

David Barlow's "Triple Vulnerability Model of Etiology"

Dr. Barlow suggests that three types of interacting vulnerabilities help explain the origins of anxiety and other emotional disorders. They include:

◆ *Generalized biological (genetic) vulnerability:* you have a low threshold for the fight-or-flight response so your stress reaction kicks in quickly.

◆ *Generalized psychological vulnerability:* you see the world as a dangerous or threatening place and believe you do not have the resources to cope or master the challenges and situations you'll face; you have a diminished sense of control that might be tied to overprotective parents and being prevented from failing and picking yourself up.

◆ *Specific psychological vulnerability:* you are taught what to be afraid of (e.g., "what would the neighbors think," "never let someone see you let your guard down", "people are really out for themselves").[7]

Constant worry about what you believe you may have to face in the future, or alternatively about past negative events (including reliving what you said or did), is disruptive. As anyone who has experienced any form of anxiety can tell you, prolonged worry actually interferes with your daily activities and saps your ability to enjoy everyday life. Not only are you tempted to give in to it, but worry and concomitant anxiety sure can take a lot out of you. The continuous looping of thoughts, with no end in sight, can be emotionally and physically draining.

Worry and anxiety are associated with persistent concerns about threat and danger, whether physical or emotional. In recent years, Barlow and other researchers have posited that worry, and, by extension, anxiety may help you avoid processing unpleasant emotions.[8] In other words, broadly speaking, anxiety has to do with emotional avoidance.

Clients frequently describe that they are feeling anxious or are "having anxiety." Therapeutically, however, I've found these words fail to adequately or accurately describe what someone is really going through. And, just as anxiety can be experienced in many different ways, people use the single word to describe varied emotional states. For our purposes, I'll use "anxiety" to represent experiences of both anxiety and worry, since any discussion of anxiety also captures the notion of worry.

Your anxiety need not emotionally paralyze you nor prevent you from pursuing your goals and the life you dream about. If you know anything about cognitive psychology, then you know that "reframing" something means looking at it from a different point of view. And that's the goal — to help you understand anxiety from an entirely new perspective.

Naming Strategies to Diminish Anxiety

Language is really important to me, and my interest in words likely stems from playful exchanges with my father throughout my childhood and adolescence. He was quick with words, and the two of us would engage in "pun fights" during my youth. As a psychologist, I now pay close attention to word choice so I can help clients use the kind of language that leads toward rather than away from the goals and dreams they have set for themselves. Which words you use can make a big difference in how you feel, and this is especially true as it relates to fear and anxiety. What you say *matters*.

Differentiating Fear and Anxiety

Though people often use the words "fear" and "anxiety" to describe what they are experiencing, I believe both words are overused and misused. In most instances, when people talk about fear or say they are "fearful," the more appropriate word would be "anxious." Fear and anxiety are different. Remember, the words you choose can influence your decisions and actions. Stating that you are fearful, as opposed to anxious, heightens the perceived intensity of threat and danger and conjures up more catastrophic outcomes associated with your concern.

You may be wondering why fear and anxiety aren't mentioned in my list of the eight unpleasant feelings, especially since they are both so prevalent in our culture. One part of the answer is found in understanding how psychologists differentiate between these two emotional states.

Fear involves physiological, behavioral, and emotional responses to a specific, imminent, or immediate danger in the moment. Fear is adaptive; when there is a real threat, your body's response signals you to escape or avoid that threat. Commonly expressed fears include riding in elevators, going over bridges, heights, being in a crowd of people, or being scared of animals, insects, or spiders; when these fears are extreme and irrational, they are considered phobias. In each situation, there is the possibility of personal harm.

Understand that your response to fear is something that is innate; if there is a genuine danger or threat present, then you're going to experience built-in feelings and reactions that are neurobiologically hardwired into you. Start by noticing what is happening around you. Is there a real threat? Is there a clear and present danger? Is it happening now? If so, then it is normal to feel the urge to fight, flee, freeze, or faint, and it means your body's stress response system is working properly.

Often, however, people experience the fight-or-flight reaction at an inappropriate time; the stress reaction occurs, but there is no real threat nor a clear or present danger. In this case, the person's response to fear is maladaptive. You can think of this maladaptive response as having *the right reaction at the wrong time.* In other words, bridges do collapse, but the chances are good that the bridge you are driving on is not actually going to break while you are on it; similarly, it can put a person on edge to fly on an airplane, though flight accidents are rare relative to the number of flights taken daily.

Experiencing the stress reaction *when danger is present* is a good thing; it's protective and that response should be fully intact when you need it. However, fear should not presage events or situations that involve things not turning out the way you want, which is why it is not included on my list of eight unpleasant feelings. Given that real danger is rarely the case, and because your choice of words influences your decisions, how you feel, and how you see and experience the world, I encourage you to use a more accurate description of what you're feeling. Anxiety is the next logical consideration.

Beyond what I described earlier, anxiety is also characterized by psychologists as a "diffuse sense of apprehension about some aversive event in the future that people believe they cannot control." Fear is distinguished from anxiety in that anxiety is characterized by *the expectation of a diffuse distress or danger in the future,* whereas fear is characterized by *a clear and specific danger in the right now.*

Similar to fear, anxiety is first felt through bodily sensations, such as a fast heartbeat, constriction in the chest, or butterflies in the stomach. It's important to determine whether you're experiencing fear or anxiety. Is the danger or threat known and immediate? Or is it tied to a broad-based concern that something bad might happen in the future, say in the next hour, day, week, or month?

Accurately name the emotion you feel. *Are you fearful or anxious?* In most situations, you are much more likely to be describing anxiety than genuine fear. Even so, like fear, I think "anxiety" is also overused and misused. Based on my clinical observations, I've found that, in most cases, anxiety is a vague description of what someone is facing. So first I direct my efforts at understanding what is really going on underneath the anxiety.

Anxiety as Unexperienced and Unexpressed Feelings

When you distract or disconnect from something that is hard to bear, feel, or know—in this case, the eight unpleasant feelings—your feelings don't just disappear; they often emerge as anxiety. You might feel anxious because you don't want to experience *any* difficult feelings, so you engage in distractions or whatever you can do to keep those feelings at bay, as described in the last chapter.

Anxiety acts as a cover, much like an umbrella. This umbrella is covering your experience of the eight unpleasant feelings. Once you are aware of and in touch with the real feelings, the anxiety dissipates or diminishes greatly. Then it is a matter of riding the waves of unpleasant feelings and making your way through them.

People say they are anxious for a variety of reasons, often claiming they are worried about a specific unwished-for outcome related to an upcoming event or a situation they need to address. What I've discerned, however, is that their worries are more superficially tied to the unwanted outcome; at a deeper level what they are really concerned about is facing the *unwanted unpleasant feelings* that might result from an undesired outcome. They are anxious because they are avoiding what they don't want to feel.

Vulnerability is the feeling people most often cover up when they say they are anxious. Vulnerability, you'll remember, involves the awareness that you could get hurt. Recall, too, that the sense that you've been exposed and feeling embarrassed are frequently linked with vulnerability. *How many times have you felt anxious when you were really feeling vulnerable instead?*

You can experiment with different words right now. Think of situations where you felt anxious, but replace the word *anxious* with *vulnerable*. How does that change your experience?

When you consciously reframe anxiety as vulnerability—that is, as an openness and willingness to learn and/or to feel hurt—these situations often become opportunities to grow, to develop confidence and resilience, rather than just to cause pain. If they work out successfully, you grow from these experiences; if they don't, but you successfully face the disappointment or frustration, you grow from those experiences, too. Either way, your choice to be vulnerable helps you develop emotional strength.

Anxiety emerges in two situations in which people are not expressing themselves. In the first, they stay distracted or avoid difficult feelings altogether and do not express themselves. In the second, they experience the eight difficult feelings, yet they keep them bottled-up inside rather than expressed outwardly to others. When people are reluctant to share or refuse to tell others the truth of what they experience (either by saying nothing or by saying the opposite of what they genuinely feel), anxiety often results. But when people express their thoughts and feelings, the experience of anxiety either significantly diminishes or goes away entirely.

Anxiety is somehow socially acceptable—as opposed to the real feelings that are harder to bear and that, if expressed, could potentially hurt others. Talking about your genuine feelings, whether pleasant or unpleasant, can seem messy and uncomfortable. The key is to become aware of the true feelings you might be experiencing in a situation, no longer use your anxiety as a cover or distracter, feel your emotions, and then express your real feelings as long as it is appropriate to do so in the given situation.

A quick conversation with Derrick, a model and actor, led to a change in how he experiences his own feelings. We were immersed in discussing a provocative movie when he started talking about how anxious he feels at certain times.

When people say they are anxious, it always catches my attention because I'm so intent on changing the way people understand, experience, and express anxiety. In Derrick's case, I asked only a couple of quick questions. First, I asked him how, what, and where he experienced anxiety in his body. He circled his hand all around his upper chest. Then I asked: "If I took all the words relating to anxiety away from you, what would you really be feeling?" Immediately he recognized his feeling as disappointment—a true "aha" moment for him. When we talked again several days later, he described how he could readily attach his feeling of disappointment to a variety of memories involving his father, who had left the family when he was a young boy—memories he had been avoiding and sweeping under the carpet for years. He had used our conversation as a catalyst and opportunity to reflect on a variety of memories, first about his dad, and then about other important people in his life. He said he realized that thinking of himself as anxious gave him a way to hide from disappointment. With this new insight about his own reactions, he found that he could think about and make sense of painful memories with much greater ease and could therefore more effectively deal with disappointments as he faced them. Ultimately he felt less anxious and more empowered as a result.

These moments of realization often become tipping points for emotional growth. They allow us to break old scripts or patterns of thinking and feeling by giving us the proper language and tools by which to define—and subsequently experience—our authentic emotions.

I was several weeks into listening to Sally and Jane, two graduate students enrolled in a group therapy course, discuss their individual experiences of anxiety when I finally wondered out loud whether it was really anxiety they were experiencing. My statement stopped them cold and piqued their curiosity.

First, I asked if they were interested in diminishing their experience of anxiety. They both responded with a resounding "Yes!" Second, I asked each to identify an experience or memory when they felt anxious and to allow themselves to feel it, adding that it wasn't necessary for me to know what memory or experience they had identified. They both chose a moment to hold in their minds.

Next, I said: "If I took all the words away from you that were suggestive of anxiety, what would you really be feeling?" Sally said "apprehensive," and Jane said "fearful." Both were suggestive of anxiety and vague, so I told them they couldn't use those two words. In their second attempt, Sally said "sad"; Jane followed with "anger." I asked each of them to go back to the memory they had identified, and for Sally to feel her sadness and Jane to feel her anger. Then, I asked if either of them could experience the anxiety they had described earlier when they recalled the difficult event. The anxiety was not present for Sally nor Jane, and they both found this change quite surprising.

I asked if the memories they had chosen involved other people. Once again, they both answered in the affirmative. Finally, I asked Sally if she had expressed her sadness and Jane if she had expressed her anger in those moments to the people involved in the situation. Both replied no. Knowing smiles fanned across their faces followed by sighs of relief and laughter.

Sally and Jane had been trying to keep true feelings out of their awareness. These are examples of unexperienced feelings or "trying not to know what you know."

If true feelings are not fully felt nor expressed outwardly, they have to "go" somewhere. They tend to go inside instead of out and often show up as the bodily sensations associated with anxiety. Once you accurately identify, feel, and express your thoughts and feelings, then the anxiety dissipates and a greater sense of calm prevails.

Below are a number of words that are commonly used when someone is feeling anxious or fearful. I find most of these words too vague and I will often ask what the word really means to the person. For instance, in a room of 15 people, I might get ten different responses to what the words "upset" or "freaked out" mean to them. Notice which of the eight feelings better represent what you really feel.

Anxiety and Worry Words		
Worried	Apprehensive	Scared
Nervous	Anxious	Dread
Uneasy	Panicked	Stressed
Pressured	Distressed	Frightened
Concerned	Strained	Troubled
Tense	Shaky	Afraid
Fearful	Jittery	Jumpy
Unglued	Unsettled	Antsy
Upset	Freaked out	On edge
Rattled	Startled	Shook up
Agitated	Skittish	Wound up

After Sally and Jane practiced feeling and expressing themselves more fully, within three weeks they looked and sounded very different, appearing far more confident and relaxed. One of the best ways to resolve anxiety, then, is to experience and express unpleasant feelings. I have since refined this technique to create a variation of the Rosenberg Reset™ called the Rosenberg Anxiety Reset™.

Here are the questions I ask my clients. Use them as a guide to help you understand what you are genuinely feeling, and to identify what you may need to be expressing to others. Grab your journal to write out the answers.

The Rosenberg Anxiety Reset™

1. Identify an experience or memory when you felt anxious and allow yourself to feel the anxiety you felt at the time.

2. If I took all the words away from you that were suggestive of anxiety, fear, or worry, what would you really be feeling? Use the eight difficult feelings as your starting point. (For example, don't use *apprehensive, fearful, panicked,* or *scared.* See the boxed list of anxiety and worry words on page 119 as a reference for which words to stay away from.)

> *If I took all the words away from you that were suggestive of anxiety, fear, and worry, what would you really be feeling?*

3. Go back to the experience or memory you identified and swap your anxiety, fear, or worry with this new feeling (from question 2). Stay with the experience for 5 to 10 seconds.

4. Can you feel or experience your previously described anxiety? (Most commonly, the answer is no; if yes, consider whether you've accurately identified the underlying feeling.)

5. Did the memory you chose involve other people?

6. Would expressing the feeling you identified have been appropriate in your situation?

7. Was this feeling expressed during that situation or soon after?

Anxiety and the "Can I, Do I, Will I, Am I?" Questions

There are a number of questions people ask themselves that provoke feelings of anxiety. These are the "Can I? Do I? Will I? Am I?" questions.

◆ "Can I really pull this off?"
◆ "Can I achieve what I want to achieve?"
◆ "Do I have what it takes to succeed?"
◆ "Will I be able to deliver a good presentation?"
◆ "Will I do a good job?"
◆ "Will I be well liked?"
◆ "Am I going to be able to complete this project?"
◆ "Am I okay?"

These types of questions foster and increase doubt, and doubt, in turn, increases the experience of anxiety. Doubt leads to a loss of personal power, a lack of a sense of resourcefulness, and less confidence.

When you prime your brain with questions, your brain naturally does its best to answer. The strategy for addressing these anxiety-maintaining questions is to turn them into statements instead. Make declarative sentences simply by switching the order of your words:

"Can I?" becomes *"I can."*
"Do I?" becomes *"I do."*
"Will I?" becomes *"I will."*
"Am I?" becomes *"I am."*

For instance, rather than asking "Will I do a good job?" turn that question into a statement and say to yourself: "I will do a good job." And if you ask a variation like "How will I...," change that question into a statement like "I will find a way to...."

The Doubter's Reset

1. Take a moment to ask each question.
2. Notice how these types of questions ("Can I, Do I, Will I,

Am I") feel within your body. Do they foster more doubt and anxiety?

3. Now for each, make the corresponding declarative statement.

4. Notice how the corresponding statements ("I can, I do, I will, I am") feel within your body. Do the statements help you feel more capable, confident, and empowered?

5. Write about what happens when you make that switch.

---

* *Companion worksheets, guided exercises, and more resources can be found at www.DrJoanRosenberg.com/resources90/*

Anxiety is Doubting Your Emotional Strength

As I noted earlier in this chapter, if you tend to experience a lot of anxiety, it may mean that you have a hard time managing the eight unpleasant feelings. If you don't let yourself deal with your unpleasant feelings or you don't manage your feelings well, then, generally speaking, you won't believe you're fully capable of handling whatever life throws at you.

You won't be resourceful, either. As I've described, resourcefulness involves feeling vulnerable, and vulnerability enables you to acknowledge your needs and limitations, reach out to others, and ask for help.

In this way, anxiety can seem almost circular. Difficulty handling the eight unpleasant feelings leads to feeling less capable, and the less capable you feel, the more anxious you become, which makes it even harder to handle the difficult feelings. If you feel capable—meaning you can experience and move through the eight difficult feelings—then there are fewer reasons to feel

> *Anxiety is doubt in your capacity to be capable and resourceful.*

122

anxious, because you already know you can handle the feelings that result from things not working out the way you want.

Self-Affirmations

Who would have thought that self-affirmations could make a difference in easing anxiety, given the tremendous amount of confusion and controversy about them? Affirmations are the positive self-statements (e.g., "I am beautiful," "I am well liked and well respected," "I am fit and in excellent health") that have often been derided as silly and useless. Yet, as psychologists Clayton Critcher and David Dunning believe, affirmations act as a buffer or cushion against outside threats. [9]

Affirmations are more helpful when you are able to see yourself as a multidimensional human being with several aspects to your identity; in this case, affirmations can help you broaden that perspective, mitigate and defuse criticism, stand up to what you perceive as dangerous, and persevere when facing challenges. If you use them already, science stands behind you. If you have never tried using them because it seemed foolish to do so, know that they can help expand your emotional and cognitive flexibility so you can more successfully handle life's challenges.[10]

Saying "I am capable and resourceful" is one example of an affirmation you can use to mitigate your anxiety. It may seem basic to say those words, yet making that switch from a question that raises doubt into a statement that conveys strength and confidence really can make a difference in how you experience yourself. Countless individuals have greatly benefited from consistent practice in using this one phrase.

Try it for a few seconds right now. And with each new or difficult situation you encounter, keep reminding yourself of your ability to be capable and resourceful. Keep rehearsing this phrase over and over in your mind.

Use Your Name to Talk to Yourself

What you say to yourself really does matter. When you talk to yourself (and most people do), and you've done something you feel embarrassed about, do you say something like, "I'm such a dummy" or "I can't do anything right"?

You might consider your self-talk mindless chatter, yet a growing body of research suggests that how you talk to yourself can make a big difference in how you handle your anxieties and fears—and even in the compassion you show yourself. More specifically, psychologist Dr. Ethan Kross and his colleagues discovered that how people talk to themselves has a significant impact on their ability to regulate their thoughts, feelings, and behavior, especially when it involves social situations or social demands.[11]

His most interesting finding is that if you talk to yourself using the pronoun "I," you are more likely to perform worse when faced with stressful situations (e.g., competitions, public speaking, or asserting yourself). Yet if you address yourself by using your first name, you increase your chances of performing better. Instead of saying, "I'm afraid of messing up my dance audition," you would say something like "Jill, you've got this; you've rehearsed for hours and know all the moves. Just chill." Rather than "I'm afraid of giving this wedding toast," you could say, "Mike, your friends love you and you know it's an honor that they asked you." Or if you say, "I'm worried about hitting my project deadline," you could say, "Brian, you know all the steps you want to take, just prioritize; you've never missed a deadline."

When you experience strong feelings, using your name allows you to take a step back and get a little psychological distance from whatever is going on. Just that little bit of emotional detachment can have the effect of allowing you to advise and reason with yourself in the same wise and gentle manner that you would use with a friend. (Fair warning, though: you don't want to use this self-talk approach to avoid your feelings. That can lead to a different set of problems.)

> *Addressing yourself by your first name can allow you to advise and reason with yourself in the same wise and gentle manner you might use with a friend.*

Dr. Kross suggests this small shift in language from personal pronoun to first name can help minimize social anxiety. Overall, it leads to less rumination, a more flexible thinking style, and better performance. It allows you to think through your own problems more wisely.[12]

Just imagine how you can use this. Need to repair a conflict with a friend you have been avoiding? Go into it saying to yourself: *"Now, Abby, go ahead and call her. You've handled conflicts with friends before and had things turn out really well. Just stay calm. And if it doesn't work out, you'll be able to deal with it. You're smart, likeable, and have lots of friends who love you and want to spend time with you. Just do your best. Abby, you've got this."* You can use this approach for a first date, making a speech, or asking for a raise—the options are limitless!

Anxiety and Decisions

Choose Growth over Fear, Anxiety, or Worry

Dr. Bruce Lipton, a well-known cell biologist and the author of *The Biology of Belief,* suggests that we are all programmed for the processes of growth and protection. He describes how cells exhibit a growth response when they gravitate to nutrients and a protective response when they retreat from toxins. He suggests we humans (who happen to be multicellular organisms) behave similarly.[13]

However, these processes (protection and growth) cannot function effectively simultaneously. Lipton notes that growth is a process that both expends and produces energy; thus, "a sustained protection response inhibits the creation of life-sustaining energy."[14] The longer you stay in protection mode (that is, anxious) the more you deplete your energy reserves, which, in turn, can compromise your growth.

Think of anxiety as internally generated stress. Long-term stress has a negative impact on the body, so being able to manage worry and anxiety is beneficial to your overall health.[15] If you consistently inhibit your growth process through worry, you significantly compromise your vitality.

What's more, you can't really be fully engaged in activities of protection and growth at the same time. That's like trying to go in two opposite directions at once. Think of it this way: living in fear leads to compromised health and a protective response from your body; living in love, kindness, curiosity, compassion, and gratitude leads to growth. Focus on holding positive attitudes to diminish anxiety. It's important, then, to pursue experiences that are fulfilling and bring you joy.

If you don't have to expend physical or emotional energy on protecting yourself, you can instead gravitate to experiences that involve growth, namely, connecting with others and being creative. Spend time with people with whom you feel nurtured, or with those who make you smile or laugh or feel enriched. Engage in activities that you are passionate about or ones that capture your interest, challenge you, or bring you a sense of peace. When you feel safe, you are more likely to explore, investigate, exhibit curiosity, and pursue experiences that elicit a sense of purpose and meaning.

Choose Ease over Difficulty

There is a tendency for anxious people to ask "what if" questions followed by negative statements, which ultimately increases anxiety. As I noted earlier, your brain will try to answer whatever question or problem you pose — so if you ask questions that suggest difficulty (e.g., "What if this will be hard?", "What if it takes a really long time?"), your brain will come up with thoughts, feelings, and memories to answer your questions (e.g., "I remember the last time I looked for work, I was so frustrated because it took way longer than I expected it to. I wonder if this time will be just as hard?"). Similarly, there is a tendency to expect that life will be difficult and painful, and that goals and dreams take a long time to come to fruition. Notice how tempted you are to make things difficult, hard, or a struggle.

As you practice asking more positively oriented questions and making positive statements, also practice anticipating that positive things can happen in your life. What if it were easy? What if everything worked smoothly? What if we had fun while working our way through this problem? What if we laughed about all the things we found challenging? Alternatively, you can turn all of these questions into statements or affirmations:

- "It will be easy."
- "Everything will work out smoothly."
- "Let's turn this into something really fun."
- "Let's just laugh at these challenges."

Consequences and Loss

Decisions, by their very nature, imply loss. One thing gets chosen, and one or more do not. Sometimes you experience anxiety over having to face a loss. Loss is tied to sadness, anger, helplessness, and disappointment. You might delay making decisions and find them hard to make so you won't have to deal with the loss nor the feelings it invokes. Instead, you just feel anxious.

Besides writing out the traditional "pros and cons" list that people often recommend in this kind of situation, here is another strategy to consider.

Visualizing Decisions

1. Set aside roughly 20 minutes to sit quietly and just focus on deep breathing and quieting your mind.
2. When you feel fully relaxed, take each available choice for your situation and run through your mind how you see it playing out, from beginning to end. Pay special attention to the feelings each choice elicits, whether pleasant or unpleasant.
3. Consider the consequences in the short term (over the next few weeks or months) and the long term (in three, five, or ten years).
4. Return to a relaxed state and take some time to absorb what your experience of loss may be if you were to make one choice over the other.
5. For each choice you considered, write down the thoughts, images, and feelings that surfaced.

---

* Companion worksheets, guided exercises, and more resources can be found at www.DrJoanRosenberg.com/resources90/

Anxiety and Taking Action

I frequently talk with people who are anxious about taking risks and are afraid of being disappointed or embarrassed. For instance, they might be disappointed about not having more friends, yet they are afraid to exert the effort it takes to make them because they fear rejection and more disappointment. By not pursuing friendships, they are already experiencing the emotion they are afraid of (disappointment).

Anxiety can present an interesting paradox. Often, you are already tolerating the feelings you are afraid of facing, yet absent this awareness you become afraid of dealing with the same feelings in the future. And given that you're already experiencing those feelings, you are actually making your way through them.[16] Realizing this might make it easier for you to go after your goals and dreams in the first place.

Taking action is one way to resolve anxiety. We don't take risks or take action because we have confidence. Instead, *in the process of taking risks or taking action, we develop confidence.* Why? Because, as I noted before, we grow either way. If we're successful, we grow in competence; if we're not, we grow by developing our emotional tolerance skills, by dealing with the frustration, and by persevering to achieve our goal.

Resourcefulness Reset™

Here's what you can do to diminish your anxiety. You'll be writing throughout this exercise, so grab your journal or laptop.

1. Write down three to five specific worries.
2. Choose one and allow your worry to play out to its logical conclusion. With your worry in mind, ask yourself,

> *What's the worst thing that would happen if my worry about the situation came to pass?* Once you have the answer, ask yourself, *If it did, then what? Keep asking these two questions until your worry can go no further.*

3. Write out every answer you have to each round of those two questions.
4. Also write down the feelings you might experience if that event or situation occurred, as well as the resources you might need at each step of the way. Keep writing until you reach a sense of completion.
5. Then, read your initial worry and, one by one, read each of your responses. Visualize each response; see yourself effectively handle the situation, whether that involves your feelings, words, or actions.
6. Address the next worry in the same way. Once you make your way through the entire list, take a moment to check in with yourself to see if the intensity of your worry has diminished.

As you face life events and situations, remember that reducing your anxiety involves handling the emotions you'll feel if something doesn't go the way you wanted or expected it to. What if you get frustrated? Or angry? Or disappointed? Or embarrassed? Start to believe you have the available resources — emotional or otherwise — to manage the situation, and then act accordingly.

So what are the resources? They start with the ability to experience and move through the eight difficult feelings. To do so, you'll need to correctly identify and describe what you are feeling, develop the ability to express yourself with ease, and take action where necessary. (Having the help of others, organization and planning or actual material goods may be other resources you may need to handle the situation.) Each of these elements will help decrease anxiety.

Remember, worry, anxiety, and preoccupation are often distracters from unpleasant feelings. Focus on the real feelings underneath, and chances are that your anxiety will greatly diminish or even dissipate entirely.

CHAPTER 6

Resolving Faulty Thinking

How you experience and express unpleasant feelings is central to building confidence, developing self-esteem, and pursuing a life you love. *What* you think and *how* you think play a role, too. As we saw in chapter 3, your thinking via recall of memories and negative self-talk contributes to the experience of lingering feelings. In this chapter, I'll talk about other undermining effects negative thinking can have on your life. Specifically, we'll address faulty thinking patterns such as cognitive distortions, "Bad Emotional Math™," worry over what others think of you, and the highly toxic practice of harsh self-criticism. This chapter is designed to show you how to clear away, resolve, or diminish faulty thinking. As you learn how to move beyond these damaging thought patterns, you can enjoy the freedom and empowerment that a healthier way of thinking offers.

Your Thinking Approach to Life

An appreciable degree of your sense of well-being is tied to what you think—the actual content of your thoughts. Take a moment. If we were to look at the content of your thoughts, what would we find? Would the greatest percentage of them be positive, optimistic, and accepting, or would we find negative, pessimistic, and cynical thoughts? Are they thoughts that suggest calm and contentment or, rather, anger, disappointment, and anxiety?

If the overall nature of your thoughts is negative and pessimistic, then you can begin reconditioning your way of thinking. Cell biologist Dr. Bruce Lipton has provided compelling evidence that your thoughts and beliefs affect virtually every cell in your body; positive thinking promotes health and better immune function, and negative or pessimistic thinking leads to deterioration of cells and decreased immune function.[1] Dr. Bruce McEwen and Dr. Robert Sapolsky are two of many researchers who have documented the benefits of a positive attitude on health and how such an attitude promotes immune system function and reduces the effects of stress on physical health. As their research suggests, negative thoughts can have far-reaching effects on bodily processes: they can interfere with metabolism and hormone release, which in turn can lead to increased inflammation, disease states, and compromised immunity.[2] In contrast, positive thoughts can release neuropeptides that help fight stress and potentially more serious illnesses.[3]

Research drawn from studies on meditation and positive psychology strongly suggest that an optimistic attitude, positive thinking, holding positive values, and engaging in attentional practices (e.g., meditation, yoga) that are good for the brain all have very beneficial effects on emotional and mental health. It's tempting to ask, "what aren't positive emotions good for?"

If we look at meditation, for instance, the benefits of mindfulness-based meditation practices (e.g., Mindfulness-Based Stress Reduction, or MBSR) have been well-documented as effective in managing anxiety, depression, and stress.[4] Those practicing MBSR report such changes as an increased ability to notice what is happening in and outside of themselves without judgment or reactivity (e.g., letting thoughts and feelings come and go with greater ease); these capacities contribute to and are a result of better emotional regulation.[5] Overall, mindfulness practices improve one's patterns of thinking, help diminish a negative mindset, and forestall emotional problems.

We see parallel benefits with positive emotions and optimism. They lead to fewer symptoms and lower levels of depression; decreased risk of suicide, schizophrenia, and bodily concerns; less social anxiety; and lower probability of drug use. Positive emotions also promote sociability. Being more social translates into more friends, and better relationships lead to greater health, social acceptance, emotional well-being, and longevity; increased energy and vitality; and greater creativity (including flexibility in thinking, originality, and efficiency at problem-solving).[6]

I talked in chapter 3 about feelings being available to us for purposes of protection, connection, and creativity, noting that "negative" emotions are involved in protection and survival. When we're not in protection mode, we can experience positive feelings, which are associated with connection and creativity. One narrows our life and focus, the other expands it.[7]

We see this idea of expansion reflected in psychologist Dr. Barbara Fredrickson's work; she developed the *broaden-and-build theory* of positive emotions, which highlights the role these feelings play in our lives. Fredrickson suggests that feeling momentary positive emotions has a cumulative effect over time of helping people build long-lasting skills, such as musical abilities, that can be used for purpose (career) or pleasure (hobbies). Likewise, positive emotions help people build or develop themselves personally— socially, intellectually, physically, and psychologically—thus broadening or expanding their world. For example, interest or curiosity

> *Positive emotions "broaden and build;" negative (unpleasant) emotions narrow one's focus and life.*

can lead to a desire to explore or try new things; with sustained interest over time, one could then develop expertise or mastery in the area of curiosity.[8]

Since all evidence indicates that mindset has a direct influence on physical as well as emotional health, let's take a look at the kind of negative thinking that undermines your confidence, health, and overall sense of well-being—and what you can do to effect positive change in your thinking patterns.

Negative Thinking

Aaron Beck, a psychiatrist well known for his work treating depression using cognitive therapy, suggested that negative thinking lies at the heart of depression.[9] In fact, negative thinking actually fosters the experience of depression.

Someone who suffers from negative thinking might repeatedly interpret her experiences of her *self*, the *world*, and the *future* in a negative way. More specifically, the attitude toward the self is one of blame; the world is experienced as filled with obstacles and unsolvable problems, and the future is seen as bleak and unpromising, thus only continued failure is anticipated.[10] Clearly, a view like this can undermine your efforts to feel good about yourself and quell your desires to pursue interests or goals important to you.

What makes this mode of thinking so challenging is that it can reinforce and strengthen memories of a difficult past. The brain is both an "associational organ" (matching present neural firing patterns with those of the past, including thoughts, memories, and sensory experiences) and an "anticipation machine" (anticipating or always preparing itself for the next moment based on what has happened in the past).[11] This means that all of your prior learning affects how you perceive and interpret the present. Learning, in this case, could also include hurtful words said to you, physical actions against you, painful memories, and pessimistic and self-defeating thoughts.

Consequently, if you are locked into recalling these types of memories or engaging in these kinds of thought patterns, you are preventing yourself from living fully in the present and from experiencing contented, satisfied, or happy states. Negative thinking only leaves you agitated about a painful past or anticipating a bad future with nothing to appreciate, look forward to, or celebrate.

Dealing with negative thinking is different from dealing with unpleasant feelings, though negative thinking is linked with and often generates many unpleasant feelings. Negative thinking colors the way you interpret everything else and, like the repetition it takes to learn a skill, it generally requires repeated efforts to train your brain to engage in positive thinking.

Journal 6: The Thoughts I Think

Take a curious, kind, and gentle look at yourself. How do you see yourself?

What do you think about? What kind of thoughts predominate? Do you notice any common themes, patterns, or trends?

Negative Thinking Tally

As a place to start, consider tracking the nature of your thoughts for the next week, and in the following week, practice changing the focus of your thoughts.

1. Make a chart with two columns on it, one labeled "Positive/Optimistic/Accepting Thinking" and the other

"Negative/Pessimistic/Cynical Thinking." Here's what the headings of your chart would look like:

Positive/Optimistic/Accepting | Negative/Pessimistic/ Cynical

2. To increase awareness of the content of your thoughts, pause every three to four hours to pay closer attention to what you think about. Track your thoughts for seven days, recording them as you become aware of them. Each thought should be put into the positive or negative column, and for each, indicate whether the focus is about *you* (e.g., your attitude toward yourself), how *the world* works (e.g., obstacles or opportunities), or if it relates to how your life will be in *the future* (e.g., bleak or bright).

3. Also note the frequency of negative to positive thoughts across the seven days to assess your thinking trend.

4. During the second week, if you catch yourself thinking something negative/pessimistic/cynical, practice a mental shift by matching your negative statement with one that is positive, optimistic, and accepting instead. Rather than saying "The event is just going to fall apart, be trashed, or won't work out," say instead something like "I'm looking forward to the situation going my way." If that feels too difficult, then just state one that is neutral, such as, "I'm not really sure which way the event will go, but I'm open to whatever happens."

5. Keep practicing this mental exercise until you have trained your thinking to naturally and consistently produce neutral or positive/optimistic/accepting thoughts.

---

* *Companion worksheets, guided exercises, and more resources can be found at www.DrJoanRosenberg.com/resources90/*

Thinking Patterns: Be Aware of How You Think

It's not enough just to notice *what* you think; you also need to be aware of *how* you think. *What* you think involves the actual thoughts and topics you think about (e.g., tasks you want to complete, someone you want to text or call, an event you look forward to); *how* you think involves your thinking patterns. A pattern of irrational thoughts and beliefs can provoke or exacerbate depressive symptoms. For instance, one kind of pattern, personalization, involves taking everything personally or seeing yourself at fault in situations out of your control. *What* and *how* you think have an effect on how you experience and express feelings, so noticing and changing both can help you develop emotional strength, confidence, and resilience.

The naming of these thinking patterns originated in the work of Dr. Aaron Beck[12], and Dr. David Burns, author of *Feeling Good: The New Mood Therapy,* expanded upon and popularized the ideas.[13] Burns noted that certain types of assumptions and cognitive (thinking) errors people make contribute to their experience of depression and leave them feeling more "bummed out" and unhappy about their lives. These thinking errors seem to foster an experience of being trapped in a downward emotional spiral, leaving one with a poor view of self, no interest in connecting with others, and no desire or energy to pursue one's goals.

Psychologists use the phrase "cognitive distortions" to describe such irrational or faulty thinking patterns. I've highlighted a few that I consistently hear clients express, though many more can be found in psychology research literature. Some of them overlap with one another, or several may occur simultaneously.

After reviewing the list below, start by selecting the cognitive distortions that describe how you think.[14] The goal is to think more positively and expansively. Choose to work on only one at a time. It will take mental effort because you have to be aware of the distortion, catch yourself using it, and then replace your old thought patterns with thinking that is more constructive and optimistic in nature (even if you don't believe it yet). After each distortion, I've added suggestions for you to follow. The more effort you put into changing each one, the sooner you will experience greater emotional freedom.

Cognitive Distortions

1. "All or nothing thinking"

Everything is either one extreme or the other. Things are either "black or white" or "good or bad" — there is no middle ground. However, life unfolds in shades of gray. An example: you're either perfect or a failure. You tend to see people and situations in "either/or" categories, thus not allowing for the complexity of most people and situations.

Adopt a "Both/And" Perspective
Our world is quite complex, yet many people view it from a much more simplistic either/or, black-or-white perspective. Determine whether you approach the world from this all-or-nothing perspective. Here's an example of what you can do:

a) Make the decision to break the pattern of either/or thinking.
b) Notice the times you only speak about or give yourself two options (e.g., *I have to be perfect on the dance floor or I'll look like a ridiculous fool*).
c) Challenge this thinking pattern by generating another possibility between those two options (e.g., *I love dancing and can dance well, so I'll just go out and enjoy myself*) and then two more possibilities between the two extreme

ends (e.g., *I may not be a great dancer, but I'll never see most of these people again; I will get out there for two songs, and if I'm still feeling awkward, I'll consider sitting back down*). One alternative breaks the pattern; generating a few more alternatives develops the skill.

d) Depending on the situation, you can also break this either/or pattern by shifting to a *both/and* perspective (e.g., *I'm glad I danced and am still a little frustrated that I wasn't good enough to win the prize for the most expressive dance*).

2. Overgeneralizing

If something is true in one case, then you apply this same "truth" to any case—even those with only slight similarities to the first situation. The tendency is to draw general rules from isolated events and to apply them across unrelated situations. For example, you see a single negative event as a never-ending pattern of defeat.

One Equals One

If your tendency is to overgeneralize, remind yourself that this one truth or situation only equals—or is true in—this one situation. Additionally, you can ask yourself if you are trying to take your results from this one situation and indiscriminately apply them to anticipated or upcoming situations. Remember, this one situation = this one situation.

3. Disqualifying the Positive

You reject positive experiences by insisting they "don't count" for some reason or another. In this way, you can maintain a negative belief that is contradicted by your everyday experiences.

Accept the Positive

When you disqualify the positive, in essence, you are reasoning away or minimizing nice things said to you. The most important action you can take in the moment is to stop reasoning away what you've heard without any further consideration. If you find it difficult to accept what is being said to you, start by simply and sincerely saying "thank you" and then let yourself think about and feel what it might be like if those words were true.

4. Magnification (Catastrophizing) or Minimization

You magnify or exaggerate details or events (your errors or someone else's achievement) or you minimize the importance of details or events (your desirable qualities or someone else's mistakes); both approaches diminish you and your value.

Track Two

If you tend to exaggerate your faults or others' successes, there's a good chance you also minimize your good qualities and others' errors. These patterns often show up together. If you notice that you engage in either one or both types of thinking, tell yourself you are not thinking realistically. Here, it's about acknowledging the truth that your errors are not so catastrophic and that your good qualities and successes are better than you think.

5. Personalization or Excessive Responsibility

You see yourself as the cause of some negative external event, for which you were not responsible. Consistent self-blame for the misfortunes of others and for everyday mishaps, or relating external events to oneself when there is no basis for making such a connection negatively impacts your experience and the way in which you see yourself.

You, Too

Personalizing is a bit of a challenge and appeals to our desire to be seen as responsible, except it adds pressure and strain. In situations where you are quick to take responsibility *and* the situation was out of your control, notice how you might have contributed to the problem yet make sure to *also* ask if you are protecting others by taking responsibility. Consider what else may have contributed to the problem and who else can take responsibility.

6. "Should" Statements

You punish yourself psychologically via critical statements that include "should," "ought to," or "must." However, use of these words often elicits feelings of frustration and anger (e.g., *You should have this project completed by Friday so you can consider yourself a productive person rather than a lazy failure*).

Expand Your Sense of Choice

Perhaps you've heard the phrase "stop shoulding on yourself." Words like "should," "ought to," and "must" are words of constraint and constriction and lead to a sense that you have fewer options available to you. Expanding your options and sense of choice starts with changing the language you use. You can:

    a) notice your use of the words "should," "ought to," and "must";

    b) replace them with "can," "choose to," or "decide to."

You might use any number of cognitive distortions. The more you use them, the worse you are likely to feel and the more you'll feel constricted, constrained, or trapped in the current circumstances of your life. You can even imagine that each cognitive distortion is like one of the circular rings of a spiderweb. The more cognitive distortions you use, the more you feel trapped at the center. These thoughts can make you feel depressed, and even hopeless.[15] When you stop using each faulty thinking pattern, you erase a circle of the web until there is an opening all the way to the middle.

Marsh, 26, came to see me complaining of depression and longer and longer periods of isolation. Though he had family and friends nearby, he had lost interest in being around them and would only go to and from work for weeks at a time, holing himself up in his apartment. He would usually back out of any plans he made with friends. He was frustrated and bored with work, stagnating in a position he didn't like. He had grown doubtful and hopeless that anything would change. I helped him identify his faulty thinking and see its effects. We were also able to identify his Bad Emotional Math beliefs (see page 150). As soon as he was aware of and able to understand the effect of his thinking on his mood, motivation, and outlook, he began to challenge his long-standing faulty beliefs. His mood lightened, and over time, he reengaged with family and friends, learned many new sets of skills at work that subsequently led to multiple promotions, and was able to return to his musical pursuits, a hobby he loved.

If you can monitor *what* you think (pessimistic/negative/ cynical thoughts and topics) and *how* you think (each of the cognitive distortions or negative thinking patterns you use), and change both, then there is real hope for long-term transformation. Remember, this type of thinking constrains and constricts your experience of life. Changing how and what you think creates options and opens up your life to be more expansive and hopeful; not only will you feel better, but you may rekindle your desire to pursue what is meaningful to you.

When you cease using these distortions, you begin to create a pathway toward a freer and more fully expressed life. Depressive feelings begin to lift, and you are freed from restricting beliefs and feelings of being trapped. You develop more emotional flexibility, an ability to be responsive rather than reactive, and the resilience to bounce back when things are hard. There really is so much more for you to experience in life; you just need to be willing to break out of the old thought patterns that are keeping you artificially constrained and distracted from what you really want.

How to Stop Worrying About What Others Think of You

One of the most common and frequent concerns people express to me is their worry about what others think of them. If this is something you struggle with, know you are in good company; some people get so preoccupied about what others are thinking about them that they go so far as to cancel or decline social events and invitations in order to avoid the situation.

Worries may sound like these statements:

- "They'll think that I'm too fat" (or too ugly, or unattractive).
- "If I answer, I'm going to sound stupid."
- "They'll hate what I'm wearing."
- "If I show up, they'll wonder why I got an invitation."
- "They're just going to laugh at me."

Let's break down these concerns. First, when you worry about what others may be thinking, you put the center of your attention and your emotional and personal power outside yourself and onto other people. You lose sight of what is important to you, including what you think, feel, sense, or need; how you experience other people; and how you experience the world.

Imagine standing in the center of a circle of people and looking through your own eyes at all the people around you.

This is your position of personal power. Imagine next that a number of people are standing around that circle looking at you—and you are trying to look through their eyes before you can look through your own. In this second situation, you are off balance; the energy is coming *at you* from *outside* the circle—as a result, you lose your sense of personal power. This is what it feels like when you are trying to live your life through others' eyes. It sort of forces you to be a human pretzel, contorting yourself in all sorts of ways to make others happy. You end up making all kinds of assumptions about what others like, need, or want. It never works and only leaves you compromising your sense of self.

Worrying about how you are perceived by others can become a preoccupation that simply dominates your thinking. Yet, this focus on what other people might be thinking about you (actually, what *you think* they might be thinking about you) is really just a distracter from feeling vulnerable. The truth is that most people worry about what *you* might be thinking about *them*!

Define or Refine?

Thinking about what (you think) others think about you puts you in a real conundrum. When you are young, you need the observations, feedback, and connection with others to help you develop, and the nature of your connections with others makes a difference in how your brain structures develop and how efficient your brain processes are. As you age, although the feedback is useful, if you rely too heavily on the views of others, you never develop enough trust, confidence, and ease to express yourself.

In the early part of your life, you need a much higher

percentage or proportion of feedback from others to develop your brain and your sense of self. That feedback comes first from your parents or caregivers, then from teachers, coaches, and other mentors. As you move into later childhood and adolescence, parents and other authority figures may take a bit of a back seat; instead, you begin to rely on peer feedback.

As years pass and you move into and through adulthood, the key is to rely on such feedback a much smaller percent of the time. The degree of influence and input you need from others (e.g., being told what to do, their opinions) diminishes as you mature because you feel more capable of making decisions for yourself. In other words, you know and believe in what you want to do and rely more on your own inner knowledge and guidance than on other people's directions for you. You can still incorporate their opinions if they are helpful and relevant, yet it is important to discern which opinions might pull you off track and which are truly constructive and can help guide some of your decision-making. Doubting, questioning yourself, and making others' opinions more important than your own compromises your ability to rely on yourself.

Think of it this way: From roughly birth to your middle twenties, you use feedback from others to help *define* yourself. After your middle twenties, you use others' feedback to help *refine* yourself.

Neuroscience offers some explanation as to why we pay so much attention to what others think about us. Paying attention to others is hardwired. Whether we are aware of it or not, we are *always* assessing others and the environment for safety, danger, and life threat.[16] So it makes sense that you might easily worry about what others think of you.

However, when worrying about how others see you becomes extreme or the dominant focus of your life, it can constrict your life and become quite debilitating. I believe this type of worry is the cause of a lot of social anxiety. But if you alleviate your worry about how others view you, or how you *think* others view you, you can experience more confidence and enjoy your life a whole lot more.

The following information may be extremely helpful for you if you:

- think others are thinking about you;
- tend to be overly concerned with what others think of you (or more accurately, what *you think* others think of you);
- are afraid of making mistakes in front of others;
- are afraid of being ridiculed or laughed at or thought stupid;
- are afraid to take risks;
- are shy;
- hate public speaking;
- can't stand using the phone;
- are afraid of social gatherings.

Let's start by having you answer a few questions:

1. What percent of the time do you think people are thinking about you as you go about your daily life? Notice how I framed this question. I did not ask: what percent of the time do people think about you? Instead, I asked what percent of the time do you *think* people are thinking about you?

2. What percent of the time are people *thinking the exact thought* you think they are thinking about you?

3. When you are busy worrying about what you think other people are thinking about you, what are you missing?

The answer to this third question should be that you miss:

a) being aware of your own experience—what you think, feel, sense, or need;
b) what you think about others and your experience of and with them; and
c) being as fully aware of the world around you as possible.

You can't really know what other people are thinking; you can only guess. You'll know if you ask—and if you ask, you'll find out the other person's focus is rarely, if ever, on you.

In short, you lose sight of your own experience. You take yourself out of the present moment and out of your own experience, which means you can't know what you think or experience about yourself or for yourself. You disconnect from what is going on inside of you.

This pattern of *thinking from the outside in* is mostly just *a cover for feeling vulnerable*. By doing this, you create and subject yourself to a false narrative rather than experience your authentic reactions. In other words, instead of allowing yourself to be exposed, you try to take control of your vulnerable feelings by worrying. Remember, this is really just a distraction from the eight unpleasant feelings, especially vulnerability and embarrassment, rather than any kind of truly beneficial thinking.

For example, let's say you put on a couple of pounds. You go to the mall and all you do is worry that everyone notices your weight gain; you believe they all are thinking that you are fat. Even though *you* are the one thinking about your weight gain, you are making the assumption that everyone else is having those same thoughts.

So what can you do? Below is a six-step strategy for diminishing your worry about what others think of you.

Six Steps to Reclaim Your Personal Power

Using the information from above, let's look at a step-by-step method to change your thinking:

1. Notice the times you are worrying or thinking about what (you think) other people are thinking about you; this is an outside-in thinking pattern.

2. Ask yourself, *What makes me think that others are spending so much time thinking about me?* Though your worry appears to be on what others may be thinking, the reality is that your worry ultimately has the focus turned back on *you*. Even if the last thing you may be thinking is that you're somehow special, this focus needs to change.

3. Recognize you are making an assumption that you know what another person is thinking, or *mind-reading*. You are projecting the thoughts you have about yourself onto other people. Once you are aware you are engaging in mind-reading, remind yourself that you are assuming others are thinking *your thoughts* about you. Then stop and ask yourself, *Is it really likely that they are thinking about me, and if they are, is it likely they are thinking the exact thought I think they are thinking about me?*

4. As you remain aware of this outside-in pattern, realize that thinking in this manner is a distraction from thoughts or feelings that are unpleasant and uncomfortable for you— and that these unpleasant thoughts or feelings may have nothing to do with the specific thoughts you displaced on others. Ask yourself, *What uncomfortable or unpleasant thoughts or feelings am I trying to keep out of my awareness?*

5. Outside-in thinking is most often a distraction from feeling vulnerable. Ask yourself, *What am I feeling vulnerable about?*

6. When you are lost in thinking about what you think others are thinking about you, you have stepped out of your experience of the present moment. Your center of power is now outside of you and located in other people. You need to redirect yourself back into both your own experience and the present moment. Actively shift your thinking style to *think from the inside out.* You can best do this by asking yourself, *What do I need, think, feel, or perceive right now?* and by communicating the answers, as appropriate, to others. This will help you regain your sense of power and control.

Bad Emotional Math™

In my practice, I have found that people often equate thoughts or beliefs that don't fit together. For instance, I frequently hear clients say that failing at a given task is the same as being a failure as a human being. Except failing at a task just means you failed at a task and does not equal or reflect your success or worth as a human being. When a client is talking about what it will take to change or grow, she may say, "Well, I've always been this way"; except behaving a particular way in the past or present does not mean she will always behave this way in the future. I call these statements "Bad Emotional Math."

Consider Bad Emotional Math a variation of cognitive distortions—thoughts that constrict, constrain, and entrap. By using Bad Emotional Math, not only do you lose belief in the possibility that change can occur so you can lead a better and happier life, you lose belief in yourself and your ability to bring about those changes. The emotional effect is that of a narrowed and limited world, absent opportunity and colored by anxiety, depression, helplessness, and hopelessness. So as long as you are taking a look at what and how you think, then consider stopping and replacing Bad Emotional Math as well.

Circle the statements below that most accurately describe your use of Bad or Good Emotional Math. Review the statements that reflect where you are engaging in Bad Emotional Math and then ask yourself what needs to change in your belief, attitude, feelings, or behavior to accomplish Good Emotional Math.

BAD EMOTIONAL MATH	GOOD EMOTIONAL MATH
One bad thing = all bad things	One bad thing = one bad thing
Always was = always will be	Always was ≠ now or future
Always has been = always will be	Always has been ≠ now or future
That's just who I am = that's who I will be	That's just who I am < who I can be
Past = present	Past ≠ present
Past = future	Past ≠ future
Present = future	Present ≠ future
"Bad" feelings = bad self	"Bad" feelings = unpleasant feelings
"Ugly" feelings = ugly self	"Ugly" feelings = unpleasant feelings
Doing = being	Doing ≠ being (i.e. mistake or failure) ≠ (i.e. I am a failure)
Who I am = what I want	Who I am > what I want
Who I am = what I have/own	Who I am > what I have/own
Who I am = what I feel	Who I am > what I feel
Who I am = what I think	Who I am > what I think
Who I am = what I believe	Who I am > what I believe
Who I am = what I do	Who I am > what I do
Who I am = what I accomplished/expressed	Who I am > what I accomplished/expressed
Who I am = what others say about me	Who I am > what others say about me
Who I am = my reputation	Who I am > my reputation
Who I am = what I show to others	Who I am > what I show to others
Who I am = how I think others perceive me	Who I am > how I think others perceive me
Who I am = my parent/child	Who I am ≠ my parent/child
Who I am = my label	Who I am > my label
Who I am = my illness/disease	Who I am > my illness/disease
Feeling suicidal = act/action	Feeling suicidal = difficulty facing unbearable pain

* *Companion worksheets, guided exercises, and more resources can be found at www.DrJoanRosenberg.com/resources90/*

Just to give you an idea about how all of this can come together, let's take a look at how Emmy, a past client, handles her work life. She described experiencing extremely high stress and anxiety, as well as a constant desire to quit her job because of fear that she would ultimately be fired. There is no evidence her position is in jeopardy, as the feedback she receives from her respective supervisors and colleagues is consistently positive and encouraging. Yet, what comes out of her mouth is always negative and self-deprecating; she is the first to describe all the ways her work went wrong; she does not acknowledge any of her good qualities or accomplishments at all. Positive feedback from supervisors and peers is dismissed or ignored.

You can start to see the problems in her approach right away. In terms of *what* she thinks, it is unquestionably negative. We can also take a look at *how* she thinks relative to cognitive distortions. First, her thoughts disqualify the positive. She expresses her thoughts in the extreme, and magnifies the negative/minimizes the positive by refusing to accept positive feedback or compliments. From a Bad Emotional Math standpoint, she also believes who she is depends on how she is perceived by others, her reputation, and what she accomplishes. She thinks she is only as good as the last project she completed well or the last sale she closed at high value.

Every one of these beliefs can be changed. To end some of these faulty thinking patterns, we started addressing the cognitive distortions first, which included helping Emmy understand how lopsided her thinking was: she would only allow herself to focus on the negative, even when there were good things happening in her life. So we looked at the evidence—a promotion, a new title, and more money; an improved relationship with her mother; dating a man she was interested in; and an established exercise routine. Once she got curious about noticing and accepting the warm, supportive responses she received and the positive things happening in her life, she could acknowledge how much her negative focus was fending off anticipated disappointment and feeling vulnerable.

As Emmy worked on her Bad Emotional Math, we spent time trying to understand how she had developed her particular beliefs. For instance, we explored how she had developed the idea that she was what she accomplished; one of the things we learned was that she would only be noticed or praised when she *did* something but would never receive love and acknowledgment simply for herself. As we proceeded to look at each belief and she could see, for instance, that she was so much more than her last accomplishment, she was able to let go of a lot of pressure she put on herself and found she relaxed with greater ease and was calmer, happier, and laughing more. Addressing each belief went a long way in relieving her high level of stress.

Journal 7: Bad Emotional Math

For each Bad Emotional Math belief you have, ask yourself how you might have developed it. Write this down and then write the benefits you have received and the disadvantages you have faced by holding this belief. Also write about what you might have to change or actions you may need to take to maintain the Good Emotional Math belief.

Changing your thinking—and thus, changing your experience—often requires untangling the layered knot that includes what you feel, what you think, and how you think. This is especially true when it comes to dealing with harsh self-criticism or negative self-talk.

End Harsh Self-Criticism

Ending your use of harsh self-criticism—what some call nega-tive self-talk—can make a substantial difference in cultivating confidence, resilience, and authenticity. Harsh self-criticism might involve telling yourself you are worthless, stupid, inade-quate, dumb, fat, unlikable, unlovable, unwanted, unattractive, ugly, or a myriad of other possibilities. It's usually tied to what you might identify as deficiencies or flaws.

Despite some people's beliefs that being mean to themselves helps motivate them, what you do to hurt yourself with these thoughts and words is profoundly damaging. Toxic, harsh self-criticism kills one's spirit, erodes confidence, saps motivation, and depletes the soul.

I use the term "harsh self-criticism" to refer to the mean, cruel, self-deprecating, self-defeating thoughts you think about yourself. Whether it involves conscious thoughts or attitudes and/or unconscious assumptions and beliefs, it is negative thinking that is singularly focused on harsh judgments or attacks on *one's self*. These may include hurtful or demeaning words others have said to or about you that you repeat to your-self and have come to believe. I think of "negative self-talk" more broadly. It can include these self-defeating thoughts along with pessimism as it relates to yourself, the world, and the future; or it can involve a frequent review or rehash of painful memories, bitterness, resentfulness, or grudges.

While most people see harsh self-criticism as a serious prob-lem in and of itself—and, it is—they do not understand that it primarily functions as a way to disconnect or distract from the eight unpleasant feelings: sadness, shame, helplessness, anger, embarrassment, disappointment, frustration, and vulnerability. For instance, sadness and disappointment on their own can be really hard to experience, even profoundly painful. They might also act as a catalyst for bigger problems (e.g., depression), but they tend not to be crippling except in unique circumstances[17]. When you engage in a realistic assessment of your skills and aptitudes—that is, in constructive criticism—these efforts are not harmful. Harsh self-criticism, however, is highly destructive; essentially, you are using your own mind to destroy your sense of self, your capacity to enjoy the present, and your hope, belief in, and pursuit of unlimited possibilities for the future.

I first understood the function of harsh self-criticism when working as a staff psychologist at UCLA, with Jeff, a client who was writing his doctoral dissertation at the time. He generally stopped working on his dissertation whenever he started feeling disappointed and frustrated, either because he couldn't find the right research, couldn't reach his advisor, or struggled with the writing itself. As we explored his difficulty tolerating frustration, I observed him go from simply feeling frustrated to calling himself a whole host of derogatory descriptors like *inadequate, unworthy,* and *undeserving.* It was striking to see his quick leap from the uncomfortable feeling of frustration to such harsh self-

> *Harsh self-criticism is a way to disconnect or distract from unpleasant feelings.*

judgments. My interactions with Jeff marked the first time I realized how people use harsh self-criticism as a way to disconnect or distract from unpleasant feelings.

It's a little circular, but follow the sequence. Jeff's disappointment and frustration left him "feeling bad"; then, because he found disappointment and frustration so difficult to experience, he, instead, described himself as inadequate, worthless, and undeserving. Jeff's experience of himself as inadequate, worthless, and undeserving, of course, leads to Jeff "feeling bad." It seems like a common process people go through. You'll feel bad either way. In this example, then, it looks like Jeff is in charge of the degree to which he "feels bad."

However, when you engage in harsh self-criticism, you

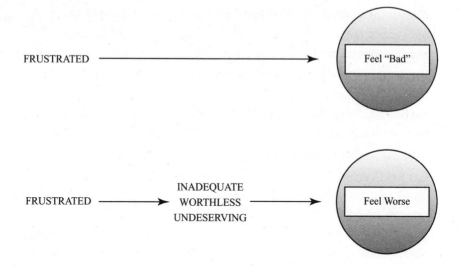

FRUSTRATED ⟶ Feel "Bad"

FRUSTRATED ⟶ INADEQUATE WORTHLESS UNDESERVING ⟶ Feel Worse

actually make yourself feel *significantly worse* than if you had simply allowed yourself to experience and move through the difficult feelings themselves. In this example, Jeff would have experienced his frustration and disappointment, and then figured out the next steps to take to address his feelings and resolve the situations.

As I described earlier, you are not in control of *what* you feel or *that* you feel until it is in your conscious awareness. Since most people don't like feeling something unpleasant that they cannot control (e.g., frustration, or Jeff's "feeling bad"), many resort to harsh, punitive, critical, or cruel self-talk or self-evaluation at the first indication of unpleasant feelings.

What's the effect of *thinking* in such a negative manner over an extended period of time? Simply put, you don't just end up feeling bad; *instead, you end up feeling markedly worse.* Initially, it seems to mimic the same kind of "bad" feeling you experience when you first start to feel anything unpleasant about your situation, but harsh self-criticism ends up taking you to a much darker and more painful place from which an exit seems long, arduous, or impossible.

Other than riding the 90-second waves of feelings once they arise, you have no way to prevent and control those spontaneous unpleasant feelings, no matter how much you would like to do so. However, you do have some control over what and how you think, which means you have control over what you think about, what you say to yourself, and how you evaluate yourself. The element to keep in mind here is that you're not in control of your feelings but you *are* in charge of your thoughts.

Let's take this idea one step further. When you put yourself down, it *looks like* you can be in control of just how bad you'll feel because you are in charge of your self-critical thoughts, when you start and stop thinking them, how frequently you think them, the intensity with which you think them, and the length of time you think them. I call this the "delusion of control," because all the ways you can be in charge of your self-critical thoughts (e.g., frequency, intensity) make it *appear* as if you are in charge of an experience (your spontaneous reaction of feeling disappointed or frustrated) that you had no control over.

Not only does harsh self-criticism act as a thought-hijack of unpleasant feelings after something hasn't worked out the way you desired, but, much like anxiety, it can also act in a preemptive manner. In this case, your harsh self-criticism shows up as *self-doubt,* thus inhibiting you from pursuing what is important to you. Due to your own doubt, you hold yourself back and are reluctant to take risks.

I see negative self-evaluation or harsh self-criticism as a rather elegant yet profoundly destructive strategy for disconnecting or distracting from the eight unpleasant feelings. Some researchers have described it as a strategy for safety and self-protection.[18] In an odd sort of way, your harsh self-criticism may protect you from the critiques of others, but it also prevents you from fully expressing yourself with others, or in life.

End Your Harsh Self-Criticism

What can you do to end your own harsh self-criticism?

1. Become more aware of your harsh self-criticism or negative self-talk. Understand that each time you talk to yourself this way, you are using harsh self-criticism as a way to disconnect and distract from painful or unpleasant feelings.

2. Use your awareness of harsh self-criticism as a signal that something harder to feel, know, or bear is trying to make itself known to you.

3. Ask yourself, *What is difficult for me to know, feel, or bear right now?* and invite it more fully into your conscious awareness.

4. If painful feelings surface, take several deep, slow breaths and then ride those 90-second waves.

5. As you move through your feelings, notice any insights that surface (e.g., realizing you are angry and needing to express your anger to resolve a conflict).

6. Make use of the insights for decision-making, to express yourself, or to take action.

7. Approach yourself with more kindness and compassion.[19]

8. Deepen your understanding by asking yourself what you can learn from what you are experiencing.

Feeling Inadequate, Stupid, Unworthy, and Undeserving

I talked earlier about the importance of the words you choose to use, and as it relates to our discussion about harsh self-criticism,

I want to make one final distinction about words that get mis-taken for "feeling" words. Specifically, I am referring to words such as "inadequate," "unworthy," "undeserving," "stupid," or other similar words people use to describe what they are feeling.

What is important to note is that these are not words that describe how one is *feeling;* instead, they are evaluative, compar-ative, or judgmental words. When we evaluate, compare, or judge, we are *thinking,* not feeling. If you use these words, the upshot is that you think you are describing how you feel, but you are really engaged in harsh self-criticism and just making your-self feel worse.

Consider the possible feelings underneath these words. For instance, "stupid" and "ugly" may hide feelings of embarrass-ment and shame. "Inadequate" may suggest embarrassment, shame, disappointment, or helplessness.

"Unworthy" and "undeserving" carry a different kind of weight with even more serious implications—these evaluative words seemingly question whether or suggest that you may not be deserving of good things or, carried to the extreme, that you may not even be worthy of life.

These words, too, often get mixed up with the experience of shame—and the *belief* that one is inadequate, defective, flawed, damaged, or bad. It's a common aspect of our shared humanity to think this way.[20] We know that these types of beliefs often orig-inate early in life and are associated with trauma, and in chapter 8, I will provide you with a framework to help you address them.

If you have these beliefs about yourself, consider:

- when the beliefs started,
- who initially said those words to you,
- whose voice you hear saying the words to you in the present
- which of the eight difficult feelings are associated with these beliefs, and

◆ whether or not these beliefs might be preventing you from moving forward in life.

If these beliefs remain active over a long period of time, we can view them as distracters that keep you disconnected from your feelings, stuck in the past, and prevented from living the life you would love to create for yourself.

There's one more thought I'd like to add here. As humans, I don't think we get to decide whether we are worthy or not; by virtue of being alive, we are deserving and worthy. I hope you'll consider this possibility.

I am encouraging you to develop a different relationship with yourself and am inviting you to be your own best friend. Negative thinking, cognitive distortions, worrying about what others think of you, Bad Emotional Math, and harsh self-criticism keep you from that goal and leave you a stranger to yourself.

You might not want to deal with these thoughts, yet engaging in consistent practice recognizing and rectifying your negative thinking, cognitive distortions, and Bad Emotional Math; centering yourself in inside-out thinking; and ending the destructive force of harsh self-criticism are necessary for creating a loving relationship with yourself.

Clearing these challenges in thinking will open a space for you to be connected to your genuine feelings. All it takes is one choice to experience and ride the waves of unpleasant feelings, and you can dramatically change your way of relating with the world.

PART III

Benefits

CHAPTER 7

Speaking Your Truth

How often are we told to speak up, whether in situations of conflict or appreciation? We sense that it's important to do so, but what is so imperative about us speaking our minds? What difference does it really make?

Speaking your mind with ease—to say what you want to say, with whom, where, when, and how you want to say it—involves using your voice by your own choice. It means speaking your truth. Having the ability to express yourself with ease is, without question, one of the most significant factors in developing emotional strength, unwavering confidence, high self-esteem, and an overall sense of well-being. You tend to be less emotionally reactive to challenging life events when you are able to speak your mind in the moment. Likewise, having the ability to be a great listener deepens your connections with everyone—and especially with the most important people in your life, whether family members, partners, spouses, children, mentors, colleagues, bosses, or close friends.

Language, generally considered tied to the brain's left hemisphere, allows you to put words to your experience, which, in turn, is tied to the right hemisphere. As this linking and crossover takes place, the brain becomes more integrated.[1] So, putting words to your experiences and feelings—whether in the privacy of your own thoughts, through words splashed on a page, or through speech expressed to others—helps you to handle your feelings more effectively. Additionally, as Dr. Dan Siegel suggests, an integrated brain leads to greater emotional health and well-being, the outcome of which is a greater sense of harmony, emotional flexibility, kindness, and compassion.[2]

Your voice is a link to your mind. It enables your internal world—thoughts, feelings, ideas, beliefs, memories, perceptions, needs, desires, and sensations—to be communicated. That's what I want you to be able to do: think about and then comfortably express your words, though not just to yourself. The people who you care about will benefit, too.

Perhaps it's already easy for you to express yourself. If so, that's great. Or maybe you are reluctant to talk because you were told, "You've got nothing to offer. Don't open your mouth and make yourself look stupid. Just sit there and look pretty." You could be someone who wonders, "Why would anyone want to listen to me? What do I have of value? What could I possibly add to the conversation?" Ironically, you may not know the answers to these questions because you haven't yet shared with others much about your life. You might not have a good read on what's significant about you because no one, or only a few people, ever had a chance to learn about and respond to your experiences.

Maybe it seems like it doesn't matter if you don't share because it's "only" your life, so what's the big deal? Yet when you think this way, you minimize the importance and effect your

You have no idea what will touch and impact other people until you open up.

experiences have had on you. Here's the point: *If it's important to you, it will be important to others.* You have no idea what will touch and impact other people until you open up.

That's exactly what happened to Renee, who was enrolled as a student in my counseling skills practicum class as part of the requirement for her master's degree. Nearly 20 years my senior, she was studying to be a professional counselor and could easily have been mistaken for the professor save for one glaring issue: Renee rarely spoke in class, and when she did, she was barely audible.

Our individual supervision sessions were the same. Even though the room was small and we sat directly across from each other, I had to lean in to hear her. How could she help clients when she couldn't be heard?

After a few sessions, I asked, "Has anyone ever spoken with you about the strength and volume of your voice?"

"No, though I've spoken this way a long time," she answered, very softly. Then she added, "I just think that what I'm saying doesn't matter that much."

I described how important it was for her to speak up and how it could make a difference to the people she wanted to help. Speaking up went well beyond speaking louder; it also meant letting people hear what she was thinking and feeling.

Renee began using her full voice only with me, starting with a basic exercise I call "Turning Up the Volume of Your Thoughts." Like other students and clients to whom I suggest this, Renee said that she wouldn't know what to say.

I rarely accept this statement outright because, in my experience, most people have thoughts in mind and know what they want to say. Countless thoughts constantly swirl inside our heads, like our own personal radio show broadcasting within. We might hear snippets of songs, provide running commentary about things we see, or replay old arguments—and that's the short list. It's not surprising that we keep our thoughts to ourselves since it's been deeply ingrained in us to "think before you speak." The trouble is we stop at the thinking part and never get to the speaking!

"Imagine that your thoughts are songs. Right now, you have the earbuds plugged in; only you can hear the songs," I suggested. "Now, to share the 'song' of your thoughts, put it on speaker, turn up the volume, and share that 'music' with others."

Encouraged, Renee made a commitment to change her volume and speak up more in class. She then took it a step further, bravely asking the class to let her know if her voice was too low or if those on the other side of the room couldn't hear her. The other students agreed and helped her learn that expressing herself at a good volume was effective for them as listeners.

Within six weeks, Renee literally sounded like a different person. She also began acting like one. She related several insights to the class, including a realization that her muted voice was just one aspect of a bigger life pattern. At the end of the semester she said, "My handwriting has always been really hard to read. I realized that messy notes were an excuse for not doing well on exams. I've cleaned up my writing and am taking responsibility for getting better grades. As the organist at my church, I also used to skip playing most of the difficult chord arrangements; now I just play through them as best I can. And speaking more confidently with my family has been pivotal; it has changed how we relate as a family and has brought us much closer."

Turning Up the Volume of Your Thoughts

1. Be aware of what you are thinking yet are reluctant to share.
2. Imagine that your thoughts are songs.
3. Without speaking, it's as if you have earbuds plugged in; only you can hear the songs.

4. To share the "song" of your thoughts, put it on speaker, turn up the volume, and share the "music" (your thoughts) with others.

---

* *Companion worksheets, guided exercises, and more resources can be found at www.DrJoanRosenberg.com/resources90*

Through all my years of clinical practice, I've found that speaking your truth is *singularly* the most important action you can take to cultivate confidence, authenticity, and resilience. The changes are profound—better brain health,[3] confidence, deeper relationships, impact and influence on others, and limitless opportunities depending on what you ask for or say. Yet it's hard to imagine any of those possibilities if you can't seem to get the words out.

> *Speaking your truth is singularly the most important action you can take to cultivate confidence, authenticity, and resilience.*

Feeling Trapped Inside Yourself

Mona, 34, was in a strained relationship with her boyfriend, Tim. She counted on a few strategies to get past difficult moments with him because of how uncomfortable she felt speaking up. She would either shut down or just ask Tim questions rather than stating what she wanted to say; she didn't believe she was important enough to voice her concerns. Both approaches left Tim confused and frustrated. When these strategies ceased to work, Mona became concerned about where their relationship was headed.

Mona didn't want to risk stating her feelings and desires. She was afraid of both being hurt by Tim and hurting Tim. Consequently, she measured every word she said, so a spontaneous, off-the-cuff, easy conversation seemed a distant goal. She counted on Tim's "mind-reading" ability to understand what she really wanted. By not speaking the truth of her experience, she was excluding the very thoughts and feelings needed to create and sustain a caring and loving relationship.

I often watch women pose their thoughts as questions rather than saying what they are really thinking and what they really mean. For example, Mona might say something like, "Tim, do you want to go to Jack and Dina's barbecue next weekend?" or "Tim, what do you think we should spend on your cousin's wedding gift?" when Mona already knows what she is thinking, wants to do or spend. Asking questions when you know what you want lends itself to misunderstandings and possible unnecessary disagreements.

It's confusing for the listener, especially for men, who tend to prefer directness. It can feel more vulnerable to make a statement and say what you want to say rather than asking a question, yet there's no way to feel whole inside or well-grounded if you keep all of you out of the relationship by not telling the truth. When you reverse that, you'll be comfortable in your own skin. When you speak your truth, you can experience remarkable shifts within yourself as well as in your relationships.

Mona slowly started letting Tim know what she thought and felt. In one of our later sessions, she told me, "Once I understood that I could say what I really meant, something lifted inside me. I felt lighter, more centered, and stronger. Tim said he had no idea of how I really felt and the impact he was having on me. Our connection has deepened. We still argue, but I sure don't feel trapped inside myself anymore when we do."

> *If you know what you want to say, consider making a statement rather than asking a question.*

For Mona, speaking up felt like too much of a risk, so she simply avoided it. The result was a strained relationship due to an absence of ease and lack of genuine emotional intimacy. Mona is not alone. Because the concept is so scary to many of us, we often try to convince ourselves that we are saying what we believe, even when we know deep down that this isn't true. So how do we know when we are actually speaking our truth, rather than faking it or even suppressing it altogether?

The Prime 17™: Signs You're Not Speaking Your Truth

You can begin to answer that question by taking a close look at what I call "The Prime 17™": 17 indicators that you are not truly speaking up, despite what you might be telling yourself. I encourage you to really study this list so that you are familiar enough with it to recognize patterns when they arise. Think of these as warning lights on your dashboard; when you notice one is activated, immediately assess the situation to see where the disconnect or incongruence between your feelings and your words might be. Circle the ones that relate to you.

1. You feel trapped.
2. You feel like you are always holding thoughts and feelings back.
3. In a group conversation, you remain quiet and seemingly unnoticed.
4. You're not sure of your own opinion.
5. You say, "I don't know," "I'm confused," "Nothing's wrong, I'm fine," "I don't care," "It doesn't matter," "I'm/everything's okay," or "It's up to you" a lot, which allows you to back away from your true reactions and responsibilities.
6. At work, school, or in social settings, there are things you want to say, but you hold yourself back from contributing to the discussion.

7. You don't share what is important to you with anyone.

8. You believe that people won't think much of what you have to say.

9. You're concerned people will laugh at you, think you're stupid, judge you, ridicule you, or ostracize you.

10. When you speak, your heart races, your body gets warm, your palms get sweaty, and/or your face turns bright red with embarrassment.

11. You hear yelling inside your head, but you do not articulate these thoughts or feelings.

12. The people closest to you don't know what you really feel, including when you're disappointed, proud, or excited about your life experiences.

13. If you're in a relationship, you "protect" your partner and the relationship from your true feelings by not speaking up.

14. You don't ask family or friends for help.

15. Even if you are clear about what you think, feel, need, or want, you ask questions instead of making statements.

16. You're disconnected from your feelings and therefore unable to express them.

17. When people tell you what a great, cool, neat, sweet, special, (fill in the blank) person you are, you say to yourself immediately afterward, "Yes, but if you only knew the real me, you wouldn't say that."

That last point is what I call the "Hollow Chocolate Easter Bunny Complex." Chocolate bunnies look so appealing on the outside, but there is only air inside. They're empty. That's how you might feel when you don't speak your truth. No number of compliments, hard work, or serving others will fill you up because *you know* the truth of who you are hasn't been expressed. You're the chocolate shell of yourself.

Perhaps this "Hollow Bunny Complex" has a familiar ring to it. You might recognize it as Imposter Syndrome, which has frequently been characterized as a pervasive feeling of self-doubt or insecurity fueled by an unrelenting fear that you will be exposed as a fraud despite countless accomplishments and extensive evidence to the contrary.[3] Difficulty, reluctance, or refusal to speak up contributes to Imposter Syndrome.

Going forward, we will build your expressive strength to help you become an authentic and whole person who recognizes the depth and substance that others see when they pay you compliments. Metaphorically speaking, you will become a *solid* chocolate bunny, which in part means being able to confront others when necessary. But first, you need to honestly examine what might be holding you back.

The Loss Factor

If you state the truth of what you feel, you may fear that others might respond in any number of relationally undesirable ways: they may see you in a less favorable light, think you're a "bad" person because of the "bad" feelings you expressed, have their feelings hurt, not like you anymore, or leave. Perhaps you are concerned about being seen as an imposter, a fraud, or an unknowledgeable person if you speak up, and you will be booted out of a significant group of friends, a clique, or a job, or you will lose your professional standing. Maybe you simply aren't sure what to say, fear being judged, or believe that what you have to say doesn't matter. Anticipating loss of any kind (e.g., relationships, connections, membership, reputation, status, prestige, money, respect, or opportunities) can become an obstacle to truthful conversations. And you might feel incapable of handling the anticipated loss. Yet if you know you can experience and move through the eight difficult feelings, you will be able to speak effectively and also be able to handle any subsequent loss.

The Importance of Speaking

Let's dispel some misconceptions. You—and your words—matter; as I described, you'll experience this when others hear what you have to say. "Bad" (unpleasant) feelings do not equal a bad self; they merely equal unpleasant feelings. Thoughts and feelings spoken in a *conscientious, kind, well-intentioned,* and *curious* manner tend to bring people closer; they don't push them away. Maybe you believe you must know yourself and be fully informed before speaking. That's not true either. These beliefs are generally linked with efforts to not feel vulnerable, helpless, or embarrassed.

It's not that you fully know yourself and then speak. Nor is it that you are confident and then you speak. Rather, *it is through speaking that you come to deeply discover who you actually are; and, as you speak, you develop confidence.* Most people don't realize these truths.

And what about concerns that others may leave you if you assert yourself? The hard truth is that *you* leave you when you don't say what you really mean.

When you don't speak up, you disconnect from yourself and become less emotionally present. You live with an experience of disappointment that shows up mostly as harsh self-criticism or self-attack, as discussed in the previous chapter. Speaking up is one way to remedy this. Also, when you don't speak up, it makes it difficult to be authentic, and to be your own best friend—much less to enjoy the kind of deep friendships where you don't question whether others mean what they say, including compliments they give you. When you say what you mean, you stay centered and emotionally present, not preoccupied with disappointment or anger at yourself or resentful and bitter toward another because you didn't speak up.

The ability to express yourself is tied to inside-out thinking, which, as I've mentioned, involves communicating *your* experience—what *you* think, feel, need, want, or perceive— while being mindful of the needs and rights of others. Outside-in thinking (worry about what others think of you, concerns about feeling vulnerable) creates a mental barrier to speaking with ease.

It feels liberating to say what you want to say, with whom, and when you want to say it. Because you are speaking what you already know and feel, you don't have to be as considered or calculated with your language. Words come easily, giving you the ability to be assertive, effective, and spontaneous. Using your voice with clear intention helps you become more of who you are, as well as who you are destined to be.

In order to speak what you know, you must make the choice to feel one or more 90-second waves of one or more of those unpleasant feelings. When you are able to effectively tolerate your unpleasant feelings and choose to speak your truth in the midst of them, you have integrated the Rosenberg Reset into your everyday functioning.

"You don't know what my mother is like," Kate, a 41-year-old high school teacher and patient said. "She's got a black belt in meanness and could teach a master class in cruelty. I call her the 'Sensei of Sarcasm.' When she speaks to me, I'm left speechless and way too afraid to reply. What can I do?"

In the ideal situation, when you are speaking to another, first and foremost, you want to direct your intent and efforts at communicating clearly, kindly, and honestly; a second important consideration is to direct your intent and efforts to understanding the other person's point of view, so you can create deeper connections. A healthy relationship involves being on the same team, not opposing sides where you are in frequent battle. If you view the relationship as oppositional or contentious, your exchanges will involve finding out who is right and who is wrong, or to whom the blame is due. As a result, conversations just become "win-lose" situations.

It can, admittedly, be a challenge to stay focused on being on the same team with the same desired outcome—increased understanding and connection—when those you speak to make the situation contentious. Others' words may cause us harm, and family members, friends, or colleagues may use what we say against us. Let's be realistic. It does make it worse when we feel we can't answer in kind.

But, as hurtful as words can be when they are leveled at and against us, they can also potentially protect us from mental, emotional, or bodily pain when we use them to speak to others. Self-defense classes even teach people to use words as a protective strategy to prevent, de-escalate, or end hurtful acts. So, it's really important to learn how to respond. Using one's voice should not be employed for any kind of mean, cruel, or hostile purpose unless you face real danger or your life is threatened. Rather, the emphasis is on *telling the well-intentioned truth* when you speak to another.

By well-intentioned truth, I mean delivering with warmth, care, and genuineness the kind of truth that invites us to be better—more than we are now. It's the kind of truth that resonates inside each of us. You'll feel calmer, stronger, and more confident when you acknowledge what you know to be true and speak that truth to another. Though it may be unsettling at times, you will feel clearer when you speak the sincere, well-intentioned truth or hear it spoken to you by someone else.

Kate kept tackling her hesitation to stand up to her mother to put a stop to her cruel comments. But she finally arranged a time to talk to her mother. As she said to me, "I finally told my mom how insensitive and hurtful her statements are. She heard me, though I'm not sure how much she took in or if she'll change. But just getting the words out left me feeling so much stronger and better about myself."

What Kate came to realize is that the actual expression of your thoughts, feelings, and needs, and the ability to handle the other person's response, builds confidence and emotional strength. When she felt able to experience her emotions fully and express them honestly, she suddenly felt emboldened to stand up for her-self and her own opinions, and become her own defender and advocate.

> *The actual expression of your thoughts, feelings, and needs, and the ability to handle the other person's response, builds confidence and emotional strength.*

I'm frequently asked how to begin to speak one's truth. My advice? Start with a respectful attitude. Be positive, kind, and well-intentioned; speaking your truth is not a license to be cruel or insufferable. While you may need to pause—to think before you speak—you'll still need to express yourself. Remember the 90-second waves. If you're really angry or upset, wait until the intensity has subsided and you're on the downside of the wave before saying anything. In the absence of danger and threat, the goal is to be respectful in your encounters; thus, to the degree that you can, you maintain the emotional integrity and well-being of each person involved in your conversation. You're not responsible *for* the other person, though you are responsible for how you treat them.

> *Before you speak, let your words pass through three gates: Is it true? Is it necessary? Is it kind?*
> *—Rumi*

Be aware that speaking what you know to be true makes your experience clearer and more real. In fact, feelings you try to hide often surface quickly once you start talking. Now you know what to do when you feel those emotions begin to rise:

ride the wave and experience your true feelings. Then, be courageous and speak up.

If your thoughts and feelings have been locked away for a long time, approach your interaction from the standpoint that expressing yourself and using your *positive, kind, and well-intentioned voice* is the number-one goal of the conversation. Speaking up can make a difference, but not always in the ways you might expect.

People are encouraged to speak up to get what they want or to garner a specific response from someone else. Even though it might seem a bit counterintuitive, *getting the response you desire is the benefit, not the goal.* The real goal is *cultivating your authentic self in the process* by being able to express your thoughts, feelings,

> *Who you become in the process of speaking up is the real goal.*

and opinions with ease, absent anxiety. Your personal growth and evolution as a human being is at the base of all your efforts.

What builds confidence, emotional strength, and authenticity is the expression of your thoughts, feelings, needs, and perceptions, and your ability to handle the response you get, not the response you desire. Most believe that it is the response that changes us, but it is actually your ability to express yourself and handle the response you didn't want that invites you to be stronger and more resilient. Effectively and maturely handling the eight difficult feelings that result from not getting what you want builds emotional strength and the sense of being capable.

The Approach

In order to feel more comfortable speaking with others, you need to be able to handle a number of back-and-forth conversational exchanges, especially if a conversation involves conflict or intimacy. That may seem obvious, yet some of what occurs between two people during these moments remains out of their conscious awareness.

You can choose to talk or not talk in any given situation. As I noted above, when you speak, your feelings become more real to you and others. If you have trouble speaking up or speaking with ease, consider that not talking may be an attempt to not know what you know or to distract from what you're feeling. *Difficulty speaking is really difficulty feeling.* The more comfortable you are experiencing and moving through the eight unpleasant feelings, the more likely you are to make the choice to speak.

Remember, experiencing your feelings requires that you ride one or more 90-second waves. If you are in the habit of distracting yourself from knowing, accessing, or experiencing your feelings, it's likely you won't even initiate the conversation. When you speak up, you have to be willing to experience the unpleasant nature of your own emotional discomfort or the bodily sensations that help you know what you feel.

Let's take this one step further. In order to make the choice to speak up, you have to be present to your own experience and be willing to experience the eight unpleasant feelings. Let's assume you can handle your own emotional discomfort—in essence, the bodily sensations that help you know what you are feeling. You choose to express yourself, and now the other person reacts to what you said. Like you, the other person must also be present to their own experience so they, too, can express themselves.

You then need to hear what the other person says, which means being able to tolerate the discomfort of someone else's emotional discomfort (their expression of one or more of the eight unpleasant feelings). If necessary, use the 90-second waves to handle your emotional reactions to what the other person says so you can stay centered, without letting their feelings overwhelm you. Then you'll make a response to the response. This is how you successfully negotiate the flow of being aware of and expressing your experience. You are tolerating your own emotional discomfort, as well as another's emotional distress simultaneously. You are able to make appropriate responses at each turn of conversation.

Every time you do this, something wonderful happens: You are able to face conflict or upsetting situations. You can also use these skills to move your life forward (e.g., "I'd like to be considered for a promotion and raise," "I have this dream and really want your thoughts and support") and toward positive intimate moments (e.g., "I like you," "I'd like to spend more time with you," "I love you"). You are secure in the knowledge that you possess the emotional and communication skills to navigate life.

The Key to Speaking

The essential key to communication and extended conversations is to be able to tolerate both the unpleasant and pleasant feelings within yourself so you can simultaneously tolerate those same feelings in another person.

Facing Challenging Conversations

Writing is an effective way to gain clarity on what you are thinking and feeling. If you're not accustomed to speaking up and you are concerned about what to say, jot down the points you want to cover in your conversation. Bring the notes with you. Let the person know how important the conversation is to you, and explain that the notes are to help you remember what you want to say. You'll likely find that people are quite open to your having them with you.

Once you've written out your initial concerns, you'll be better prepared for the face-to-face conversation. Remember the Reset: one choice, eight feelings, 90 seconds. If you are willing to handle the eight unpleasant feelings, make the choice to stay connected to your truth and then speak (e.g., state an observation, address long-held pleasant or unpleasant feelings, or confront someone over something you didn't like). Speaking up can become a turning point for developing confidence. I don't see it as a one-time effort. Like any skill, you have to practice over and over and over again.

Go into the conversation reminding yourself that you'll handle the conversation, however it turns out. Hope for the best; yet, if the conversation doesn't go well, be prepared to experience one or more of those eight difficult feelings.

Speaking Prep

- What is the message you want to convey?
- What is important for you to say and for the other person to hear?
- What would be the ideal outcome of the conversation?
- What might you realistically expect?
- What response are you most likely to get?

The Preemptive Bid™

Remember to approach any tense conversation with good intentions and goodwill toward the other person. Wrap anything that is hard to say in softness by speaking more slowly, using a less intense and slightly deeper voice. Be aware of your inflection and tone. Here's how you handle that conversation.

1. Acknowledge that you are bringing up the difficult topic because you want to prevent a situation from going bad and thus straining a good connection, stop a situation from getting worse, or repair emotional distance that already exists.

2. Acknowledge your caring or loving feelings for the other person. With people you don't know, especially in customer-service situations, convey your anger, frustration, and distress while simultaneously stating (if it's true) that he or she was not the cause of that distress. Even with strangers, you can express frustration and still approach them in an empathetic manner. Even if you don't like where things are headed or the end result, tearing someone down is cruel. Behave in a way that helps maintain everyone's integrity.

3. Acknowledge your concern or worry about the other person's reaction (e.g., laughing at or ridiculing you, dismissing or diminishing your concern, or walking away). There may be reasons you didn't start the conversation earlier, so address that hesitation up front before you even raise the issue that most concerns you. When you are preemptive by openly discussing any obstacles holding you back from speaking, it invites the other person to listen more closely to what you have to say, with less chance they will behave in hurtful ways.

Here's a generalized script that might help you formulate your thoughts:

"[Name of person], something's been on my mind for a while, and I thought I could get past it, but I've realized that holding my feelings in is causing distance between us, and I don't want the distance to continue. I love you, and I'm really glad we're sitting down to talk. I want us to be closer. I've held back from saying anything before because I'm worried that once I tell you what's upsetting me, you'll make light of it and think it's no big deal. Or you'll laugh it off or make it seem like nothing. But it's a big deal to me, and I want you to know that."

Imagine if your partner or a dear friend approached you like this. Wouldn't you be more inclined to listen closely and be responsive to their concern?

If you are angry, hurt, or frustrated, express the feeling by naming it and not acting it out. Yelling and screaming are expressions of anger and frustration but not very effective ones. An escalating voice may be an attempt to get the other person to feel as you do, as if the louder voice will help them hear or understand you better. But think about the last time you heard someone raise his or her voice or yell. Or recall when you screamed or raised your voice in an effort to be heard. How well did that work?

Your listener is going to pay more attention to the fire and heat in a message than the message itself. The louder you scream or yell, the less safe your listener will feel. Consequently, that person will be less able to connect with what you're saying. Lose the fire and heat and, if you can, say what you mean from a calm place, on the downside of the 90-second wave. Don't escalate to evoke a response so someone will feel as you do. Speak your words; don't act them out.

Journal 8: The Preemptive Bid

Think of someone with whom you have been fearful, reluctant, or refused to talk. Using the Preemptive Bid script above as a template, take some time now to write out the beginning of your conversation as if you were preparing to talk with him or her in three or four days.

The Super Vital Hidden Stuff of Conversation

When you interact with others, your focus is rightly on the words, content, issues, or topics of the conversation. But what is often ignored is *how* you actually relate to one another. Understanding the *how* brings richness, depth, and intimacy to relationships. The *how* of relating often impacts you more than the actual words someone says. Just think about how eye rolls, sighs, a sarcastic tone, or outright mocking has made you feel in the past, and you can see how potentially damaging these kinds of reactions can be to relationships of any kind. These dismissive, hostile, or contemptuous behaviors often elicit anger or trigger a desire to withdraw from others. It's crucial that you learn to talk about both the words being said *and* how they are delivered as part of your everyday conversations and connections with others—especially those with whom you are close.

Sarcasm Is Not a Communication Tool

Sarcasm delivers a mixed message. Essentially, there are two kinds of sarcasm. One is playful and flirtatious and disguises vulnerability and embarrassment, while the second disguises anger, frustration, sadness, or disappointment. With the first kind, you can be clearer by being more open and direct with your caring feelings. With the second, you can be more open, direct, and honest about any feelings that leave you angry or upset. The direct approach lets your listener know what you really mean.

Conversation or Confrontation?

Confrontation is a unique, expressive skill; it's one that most people are reluctant or find difficult to develop. Reasons for not confronting others usually sound like: "Oh, I could never say that," "I have a really hard time speaking up," "I don't want to talk about stuff that upsets me," or "I don't want to hurt that person."

There will always be difficult conversations, unpleasant events, and challenging or upsetting situations. There will also always be conflict, whether it's as personal as a tense Thanksgiving dinner with a racist in-law, a request for a promotion or a raise, or an encounter with someone who is hard to work with, or as anonymous as a customer-service interaction or a parking lot fender-bender.

Conflict is a normal part of life, and the ability to confront others is a crucial life skill. It will help you feel more confident, capable, and empowered. But rather than the kind of confrontation intended to empower, you might have only experienced heated conflict, the kind characterized by hurtful or explosive arguments or behavior.

Let's change your perspective. Think of confrontation simply as describing your experience to another or stating what you observe. It may be the deepest form of empathy you can offer.

Confrontation Prep Checklist

- Come from a place of kindness. Be well-intentioned.
- Approach with empathy. Confrontation doesn't demand any kind of heated exchange.
- Be calm and direct. It's not necessary to raise your voice or be sarcastic. (When you approach in this manner, you can say what you need or want to without all the extra heat attached.)
- Simply state what you observe.
- Take ownership. Be responsible. Use "I" in front of whatever you describe or experience. (Never use "you" to

describe your experience: use "I'm angry" rather than "You make me so angry.")

◆ Along with talking about the issue that concerns you, describe what you observe about the behavior, thoughts, feelings, meanings, contradictions, discrepancies, incongruities, or mixed messages in any aspect of your conversation.

◆ Also talk to the person about *how* he or she is relating to you (e.g., rolling eyes, turning away, or using an angry or sarcastic tone).

If you start your conversation from an explosive or highly reactive place, not only will your message be harder to hear, you may never be able to determine why the conversation went in the direction it did. As I said earlier, when fire and heat are present in the way you speak, *that* becomes what other people pay attention to and the message ends up getting lost. There's no way you can have clarity about the problem if you start charged up, heated, or unclear from the outset.

When you gently yet firmly state your observations, you remove the emotionally loaded charge from your words. When it's appropriate, speak about the issue and, when relevant, how the issue is being expressed. You can potentially deepen or change your relationships for the better when you describe *how* you talk with each other and not solely the topic at hand.

When people feel safe and an experience is truly collaborative and well-intentioned, the truth can be shared and heard. Truth vibrates and resonates within and, far from being unsettling, it's actually calming; consequently, people generally experience relief when the truth is expressed. Still, it involves a willingness to be fully present. It is in the telling *and* receiving of truth that each person becomes able to live more authentically and becomes more fully themselves.

Inside vs. Outside Conflict

When we tell our truth and speak up, a conflict, disagreement, or misunderstanding with the other person can sometimes result. Difficulty tolerating the eight unpleasant feelings, fear of losing a relationship, or fear of making others uncomfortable are often reasons people choose to remain silent and instead turn the conflict inward.

Yet the challenge with not expressing yourself is that the conflict doesn't just go away. The issues remain; the only change is where the conflict resides. Too many times an "outside" conflict (conflict with another individual) is kept inside and leads to "internal" conflict (increased anxiety, feeling sad or angry).

I was talking with Brin, a client, about speaking up and the nature of conflicts. She was upset about her partner, Jayce's, humorous and "playful" comments about her 15-pound weight gain. However, she hadn't voiced her anger and disappointment to Jayce about these comments. She had been finding it increasingly hard to spend time with him. That's when I reached for a tissue and threw it on the floor between us; the tissue represented the ongoing conflict between Brin and her partner.

For the purpose of this exercise, I started as the stand-in for Jayce. As she was telling Jayce (me, in this case) that she was upset and hurt and wanted him to stop making those comments, then the conflict remained where it belonged: between us, observable and known to both, where it could be dealt with openly. Then I was the stand-in for Brin. I reached for the tissue on the floor (the conflict) and stuck it inside my shirt where it couldn't be seen. This gesture represented the active conflict, though it was now "located" inside Brin because she hadn't said anything to Jayce yet. A conflict between them that belonged on the outside was instead being harbored inside of Brin where it couldn't be seen or responded to because Brin hadn't spoken up.

Feelings and conflicts don't magically disappear; the only change is where they reside. I want issues and conflicts between people to be out in the open. That way, they can be responded to and resolved rather than being harbored inside where there is a greater likelihood that they will fester and grow into toxic feelings and emotional distance.

Difficult Recurring Conversations

I recently spoke with my friend, Stephan, who said he becomes reactive and upset every time he has to speak with his ex-wife, Bianca. He described her as demanding, erratic, irresponsible, and unpredictable in behavior and in conversation. Because he is concerned about the care of and effects of her behavior on their 11-year-old child, he often defers to Bianca's wishes (e.g., regarding changes in schedule and plans) in an effort to minimize conflict with Bianca. This means Stephan frequently juggles his own plans to make sure his daughter faces the least disruption and the fewest disappointments possible due to the unpredictable behavior of her mother. Yet these decisions leave Stephan feeling angry, resentful, and used. He feels helpless and upset each time he has to engage with Bianca because he anticipates the same kind of conversation each time.

You might have people in your life just like Stephan's ex-wife. It could be a spouse, a partner, a family member, a friend, a coworker, or a boss. If you have to speak with someone who often seems to make things more complicated for you, consider the next couple of points. First, remember that difficulty speaking is really difficulty handling your feelings. A conversation requires you to tolerate the unpleasant feelings within yourself and those same feelings within another person.

If, like Stephan, you find certain conversations highly stressful and just the thought of having such a conversation elicits an experience of dread, it's possible that you are not dealing well with your own unpleasant feelings, are anticipating having to experience the other's unpleasant feelings, and/or find it difficult to respond to his/her disrespectful and hurtful responses to you.

Go into the conversation knowing you have to tolerate the discomfort of the other party's unpleasant emotions with clarity about how *you* want to respond (e.g., saying no, setting clear boundaries) and with an awareness that your response may elicit more unpleasant reactions from them. Know that you don't have to stay in the conversation if things get mean; politely end it if it begins to escalate.

For particularly straining situations, there is another option for you to consider. If the other person is someone you have frequent contact with and you can predict the kind of responses you are likely to get from him or her, create a grid like the one below of those possible responses before you have any more interactions. Then, complete the grid following any conversations or interactions. (You can download a grid at www.DrJoan Rosenberg.com/resources90/.)

What ends up happening is that you stop personalizing the responses, and as a consequence, you become less affected by them. When you can predict a behavior and tally it, you are one step removed from it. This approach allows you to establish a greater sense of emotional control—not over the other person's behavior, but over your own reactivity. Not only does it help you get clear on how you want to respond, it also helps you become able to observe how the person "triggers" you.

Difficult Conversation Grid

	6/12	6/14	6/19	...								
Accuses me of not caring	✓✓		✓									
Blames me		✓✓✓	✓									
Changes what s/he said	✓		✓✓									
Repeats her/himself		✓✓										
Calls me names			✓									
Escalates (screams, yells)	✓✓	✓✓✓	✓✓									
Lies directly or omits info			✓									
Refuses to take responsibility			✓✓									

How to Set Boundaries Without Being Rude

Serena was out with her new puppy for an early morning walk and was looking forward to a relaxing Saturday. Mentally she was running through her plans—the walk, watching a missed television episode, a phone call to her mom and another with her best friend, a leisurely bath, and then brunch with a friend—when she ran into her downstairs neighbor, Lonnie. Figuring she had 20 minutes to chat, she started a conversation with her. They got into some serious topics, and after two hours, Serena finally put a stop to the conversation. As she walked back to her apartment, she was frustrated that, yet again, she had deferred to someone else's (presumed) needs and had ignored her own desires and intentions. Now she had time for only a quick shower before brunch.

Do you find it hard to set boundaries with others? If so, you might be getting caught up in how you think you'll be perceived by others ("outside-in thinking") or you might be concerned with hurting someone's feelings if you set limits.

Next time you find the urge to "people-please" or to put someone else's needs before your own, stay centered and notice your own needs and feelings; approach the other person from a positive, kind, and well-intentioned place; then simply state the truth of what you need to convey regarding boundaries, limits, or needs. In this case, Serena could have said something like: "Hey, Lonnie! How are you? I've got about 20 minutes to chat, but I wanted to catch up with you. Let's plan something fun later when we can really talk."

Listen Deeply with Compassionate Attunement

Finally, learn to listen deeply with compassionate attunement. You know you're attuned when you accurately perceive the experience of the other person. This means that when you respond back to the speaker you are able to show that you've made sense of what they've told you and understand what they've said, especially in terms of what it means *to and for them*. Likewise, your responses would be well timed (close to when someone spoke versus ignoring what you heard). These would be high-quality responses, ones that could be described as "contingent communication."[4]

The following is my interpretation and practical application of psychologist Allen Ivey's "microskills" approach to listening, which was initially designed to teach counseling skills to novice practitioners.[5] These skills help you become an empathic listener and can significantly enhance your ability to attune to the thoughts, feelings, and needs of another person.

Attend to the Other Person

This might seem basic and natural yet is worth a reminder. When you attend to another person, simply look at him or her, make eye contact, and engage through facial expressions, head nods, gestures, or simple statements like "uh huh." Lean in. Use body language that expresses interest, connection, and engagement. All of these behaviors show the other person that you are paying attention and closely following what is happening between you.

When you pull your attention away, for example, by checking your phone or looking at the television, or when you fail to make any kind of response that shows you are *fully* present and actively listening, you are no longer attending to the other person.

Open-Ended Questions

Unlike yes-or-no questions, open-ended questions invite an infinite range of answers. "What do you need right now?" or "What can I do to make our relationship better?" requires an answer beyond a simple yes or no. Employ the journalistic techniques of *who, what, where, how,* and *when.* (Avoid the *why* questions since they tend to invite defensive responses.) *How* and *what* are usually the best openers.

Summarize the Facts

Even though a person may be talking about his or her feelings, the focus here is to get clear on just the facts. Either paraphrase what was said or use the other person's actual words to summarize the facts you were told.

Reflect Feelings

Always respond to *feelings first*, e.g., "I know how sad it is to lose a pet. I know your cat, Moonbeam, meant the world to you." Or, "Wow, that is so exciting that you get to travel to Stockholm to speak on behalf of your company." It could even be as simple as "That sounds so frustrating" or "I totally get why you're disappointed."

The notion here is that you respond to the feeling, or feeling tone, whether it is directly stated or not. If it is an unpleasant feeling, *never* suggest they "should" be feeling something else; similarly, do not tell them to "move on and just get over it." Those responses invite defensiveness, pushback, withdrawal, or shutdown.

If you sense what someone else is feeling, say what you observe, even if it seems like an obvious statement. Noticing someone's pain can be the very act that helps relieve that pain. Your words invite calm because the person's experience has been recognized, whether or not you agree with him or her.

When the other person feels heard or felt (meaning, they understand that you have a good "sense" of them), he or she experiences being *noticed* (I'm not alone and someone cares that I am here), *validated* (my experience is important to someone else, which helps me make it important to me), and deeply *understood* (I feel more connected with myself *and* connected with you). A sense of calm and vitality are generally the most immediate effects, often followed right away by more emotional closeness between the two parties.

Then, and only then, can you move on to problem-solving. If you try to problem-solve first, unpleasant feelings remain unresponded to, thus they tend to linger. If you are making efforts to problem-solve without responding to the feelings first, women, especially, may feel dismissed and then be less attentive and

> *If you want to have high-quality conversations, remember to respond to feelings first.*

engaged in the conversation. So always remember: *feelings first.* Using a feelings-first approach can work for every type of relationship, from personal to professional.

Equally important is to notice positive feelings. Acknowledging risk-taking, efforts, and accomplishments with, for example, "Great job!" and "I'm excited for you" can make a big difference in someone's life. Genuine appreciation and recognition has a very positive effect on the individual and on your relationship.

Learn to Allow Silence

Permit silence so that others get the chance to absorb what you're saying, and vice versa. You don't have to fill the space with talk nor rush in and rescue a conversation. Simply take your time.

Corporate or Workplace Applications

Though many concepts discussed throughout the book can have a positive impact on the culture of a company, how individuals relate to one another within the company itself, can have a major impact on how well a team or division operates and succeeds. Whether you are a supervisor providing feedback to others, dealing with collegial relationships, or an employee dealing with customers, your peers, or your boss, consider how you can apply these concepts centered on speaking and listening and how this approach could change the company culture and responses to clientele. Keep your role and responsibilities in mind as you read through these ideas. Here are just a few to consider:

- Approach each other in a positive, kind and well-intentioned manner
- In conversation, do your best to maintain each person's integrity
- Especially if you are angry or frustrated, speak *only* when you are on the downside of an emotional wave
- Speak calmly and firmly minus emotional heat, fire, and devaluing—that way your message can be heard
- Listen closely by responding to feelings first and by asking open-ended questions with an intent to solve problems, not to assign blame

For the Man or Woman in Your Life

"Jake loves to solve problems. Give him an opportunity to fix something and he's a happy man," Melissa, 38, said. "Whenever I want to run something by him, he always tells me what I should do to fix my problem. I tell him, 'I just want you to listen to me. No solutions.' He thinks he did something wrong and then he withdraws."

At the session, Jake, 41, added, "Yep, that's true—I get confused by your tone, so I'm just not sure what to do. That's when I shut down. And then we end up at an ugly impasse."

Men want to solve problems and do the right thing, yet they often hear feedback as criticism as opposed to information, which initially results in their thinking they've not done enough or they've "done bad." This subsequently leaves them believing they are "not enough," then "feeling bad." Feeling bad sometimes gets translated into "*I* am bad," and is followed by a tendency in men to distance themselves emotionally.

When a man expresses problems, ask what he thinks about a situation and you will usually be able to hear or sense his feelings as he talks about what is going on. Once you get an idea about his feelings, reflecting them back is valuable for his sense of self and well-being.

Melissa, on the other hand, is frustrated by Jake always offering solutions to her—he gets upset that she doesn't like the options he suggests to solve her problem; she gets upset that his solutions to go do something and "fix" the problem don't register with her as being listened to. Melissa wants Jake to just say something like "what a bummer," "that's so disappointing," or "I get why you're frustrated."

When women ask men to listen, they often want a response to their *feelings first* and nothing more. So men, when a woman expresses problems, respond to her feelings first...that is "the fix"! Once this is accomplished, you can see if she is ready to hear specific solutions.

> *Go and love someone exactly as they are. And then watch how quickly they transform into the greatest, truest version of themselves. When one feels seen and appreciated in their own essence, one is instantly empowered.*
> — *Wes Angelozzi*

If you remind yourself of the importance of speaking your truth—and allowing other people to speak theirs—as the major step toward building self-confidence, you will go a tremendous way toward fostering healthy and emotionally fulfilling relationships.

The Next Step

Your ability to speak with ease has *everything* to do with your capacity to be aware of and in touch with your moment-to-moment experience. And the more you are able to be attuned to and embrace your emotional experience, the easier it becomes to speak and welcome someone else's emotional experience through listening.

Remember: *Your self-confidence is derived more through your well-intentioned act of speaking and your ability to handle the response you get than from the response you desire.*

If there is one message I want you to take away from this chapter, it is how *critically important* it is for you to develop the ability to speak with ease. Use the Rosenberg Reset to make the one choice to be aware of and in touch with those 90-second waves of the eight difficult feelings, and then speak your truth.

If we put those two elements together, here is how confidence seems to progress: Once you can tolerate those eight unpleasant feelings, you then have the capacity to speak your truth. As you speak your truth, you come to know yourself better and develop confidence through the act of speaking up. And as you develop confidence, you speak more, which then helps foster resilience, since you know that you can handle the feeling outcome of any conversation.

Speaking up allows you to believe in yourself. You are no longer hiding from yourself nor are you hiding from others. You may also start to like or even love yourself more because you have now become more believable to yourself. Loving yourself is part of building a life you love.

The other crucial element here is that speaking your truth leads to greater authenticity. As you continue to speak your truth with ease, your words now match your thoughts and feelings. And when your words and actions match your thoughts and feelings (and beliefs and values), then you are "in-sync" with yourself—living as an emotionally strong, confident, and authentic person.

We've touched on feeling and expressing the truth of your experience. Now let's help you face down obstacles like fear of failure, difficulty trusting, and unresolved grief—things that stand in the way of living a fully authentic and genuine life. Once these obstacles are out of your way, you will continue cultivating the skills that help you not only love yourself more but also create a life you love. And that, ultimately, is the goal of the Rosenberg Reset.

CHAPTER 8

Moving Through Grief

I hope that by now you've discovered that you can successfully make your way through everyday-life experiences by riding one or more 90-second waves of the eight difficult feelings. However, as soon as you start to move toward the eight unpleasant feelings rather than away from them and use your voice to speak up, you will likely face a new challenge. Relevant and related painful memories that kept you from feeling your emotions and speaking your truth may emerge and bubble up to the surface for processing. Don't worry; that's common.

Many important and positive changes will unfold as you live more fully present and connected to your moment-to-moment experiences. When you allow yourself to "know what you know" and "speak what you know," your whole sense of self begins to transform and change.

Healing Old Wounds

As you feel emotionally stronger, you'll become more effective at handling your unpleasant feelings. In turn, you'll become more skilled at managing the day-to-day challenges and will begin to heal old wounds from the past. Memories and grief emerge naturally and spontaneously to be resolved. Emotional baggage seems to surface organically and is a natural outcome of your increased awareness and growth. Yet making your way through these earlier memories and pain requires more than riding 90-second waves.

You might feel singularly angry, sad, helpless, or disappointed about what you went through either as a child or an adult. No matter what the event or situation was or is, if these feelings are present, you're grieving.

You might even be frustrated or upset that these memories are surfacing as you stay in touch with your moment-to-moment feelings, and you may wonder why painful memories and feelings are showing up at a time when you're actually feeling better. Might feelings be triggered by these memories? Absolutely. You will face painful thoughts, feelings, or memories for a while, though it's not permanent. When you allow yourself to move through these feelings and experiences, you are then able to gain insight and wisdom.

Loss

Loss is an interesting phenomenon. It is common that when you lose something unexpectedly, or someone you love dearly, the loss itself quickly and easily brings up memories of prior losses. Other than your sense of smell, which is known to activate memories rapidly, my professional experiences have shown me that loss and separation elicit memories of prior losses faster than anything else.

Most people associate loss with that of a relationship: loss of a spouse, partner, parent, grandparent, brother or sister, caregiver, boyfriend or girlfriend, cousin, or friend. Loss of relationship may also mean the loss of a pet. Yet, it's really important to think of loss in much broader terms. Loss can also include the loss of less tangible aspects of life, like health, mobility, employment, finances, financial status, home, safety, prestige, reputation, status, or opportunity.

Loss, then, also often involves facing what your childhood was (or was not) or even what your adulthood is (or is not) — and recognizing the difference between what you needed, wanted, and dreamed of and what really occurred. Dealing with this gap involves grief.

Grief may not surface as only one single 90-second wave. It may come as waves of waves. Maybe you are tearful one moment, okay for a while, and then unexpectedly and spontaneously moved to tears again. As before, ride the waves. Over time, they will decrease in frequency and intensity, and they will always subside. Always.

Disguised Grief™

As I've said above, most people associate grief, which I typically describe as *sadness, helplessness, anger, or disappointment,* with more immediate or present-day losses like relationship losses or the death of a human or pet. Yet I believe there is a deeper level of grief that is connected to our life experiences during childhood and even through adulthood. If this type of grief remains unaddressed by being pushed back into the recesses of our minds, it can lead to such feelings as bitterness, resentfulness, grudges, and, eventually, soulful depression.

I am proposing resolving a different kind of grief — one that most people don't talk about or don't realize they experience. It's what I call Disguised Grief™. Disguised grief might appear as *leftover anger, bitterness, blame, cynicism, grudges, hostility, jealousy, negativity, pessimism, regret, resentment, desire for revenge, sarcasm, self-hate, or some other long-standing pain.* As I mentioned above, it also involves facing what your childhood was (or was not) or what your adulthood is (or is not) and dealing with the difference between what you needed, what you wanted, what you dreamed of, and what really occurred.

After many years of clinical practice, I started to realize that when clients described memories associated with that difference, or gap, or used any of the 14 words listed above, both the memories and the words acted as signals that guided me to the "emotional stuff," or unresolved pain, hiding behind their experiences, feelings, or reactions. When I followed the signals, they led me to the pain—pain that I have since identified as grief: disguised grief.

If you stop to think about it, bitterness or resentment, for example, may be more toxic versions of grief (sadness, helplessness, anger, and disappointment). It's as if you are blending one or more of the eight difficult feelings with some degree of ill will or hostility.

Grief Signal Words

Gently but honestly, think about whether any of the following words capture your feelings or reactions, whether this is a frequent state of mind, and whether it's about something specific, or your reaction is tied to something happening in your life right now: *leftover anger, bitterness, blame, cynicism, grudges, hostility, jealousy, negativity, pessimism, regret, resentment, desire for revenge, sarcasm, self-hate, or some other long-standing pain.* Each word in the list represents a different way in which disguised grief can manifest itself. If any of these words resonate with you, then:

1. Write down the words.
2. Think about the memory or memories attached to each word in your list and capture the memory briefly.
3. With each memory, consider the possibility that grief may be hiding underneath. It's much better if you can

stay with less toxic versions of feelings. Using the eight feelings as your reference point (sadness, shame, helplessness, anger, embarrassment, disappointment, frustration, and vulnerability), identify which of the eight may be associated with each memory you jotted down. Write down those feelings, too.

4. Write down any thoughts or observations you have while completing this exercise and what difference it makes to you to see what you are experiencing as grief, rather than resentment, for instance.

Using the Reset to ride waves of sadness, helplessness, anger, or disappointment won't fully address grief or disguised grief. You also need to make sense of your experience so that you can move through grief and release the enduring pain. Both are necessary. That's where we are headed now.

Making Sense of Your Life Experiences

Life is not absent hurt. How we are able to experience, make sense of, and bounce back from those hurts is the essential element of self-growth. Although it may be painful to do so, it's helpful to reflect upon how these hurts and experiences have shaped your character, reactions, and beliefs.

Making sense of your life experiences starts by acknowledging that some life events or situations remain unresolved and that feelings of grief may still be attached to those memories. The essence of this approach is to:

- understand the impact and meaning these experiences had upon you across time,
- forgive yourself and others,

- let go of how you've seen yourself in the past, and
- forge new images of who you want to become.

Moving through these feelings of grief can help you transition from a life of reaction to a life of creation —a life you love. It is shifting from living a life by default to a life by design.

Journal 9: Disguised Grief and Grief Reset Protocol

There are several questions to consider as you move through this chapter. I would encourage you to keep your journal close at hand and capture your thoughts as you read, and especially as you reflect upon and answer the questions raised over the next few pages.

Releasing painful memories and outdated stories takes several steps, the first of which involves taking an honest look at your life.

By acknowledging within yourself the truth about what you *actually* experienced, you continue down the path of genuine healing. Reclaiming those truths helps you release negativity, hostility, toxicity, bitterness, resentments, self-hate, blame against yourself or others, and grudges you may have harbored. In order to fully move through these, there are five main—but often overlooked—aspects of disguised grief that can help you understand why you are feeling what you are feeling. What is actually at the root of these feelings usually falls into one of these patterns or categories of grief:

What you got and didn't deserve
These are mostly negative things in life, such as parental or caretaker absence, harsh criticism, responsibilities well

beyond your chronological age, taunting and ridicule, neglect, abuse, violence, threats, or a misunderstanding of and mis-attunement to your real needs.

What you deserved and didn't get

These are generally the positive aspects of life we both need and desire, like consistent love, attention, acknowledgment, praise for work well done, and celebration of important life events.

What never was

This means recognizing your life circumstances for whatever they were, including the parents, home life, finances, friends, education, health, or opportunities you needed or wanted in life but that were never available to you.

What is not now

This means acknowledging your life circumstances for whatever they are now.

What may never be

This might be a parent, caregiver, partner, sibling, relative, or friend who may never see things as you do or who may never change in ways that are positive and supportive of you; or circumstances from the past that will never be what you want them to be.

The Grief Reset Protocol™

People often get stuck in grief if they don't accept that what was done can't be undone, and what was left undone can't be done.

To help guide others through their experiences of grief, I developed the Grief Reset Protocol.

Think about what remains emotionally unfinished in your life. Choose an experience you would like to resolve, forgive, be released from, or gain some relief around and follow the steps below. While many reactions such as bitterness, hostility, and resentment suggest grief is present, notice feelings of sadness, helplessness, anger, and disappointment in particular as signs that you're grieving.

G: Let your genuine feelings be present and **grieve** over:
- What you got and didn't deserve (the bad stuff—abuse, chaos, inconsistency, neglect)
- What you deserved and didn't get (the good stuff—acknowledgment, praise, support)
- What never was (the facts, circumstances, and missed opportunities of your life)
- What is not now (the facts and circumstances of your life now)
- What may never be (accepting that certain changes or responses may never come)

R: **Reflect** by identifying an important or high-impact memory or grief to resolve.

I: **Inquire more deeply.** Make sense of your life history by understanding the impact, importance, influence, meaning, relevance, and/or significance of your experiences across time.
- Who did you become because of these experiences at the time of the event? / in childhood? / in teen years? / in adulthood? / now?
- How did the experience shape you and your outlook or personality?

E: **Explore and extract** the positive learnings.

F: Free yourself: Let go of the "old story" you have described about yourself.

Forgive others and yourself for what they/you did or did not know, or did or did not do.

Forge new images of who you want to become and start living that new story.

In order to understand how this process works to help you make sense and let go of old griefs, let's delve into each of these steps a little deeper.

The Grief Itself

Once you identify memories that you still have a lot of feelings about—memories that easily trigger you—you can start to make sense of those experiences using the Grief Reset Protocol outlined above. You won't have to do it for each of your memories; once you start with one, there is a domino effect. Making sense of one life experience often enables you to understand many life experiences simultaneously.

It's complicated dealing with feelings involving someone who hurt you. Love and a desire to protect the person may be mixed in with sadness, anger, disappointment, bitterness, or resentment. Even vengeful feelings can emerge because you want the person to experience the same degree of hurt and pain that you experienced. Remember, however, that the focus here is on you—making sense of *your* experience. Thus, experiencing and talking about the unpleasant feelings involved with those painful life situations is really in the service of your health. Even if you never speak about the situation or your feelings to others or to the people who hurt you, it's still important to acknowledge the truth of your experience within yourself, to yourself.

Going forward, as you face this truth and your awareness

increases, your memories surface, and your feelings unfold, experience as much of each moment—your thoughts, feelings, needs, and perceptions—as you can. It's a time to release your feelings. If you're sad, be sad; if you're angry, be angry; if you're disappointed, be disappointed. Ask yourself: "What am I sad, angry, or disappointed about?" so you can link whatever you are feeling to the experience itself.

Reflect on the Memory

The next step is to reflect on the memory. Reflecting on the memory takes you into the memory. When you create the mental space to consider your past, understand that more details about specific memories or other memories may come. Stay open as these other memories are surfacing for processing and release. If you think about your overall experience as you move through what you are feeling, it helps you achieve the greatest degree of resolution.

Inquire More Deeply

The next step, inquiring more deeply, has to do with understanding the impact of your experiences across time. Consider that your life experiences exist for your overall growth and evolution as a person. Rather than asking yourself "Why did this happen *to* me?" consider asking "Why did this happen *for* me?" The nature of your answers may differ depending on which question you ask. Your focus here is to think about the *importance, impact, influence, meaning, relevance,* and/or *significance* the life experiences had *on* you or *for* you when they occurred and how these events have shaped your life.

When you go through difficult and painful experiences in life, you often develop beliefs, hold attitudes, and make decisions about your life that came about because of the pain. Sometimes those beliefs, attitudes, and decisions cause you even more pain, beyond the experiences themselves. What meaning did you attach to the experiences? How did that change how you viewed yourself, your character, your capabilities, or your deservedness? Did you, for instance, withdraw, stop trusting others, or start behaving in a rude, mean, or aggressive manner? Did you become more thoughtful and kinder? Did you look at how you used your time differently? As you consider the questions that follow, simply be an observer, absent judgment. Be gentle with yourself. The key questions relative to all of these aspects are:

- Who did I become, because of what I went through, at the time of the events?
- Who did I become as a child or adolescent as a result of the experiences?
- Who did I become as an adult as a result of the experiences?

Consider first the impact the experiences had on you as you grew up—as a child or youth—and second, the impact those early experiences had on you as an adult.

- How did the experiences impact you when they occurred?
- How have they been relevant as you have aged?
- What is the significance the experiences have had on your life today?

Another way to look at the effect of what you experienced is to consider the beliefs you developed about *yourself,* about *others,* about *the world,* and about *the future.* Again, it's good to think about how your perspective on those four elements may have changed from the time of the events, and then across time. Did your perspective change for better or worse?

Let's approach understanding your experiences from one more angle. Here, then, are the kinds of questions you want to ask yourself:

- How did these experiences change the attitudes you hold?
- How did these experiences change what you believe?
- How did these experiences change the decisions you made?

Explore and Extract the Positive Learnings

As you think about the impact and meaning these experiences had on you, think about what positive things you can learn from each one. For example, saying that you should never trust anyone again does not count as a positive learning.

It's common for children who grow up amidst the chaos of one or both parents abusing substances (e.g., alcohol, cocaine, meth) to get out of the house as quickly as possible and find refuge in the structure and stability of school. These children often become high performers, pouring themselves into academics, extracurricular activities, and leadership positions within the school, a strategy that helped them achieve great success and stay away from home simultaneously. As adults looking back, reflecting on, and experiencing the pain of multiple disappointments and periods of embarrassment and vulnerability within their childhood homes, they are often able to describe how their tenacity, diligence, and ability to focus emerged from that pain and, over time, became the same character traits that led to opportunities and successful careers.

If we can glean a positive learning from painful life experiences, we begin to sculpt our character and life in important ways. You can see that in Maya's, Natalie's, and Ronnie's lives.

Maya, an only child and now a successful 29-year-old director of human resources, initially sought therapy to deal with anxiety and dating relationships that were short-lived. Maya had witnessed a lot of arguing between her parents, even after they divorced, when she was 12. It wasn't that they yelled or screamed a lot when they fought; instead, the combination of silence, sarcasm, cutting remarks, and innuendos kept Maya anxious and emotionally off balance. She learned at a young age to read sub-tleties in both of her parents' moods as she tried to negotiate and understand her connection to each of them as well as her place between them. We discussed the effect her parents' com-munication styles had on her as she grew up and how, as an adult, she would be so focused on the men in her life and how they responded to her that she couldn't comfortably settle into a relationship with anyone she dated. As she dealt with the nega-tive impact her parents' behaviors had on her, her anxiety decreased and she was able to gain more confidence and trust in what she wanted, especially in relationships. As emotionally challenging as her childhood was, she recognized that her abil-ity to read subtleties in nonverbal communication and voice tones had contributed greatly to her effectiveness in negotiating contracts, mitigating professional conflicts, and serving her business clients' needs.

Natalie, 43, a high-powered attorney, came to therapy feel-ing overwhelmed by a rapidly growing case load and high stress in her law firm. As I learned about the demands she faced at work, at home, and in her community (she was a volunteer and leader at church, in her children's school, and in professional organizations), it was easy to understand her sense of over-whelm. Her capacity to organize and her effectiveness in all areas of her life were also easy to understand given her status as the oldest child in her family and the fact that both her mother and father leaned on her for parenting of her younger siblings, peacemaking, and her wise counsel despite her youth. She rec-ognized her anger at her mother and father for the loss of her innocence and childhood. Yet, like Maya, she expressed grati-tude that those early life demands helped her develop into a sensitive caretaker and highly effective professional who has been successful throughout her life.

Ronnie, 37, described going through an excruciatingly pain-ful breakup in his early twenties with someone he considered the love of his life. His partner had cheated and heaped one pain on top of another by lying to Ronnie's close friends, something that took months to repair. Given the mess and his heartbreak, Ronnie knew he could be bitter and could back away from relationships, but he realized that choice would hurt only him. Instead, the loss of the love of his life strengthened his conviction about staying open to new relationships. He knew what the best parts of his former relationship felt like, and if he could love so deeply that first time, he could surely do it again.

To help you gain insights, consider these questions:

- How did you change because of what you did (or did not) experience?
- Did you develop certain attitudes, skills, habits, or traits that helped you lead a more satisfying, productive, successful, and/or happier life?
- What positive learnings can you glean from those experiences and apply now in adulthood?
- Have you already applied something positive you weren't aware of?
- What can you learn from these experiences that can help you become the person you most want to become?

These are the insights you want to take away.

Forgive Yourself and Others

One of the most important steps in the Grief Reset Protocol is to forgive yourself and others. Forgiveness does not imply or suggest that you agree with, approve, or condone what happened. It simply means acknowledging and accepting the truth that the events or experiences occurred. Mary Morrissey, a premier personal development expert, often says that forgiveness removes a barrier within yourself to love's presence.[1] By grieving, understanding the impact of an experience, and harvesting the lessons, you can move to forgiveness, which allows you to let go of the past and live more fully in the present. Approach this process with a gentle loving heart, absent judgment.

Forgive yourself for what you did and did not know, and for what you did or did not do. Do the same with others who hurt or wronged you, knowingly or unknowingly. This may take conscious practice over time.

If, at this point in the process, you are still finding it difficult to accept the circumstances and experiences of your life as part of your overall evolution, and you have diligently considered the variety of questions intended to help you forgive and move forward in your life, then ask yourself this last question: *What would need to happen for me to feel totally resolved about this experience/event/situation?* If the answer is something that is not possible, then it is time to move to a place of acceptance. It is time to accept that truth and finally forgive yourself and others.

> *Forgive yourself for what you did and did not know, and for what you did or did not do. Forgive others for what they did or did not know, and for what they did or did not do.*

We all get hurt. We just don't want the effects of the hurt to diminish how we function or who we can become. I have watched many people who were hurt by one or two individuals early in life use how they were treated at that age as the model for how they relate with others many years later. Sometimes relating this way is intentional; most times it is not—we just behave with others in an effort to protect ourselves from being hurt in the same way again.

Picture it this way. Imagine how you were hurt 30 years ago as a blueprint. You handed that blueprint back and forth in childhood with the people who hurt you—same reactions, same pattern each time. You took that same blueprint and kept handing it to other people when you were 19, or 25, or 31, or 40 years old and said, "Here, new person, use this 9-, 15-, 21- or 30-year-old blueprint because I expect you to relate to me like those other individuals did when I was 10." That old blueprint, however, is not relevant to each new person you meet, each of whom could respond in an entirely different and more appropriate way.

New person, new blueprint. Every time.

It's important to recognize that, as a child, you were never the "cause" of whatever abuse or neglect you experienced. Nor was what you experienced "about you" (even if you were told it was). You were, however, impacted by these people and situations. As a child, you can be victimized. As an adult, the goal is to be neither a victim nor a perpetrator; it involves coming to the realization that your parents did the best they could for you given their own levels of function. The truth is we all have a story to tell, and that involves learning that your caregivers, or other important people in your life, had a story to tell as well.

As you move through this process, you start to see your parents, caregivers, siblings, and other mentors in a different light, understanding the limitations they had before and the limitations they may have now. You see them more clearly for who they really were and for who they are. If they are still alive, thinking through your experiences gives you a sense of what you can or cannot ask of them based on their own limitations. You learn that you can set certain boundaries around attitudes or behaviors you will tolerate or the amount of time you spend with them. Who they are and what you experienced has a lot to do with who you have become; fortunately, they have far less impact on who you can yet become.

By using this grief framework and working through to forgiveness, you can free yourself from your old life story—a story that was built on memories of what you experienced. Let go of

> *Who you were then
> is not who you are now.*

them. *Who you were then is not who you are now.* You can now choose different attitudes and beliefs.

You can make new decisions. And if you do this, you get to create and live a new life story.

Telling Others

It's so very common for children not to tell their parents or caretakers how they are being hurt. The child is at a loss, experiencing what Dr. Dan Siegel calls "an unsolvable bind," if the parent, who should be creating a safe haven, is the same person causing pain.[2] In this case the child may believe there is no one to turn to.

Even when parents aren't the source of pain, children may not discuss with them how others are hurting them. These omissions may occur because the child is engaging in grandiose thinking. In this case, a child sees him- or herself as much more emotionally capable of handling hurt or pain than his or her parents. As a result, the child may never mention the situations, diminish the impact the situations may be having on him or her, or, if asked, may deny outright that it is even taking place—all in an effort to protect parents from pain.

Reasons adults give for why they didn't talk as children usually run as follows: a) because the parent wouldn't take it well or take responsibility, which means it was on the child to deal with the emotional discomfort and issues of the parents; b) because they "didn't want to hurt the parent"; or c) because the child was hurt and didn't want to talk about it. I've also found adults didn't talk as children because they were projecting their own experience onto the parent; in this case, the child believed that the parent couldn't handle the information, when it was really the child who couldn't handle the painful experience or the process of describing what happened. Believing there is no one to turn to at times of such distress just compounds the pain; it wasn't the child's fault and now it seems there is no one to tell.

Children may choose not to tell other adults because they have been told either not to share the "family business" or to promote favorable images of the individuals involved. Finally, silence is the hallmark of being hurt; sometimes keeping one's experience quiet keeps the pain at bay, and it can seem as if by not saying anything the child is preserving good feelings toward someone who has hurt him or her.

At a conference lunch a few years ago, I sat next to Paul, a man in his 70s, who politely asked what I did professionally. After I briefly explained my work involving unpleasant feelings, he paused just a moment before telling me about his love of singing and about an experience that occurred his senior year of high school. At his final high school concert, he sang two solos in front of 2,000 people. After the performance, Charles, a close friend, said: "Paul, you sang flat. You should be embarrassed. You shouldn't ever sing a solo again." And that's what happened. But Paul actually took it one step further—he never sang, in a group or as a soloist, in public again. Ever.

Paul decided to stop doing something he absolutely loved, yet he carried grief over what never was, what was not now, and what would never be—a life filled with singing. I could only imagine how much more rich, joyful, and vibrant his life might have been if he'd had the awareness in his 20s, 30s, 40s or even later to resolve his grief and make other decisions to bring singing back into his life.

Paul never told Charles about how hurtful his comment was nor the painful effect it had had on his life. Paul's experience offers an example of how a simple, common, everyday-type comment or occurrence could strongly impact at least one important aspect of your life. Yet, consider what might have unfolded for Paul if he had talked with his friend, his parents, or his singing teacher about what had happened even days, weeks, or months after the incident occurred. A sincere apology from Charles, supportive and encouraging remarks from his parents, or problem-solving and practice with his instructor could have opened this enriching experience back up to him again.

Talking about painful experiences with those who hurt you or those who knew what was taking place is never required and should never be forced. It comes from you and only then from a place of readiness and desire. If the individual with whom you want to speak is alive and available, then it's important to consider that person's capacity for responsiveness. For instance, if you've tried to talk directly about your experiences many times before and just gotten blown off, yelled at, or faced blatant denial, then you may have to do the emotional work yourself, without the benefit of a conversation. If, however, the person has the capacity to respond, hear it, take in what you say, and take responsibility, then the conversation is worth considering.

Why tell? Remember, you're not telling them to get a specific response from them; that's the benefit, not the goal. *You are telling them because the telling changes you.* You might not get the response you want, and your ability to handle that undesired response (e.g., anger, denial, no responsibility-taking, lots of other unpleasant feelings to tolerate) speaks to your growing emotional strength.

Before telling parents, caregivers, siblings, etc., remember first to consider:

a) What do I want to say, or what do I want them to hear?
b) What do I ideally want to have happen?
c) What can I realistically expect?
d) What am I likely to get?

You can frame the conversation this way:

"I want to talk about some aspects of my experience growing up—it's information I want to share with you so I can continue to grow and so that you can know me better. I'm telling you, ultimately, to work on or work through my own emotional concerns because I have the desire to feel closer to you, and so I can become more in-sync with myself and comfortable in my own skin."

How to Know When Grief Has Resolved

There are aspects of grief that may not ever fully resolve or go away. In some situations, you may continue to experience a degree of sadness or tinges of the losses or pain—waves of feelings. As you repeatedly engage with the questions that are part of the Grief Reset Protocol, the way you experience a particular memory, the intensity of how you experience it, and the overall effect it has on your life changes. Generally, the grief ceases to be debilitating and stop you in its tracks; it's no longer disrupting or overwhelming. Instead, you can acknowledge the memory and bear the sadness or other feelings that wash over you. The grief will have shifted from overwhelming emotional pain or distress to a gentler reminder of the experience—a nod to the pain or loss. Then you can move on with your focus on the present.

How, then, do you know when grief is resolving about several memories or when working with a given memory feels more complete? You may have:

- Moments of recognition where it feels like things are lining up or falling into place.
- Moments of insight that bring tearfulness, or a sense of calm, signaling that your understanding and experience are integrating.
- Decreased frequency of triggering episodes.
- Decreased intensity (mild, tinge) of your emotional reaction to either the memory or to a parallel experience in the present.

- The capacity to respond instead of react when you are either "triggered" (by people or situations) or when you identify a script/theme from the past showing up in the present.
- The ability to laugh in a kind and compassionate manner at yourself and your life experiences.
- The ability to identify some of your life scripts or themes (e.g., in a new situation with new people you are able to notice an old script or concerns).
- The kind of response in adulthood that you were unable to have as a child if the situation occurs in the present (e.g., an ability to set boundaries on how someone can talk to you).
- Greater awareness and insight that your painful experiences have helped shape the person you are or are evolving into.

The Unexpected Riches of Grief

Moving through grief means making sense of memories—your life stories—and the pain connected to those memories. Once you make your way through emotional pain, it shifts from a life event, situation, or episode from which you may have distanced yourself to an experience that is more meaningfully integrated into the overall narrative thread of how you tell the story of your life. The very feelings you tried to push away when those life events first occurred are ultimately the same ones that can help you move to a place of forgiveness.

Yet you can't make pain disappear simply by saying to yourself, "Let's just get rid of the bad stuff"—as if you're just taking out the trash without a second

> *In order to really move through grief, you have to come to grips with the fact that you can never undo what was done, nor do what was left undone.*

thought. In order to really move through grief, you have to come to grips with the fact that you can never undo what was done, nor do what was left undone.

Making your way through this grief, then, is a crucial step as you move toward greater emotional well-being and emotional mastery. You are able to release anger, bitterness, grudges, and resentment and can, instead, be less emotionally reactive and become a compassionate observer to what used to trigger you. You'll notice that you naturally become more spontaneous and present. You become self-aware and self-attuned. You possess the ability to feel and live in (and with) your moment-to-moment experience.

Use the Grief Reset Protocol. I know from my practice what it can do to change people's lives. When you deal with such grief, you open yourself up to laughter and joy. When you forgive, you open to deeper connections, with yourself and others.

> *When you deal with grief, you open yourself up to laughter and joy. When you forgive, you open to deeper connections, with yourself and others.*

Know that facing the truth within yourself is the only thing that puts you in a right relationship with yourself—leading to a sense of calm and inner peace—and it is the only thing that can lead to love within and for yourself. The more you stay present to the truth of what your life was, the more you free yourself to create a life you love.

CHAPTER 9

Upleveling Confidence and Resilience

I was speaking with Tasha, 38, who recently started a new, high-stress, high-profile management position. She was discussing the intensity of her anxiety and how it gets in the way of her work and relationships, when she said: "I hate change and I hate taking risks." I explained to her that by insisting that everything remain the same in her life, she was actually increasing her anxiety and reducing her emotional flexibility; she was seeking to achieve the impossible. Tasha refused to shake loose the idea that her stress would decrease if she could just maintain the status quo with her circumstances. Finally, I said: "There will never be a moment in your life that will repeat, and you can never fully reexperience a moment that you have already lived. So life is really about change. Life involves solving the various challenges and problems you are faced with on a daily basis; it is about handling the constancy of change, not the constancy of routine." That finally enabled Tasha to begin to shift her perspective from one of rigid immovability to one that was more open to uncertain and ever-evolving circumstances.

Tasha's anxiety was likely a distraction from the eight difficult emotions. As discussed in chapter 5, facing the unknown and uncertainty means tolerating the unfamiliar and unexpected, and in Tasha's case, feeling vulnerable and dealing with anticipated disappointments. With regard to the latter, she wanted to have mastery over disappointment that had not yet occurred. Once Tasha realized vulnerability and disappointment were upsetting her balance, she was able to think about change in a different light.

Choosing Resourceful Attitudes

That shift in thinking that Tasha made is essential in the move from a life lived by default to a life lived by design. "Living by design" does not mean that everything will happen exactly the way you plan it to; it means that you will have ideas about what

> *Life is about handling the constancy of change, not the constancy of routine.*

you would love to create, you'll be willing to take the risks to go after it, and you'll be strong enough to build something meaningful out of whatever happens. And in order to do that, you must be flexible and adaptive.

Be Flexible and Adaptive

Most people seek stability in their lives, and they find that the predictability and consistency of routine they experience helps them feel safer and more secure in the world. Yet there are expected changes that follow the natural order of life: watching children grow up and leave home for camp, college, work, or marriage; changes in relationship status and employment and career paths; and the loss of parents or other loved ones.

While most people want and appreciate periods of stability, the absence of significant changes can lull you into a false sense of security. When things remain stable and predictable over long periods of time, it is easy to believe that the status quo is the default setting for life. Take a few moments to think about how life can change on a dime: unexpected accidents and illness or disease can change the course of your life; natural disasters such as tornadoes, earthquakes, fires, and floods can destroy a home or take a life; and man-made insults and injuries can wipe out everything you have worked for or have known. Everything can change in a matter of seconds.

I've had this experience. In fact, there was one particular period in my life where I felt like everything that I had counted on for stability and a sense of normalcy was gone. The university I was working for had restructured my division, resulting in the termination of three positions, including mine. The loss of my job was challenge enough, yet it was further complicated by a relationship breakup. Since I lived with my partner at the time, the end of that relationship also meant that I was now without a place to call home.

All the key ways we typically identify ourselves—work, relationship, and home—had suddenly disappeared. I realized three major things at that point. First, that change, not stability, is the constant. Second, that security is an illusion. The wisdom of trusting in or relying on external aspects of my life to always be there was called into question. Third, since I had no one thing on which to hang my identity, what you saw was what you got. In other words, all I had was the present moment and myself, exactly as I was, to give.

> *Security is an illusion.*
> *Virtually anything in your life can change in a matter of seconds.*
> *What can you do to trust and rely on what is inside as opposed to outside of you?*

Having stability and predictability in your life is great. It's certainly my preferred way to live. Even so, to successfully negotiate life challenges—painful ones in particular—you must develop your capacity to experience and effectively manage uncertainty and change; that often requires confidence and resilience.

Be Open and Curious

Resilience, which we can think of as emotional elasticity or flexibility, is one of the primary outcomes of the Rosenberg Reset. It's a "bouncing back" to original form,[1] though this is somewhat relative to the variety of resources you bring to a given situation (e.g., emotional, social, financial) and the degree of difficulty, frequency, and recency of the life circumstances (e.g., trauma or tragedy) you've experienced early in life and into adulthood. Resilience can also be thought of in a broader context, however, as this ability to bounce back is essential when one is facing adversities or challenges, such as the pursuit of a long-term passion, goal, or dream. Resilience can help you develop the capacity to experience and effectively manage change so you can make the desired choices and the necessary risks for moving your life forward.

The first element of resilience involves your attitude about the dynamic nature of life. My emphasis? Approach life with an open and curious nature that is always respectful and conscious of change, with an intent on developing the resources you need to meet, face, and effectively manage the vicissitudes of life. Know that the greatest sense of stability and security is achieved when you feel resourceful *within,* not just when your life is filled with resources (and things) outside of you.

> *Your greatest sense of stability and security is achieved when you feel resourceful within.*

Holding this open and positive attitude helps you develop emotional flexibility, emotional strength, and a sense of resourcefulness in the face of constant change. By all means, experience and enjoy routine, predictability, and stability—just remember that it is not permanent. Accept these calm, quiet periods with grace and gratitude, but know that you will be the most effective when you can accept the inconstancies of life. Put your energy into maximizing your capacity to

> *Accept periods of quiet and stability with grace and gratitude.*
> *Develop the capacity to be flexible and adaptive in the face of change.*

approach life with curiosity so you have the most effective attitude to handle whatever challenges you might face.

We all face difficult circumstances in our lives and, as we age, we find we can add more and more tragic or traumatic experiences to the list: sudden and unexpected death of friends or family; losses involving finances, health, home, or relationships; devastating diagnoses. None of us remains unscathed. But how do you bounce back from such experiences? How do you have the resources and resolve to face another day—or even to take another step?

There is an extensive body of research on stress and coping that spans decades. In recent years, fueled by the positive psychology movement, psychology researchers have been exploring the more positive side of our nature, such as character strengths, virtues, hope, engagement in life, and well-being. They've weighed in on a number of different attitudes and skills that contribute to or cultivate resilience.

Their focus ranges from positive emotions[2] to hardiness,[3] from a growth mind-set[4] to having grit,[5] yet if we take a closer look, the majority of these psychologists speak to elements that have to do with attitude, how you think (e.g., optimism), and how you move through what you are facing. One researcher suggested that positive emotions (e.g., hope) help broaden one's mind-set[6] and contribute to growth and resilience, yet she noted there may be even greater growth and resilience by finding "benefits within adversity"[7] or, like other researchers, finding positive meaning in adverse situations.[8] This same idea is echoed in research on hardiness where the focus is on understanding who collapsed and who thrived when faced with stress. Once again, what makes the difference is staying engaged in problem-solving, an openness to new ideas, and seeing change as a positive challenge.[9]

A growth mindset means believing you can improve. People with a growth mindset tend to persevere when facing difficult tasks and push themselves outside their comfort zones; they stay more engaged when their efforts are rewarded.[10] A growth mindset helps you develop what psychologist Dr. Angela Duckworth calls "grit," a long-term fascination with and engagement in an enduring goal that is meaningful and purposeful to you. Grit, she notes, is embodied by passion, perseverance, and daily practice; it can be observed by a "stick-to-it-iveness" that lasts day in and day out for years.[11] It is a dogged determination—a tenacity—to keep at a certain task or pursuit, allowing nothing to distract or dissuade you from accomplishing your goal.

Clearly, a great deal of resilience depends on your attitudes and your ability to reframe what you experience. George Bonanno, a professor of psychology at Teachers College, Columbia University, suggests that how you conceptualize an event (as a trauma versus an opportunity to learn and grow) is a key aspect of resilience.[12] In fact, he calls painful life experiences "potentially traumatic events," depending on whether you identify them as traumas or opportunities. He also suggests that the ability to rebound is the norm throughout adult life. That's good news for most of us; we can learn how to make ourselves less vulnerable by learning how to think more positively.

As the research suggests, the attitudes and skills that comprise resilience can be learned. Rather than one specific trait, resilience is a set of skills that can be studied, practiced, expanded, and cultivated; like any skill, the more it is put to use, the stronger it becomes. Positive emotions, hardiness, grit, a growth mindset, the ability to purposefully reframe experiences and events—these are all related to the basic idea of resilience.

Attitude Reset

In order to cultivate resiliency, it is necessary to reframe your experience to change your perception of it. If you believe everything is terrible in the present and will remain terrible in the future, there is no reason to persevere beyond disappointments, frustrations, pain, or other difficult experiences. If you deliberately shift your thinking, however, so that you acknowledge the possibility of growth, opportunity, and positive developments resulting from these life challenges, you will be better poised to develop the necessary resilience to face whatever obstacles are in your way.

In the face of painful challenges, let's incorporate the attitudes, intentions, and actions that can make a difference in your capacity to be resilient and your ability to rebound to an even better place than before a setback. These same resources can help with perseverance as you pursue a long-held goal or dream.

Resilience Attitude, Intention, and Action Checklist

Each item on the list below is a recognized characteristic of people who are resilient. Note which ones you already hold with an *H* and those you want to develop with a *D*.

- Every experience in my life is or can become a learning opportunity.
- I have a "growth mindset"—that is, the belief that I can improve.

225

- Growth is my focus, and every challenge I face is an opportunity to learn and grow.
- I know I can reframe my setbacks and view them as positive challenges.
- I am willing to experience the unfamiliar, uncertain, unpleasant, and uncomfortable in life.
- I challenge myself to take thoughtful risks outside my comfort zone.
- I understand that pain is part of my growth and evolution; though I don't like it, I welcome the growth that can come from it.
- I believe my efforts and my journey are just as important as the successes I achieve.
- Failure is something that didn't work out; failures are simply opportunities to learn and are part of the path to success.
- Mistakes and setbacks are evidence I'm taking action, signs of progress, and a test of my commitment to what I want; they are not signs of inadequacy or failure.
- I know I have faced other difficult life circumstances, and I can draw on my experience of having successfully made it through them to face my current challenges.
- I approach life with curiosity and openness; curiosity, not criticism, is my go-to response.
- I hold an optimistic point of view.
- I spend time with people who are positive, upbeat, and/or optimistic.
- I have a sense of humor and an ability to use it when facing difficult life events or situations.
- I am able to draw on my cultural, religious, or spiritual beliefs as a source of support.
- I approach people from a positive, kind, and well-intentioned place.

- I know change is the constant in life; my intent is to be flexible and adaptive in the face of change.
- I have planning and problem-solving skills.
- I am doing something I consider meaningful.
- I have a purpose that goes well beyond my individual needs.
- I have a vision of what I would love in the future.
- I'm committed to goals and dreams that require discipline, patience, and endurance.
- I'm committed to pursuing excellence and mastery in my chosen endeavors.
- I feel capable and trust in my ability to experience and express unpleasant feelings.
- I am resourceful—I have family, close friends, and colleagues that I know I can turn to and ask for help.
- I can provide support to others as a means of boosting my own resilience.
- I use resources such as meditation, journal writing, music, or prayer to help me.
- To achieve my goals and dreams, I hold a "never give up" attitude.
- I will persist and persevere because those are integral aspects of facing challenges, being successful, and achieving my dreams.

---

* Companion worksheets, guided exercises, and more resources can be found at www.DrJoanRosenberg.com/resources90/

The Practice of Perseverance

Corey, a 25-year-old college graduate working in the technical side of the entertainment industry, came to my office because he was struggling with high anxiety and panic attacks. This was the second period in his life facing them; as we talked, I learned they occurred the first time in the months between graduating from college and working at his first job. During those months, there were days he wouldn't make it into work, go on business trips, or take vacations with his family because the panic attacks were so distressing and upset his sense of well-being so greatly. He had reached out to me for help because he started missing a few days of work and he didn't want that pattern to continue or for things to spiral out of control. As we worked together, I addressed his ability to experience and move through difficult feelings, and we followed a number of other strategies, but there were still aspects of Corey's anxiety that seemed unrelenting.

At one point, I asked Corey if he ever skied or snowboarded. He smiled and answered a resounding "Yes!" I followed with a question about his experiences doing both. Corey started skiing at the age of 4; once he turned 12, he engaged in competitive skiing and snowboarding and had participated in events throughout his teenage years.

"Did you ski or snowboard double black diamonds?" I asked.

To this question he emphatically answered with another resounding "Yes!"

Then I asked him, "Where's *ski dude*?"

Here's how to understand what followed: I helped Corey learn to draw from empowering experiences that were well known to him and that he loved—experiences lived by his fearless self, not one who was afraid or anxious. He could tap into an already confident, resourceful, and resilient self that felt strong, alive, competitive, driven, excited, and adventuresome. When Corey would start to feel anxious, he could reclaim his "ski dude" self and face down the anxiety and panic with the same fearlessness he embraced when he competed on the mountains.

The key is to reclaim your empowering life experiences as part of you—something you can draw upon and use in your everyday life—as opposed to playing down aspects of who you were. Sometimes, our brain may seem as if it is too panicked to prompt us to act. When that is the case, it is important to remind ourselves of times when we were able to push through, no matter how minor those instances may seem. *Your past instances of emotional strength can help fuel your current resilience.*

> *Your past instances of emotional strength can help fuel your current resilience.*

Kiera, a 22-year-old college senior, was collapsing under the weight of demands to complete her senior thesis on time. She was feeling emotionally paralyzed in her writing and finding it difficult to follow through with even simple everyday tasks. Like Corey, Kiera was a competitive athlete—a swimmer and martial artist—throughout her childhood and adolescence. By drawing on this life experience and the energetic rush she felt while participating in these sports, she identified her history of perseverance and competition, which helped her refocus to overcome her sense of overwhelm. This allowed Kiera to jump back into her writing and complete her thesis. Her memory of her own ability to persevere through difficult and demanding tasks helped her spring back to life.

For those of you without such experiences in your background, here is one of my favorite teaching stories from Mary Morrissey.[13] Do you remember first learning how to walk? It's unlikely most of us have clear memories of learning that skill in our early toddler years. What is likely, however, is that you fell down an untold number of times before you learned the distinction of balance and how to coordinate your legs so you could move on your own from place to place. Here's the beauty of all those falls and your subsequent getting up to try again: never did you say to yourself, "Well, I guess I'm just not destined to be a walker!" Instead, you got up and stayed with it until you learned how to walk. You can always think about your determination to walk as a resource to apply to other aspects of your life. You are destined to be more than you are now.

Journal 10: Your Adventurous, Competitive, and Persevering Traits

What identity did you have in early life that showcased your curiosity, adventure, risk-taking, strength, competitiveness, or never-give-up attitude—no matter how many falls you took? Think about important challenges or pursuits you completed (even completing high school counts). Access those memories. Experience what you felt then. Write about that person and identify your best traits from those times. How were you able to persevere and be resilient? How will you apply those strengths, attitudes, and traits going forward in everyday life now?

Reframe Failure, Risk-Taking, Feeling "Stuck," and Perfectionism

Much has been written about failure and how to think about it—especially as it relates to achieving the success you want in life. Brian Tracy, a well-known professional speaker and trainer in the areas of business and personal development, likes to say that if you want to become successful, then you must "fail as fast as you can." Of course, he, like countless others who speak on success and motivation, under-

Failures = Learning Opportunities

stands failures are more like mistakes that come with lessons. Failures, then, are just learning opportunities.

What stops people in their tracks from initiating and pursuing goals, however, is often what they describe as fear of failure. This "fear," more correctly identified as anxiety, I consider a feeling of discomfort with the experience of vulnerability rather than true bodily fear or anxiety. This discomfort is made so much worse when people who fail to achieve or complete something move from saying "I failed" to "*I'm* a failure."

These statements are problematic on multiple levels. First, is the misuse of the word "fear"; in all likelihood there is no imminent danger or threat. Second, when the statement moves from "I failed" to "I am a failure," the individual is engaged in faulty thinking, bad emotional math, emotional avoidance/distraction, and harsh self-criticism—a "bad" action does not equal a "bad" self. The most common outcomes follow: feeling worse and withdrawing from one's intended pursuits. This type of thinking limits the possibility of building confidence and resilience.

At its simplest, failure is commonly understood as not achieving what you set out to achieve. However, lots of people stop pursuing their goals if the first attempt to achieve the goal doesn't work. So, we can re-craft the definition of failure to not achieving what you set out to achieve, especially the *first* time you set out to achieve it.

Neither the first nor second definition truly captures the essence of failure, however. Concerns (or fears) about failure are less about the actions you need to take toward the goal and more about the undesired feeling outcome or feeling results of taking action. The truth is, I see *failure as difficulty tolerating the unpleasant feelings that are elicited when you don't achieve what you set out to achieve,* especially the first time you set out to achieve it. You stop trying because you don't want to face the feelings that will result if you don't succeed. That takes us right back to difficulties tolerating the eight difficult feelings. As with other challenges such as anxiety or speaking up, use the Rosenberg Reset and ride the 90-second waves of those unpleasant feelings. Each time you use the Reset, it will help you develop that sense of being capable and resilient.

We simply can't get away from the fact that the path to success in any domain or for any dream is laced with failure. It's up to each of us to be able to repeatedly and positively reframe our disappointments and frustrations into the markers of our forward movement and growth.

Periods of frustration and loss can stimulate growth. When you can hold the perspective that adversity is a positive challenge rather than an insurmountable obstacle, you become more flexible in addressing the problem, better equipped to deal with the adversity, and more able to learn and grow from the experience.

This reframing is important because if the hardship is seen as a threat instead of an opportunity, the event or situation tends to be drawn out longer, and the individual experiencing the situation is more likely to be negatively affected by the experience.

Develop confidence and emotional resilience by handling the unpleasant feelings about outcomes or results that you didn't want, and you effectively handle failure. If you can experience yourself as capable of handling sadness, shame, helplessness, anger, embarrassment, disappointment, frustration, and vulnerability, you can go after anything you want in life without concerns that a failure will stop you.

A person's capacity to take risks or stop feeling "stuck" and overwhelmed by life events functions in a similar way. Many people avoid taking risks because they might result in unwanted outcomes and feelings that are hard to bear. If you think about it, risk-taking and persistence imply an ability to face anger, disappointment, and frustration. Clearly, your capacity to handle unpleasant feelings is central to your ability to pursue your dreams, to initiate action, to take risks, and eventually to persist until you reach the desired goal or goals. Your willingness to put yourself out there and risk being hurt is one of the personal characteristics that enables you to bounce back from setbacks. That's also true of your capacity to see everything as a learning opportunity, especially when confronting obstacles. I realized long ago that what didn't work out the way I wanted was often a good story to tell later on. That realization helped me stay the course on whatever I was pursuing.

Perfectionism is similar to fear of failure and feeling "stuck." Many people desire to be perfect or say they are perfectionistic, yet when asked what being perfect means, they can't describe what it looks, sounds, or feels like. They are pursuing an undefined, amorphous ideal. Think of a dog chasing its tail—it will never be caught. Except, once again, the attempts at perfection are efforts to not feel sad, angry, disappointed, frustrated, or embarrassed. What if, instead, you could pursue mastery or excellence, or put your focus simply on doing your best? And then making that best even better?

Experiment. Explore. Be curious. Be willing to feel vulnerable or embarrassed or ask for help. Risk a little more. Watch what happens. Go after what you want. And don't stop.

How does emotional resilience help you to actively *create* and have a hand in building the life you want? By living in harmony with your most difficult emotions, you know you can bounce back from any action you take—no matter how it turns out. These qualities are the necessary fuel that empowers your efforts at building a life of your own design—a thriving life you love.

Thriving

Dr. Joe Dispenza, a scientist, lecturer, and author, likes to say that over time we get into so many patterns of ritualized behavior (e.g., your morning hygiene routine) that we feel the way we think and think the way we feel. We do this so often that, in essence, we get in the habit of being ourselves. Growth and change, then, requires that you think beyond how you feel[14]—imagining who you would like to be *more* than who you are currently. This enables you to break those long established patterns of behavior that represent who you are now.

You don't want to let the feelings and habits of who you are now and how you have lived and behaved up until this point hold you rigidly in place in a familiar and comfortable version of yourself. Take a few moments and think of who you *have been*. Have you been a person who has avoided your feelings and been lost in negative thinking? If so, then, for better or worse, this is the person that you have become familiar with and are comfortable being. This is the *you* that you have embodied. Literally. Right down to brain-firing patterns.

Is this who you want to remain—someone in the habit of repeating the past over and over again? If not, the great news is that any new thought, feeling, or behavior essentially invites you into a new you. A thriving you.

If you consider thoughts the language of the brain and feelings the language of the body, as Dispenza describes,[15] then changing your thinking and how you experience and express your feelings is vitally important to resculpting a new you. It takes thinking new thoughts, feeling new feelings, and engaging in new actions and experiences. Know that the new choices you make may initially feel unfamiliar and uncomfortable. But each time you experience and express your truth and face down old negative thoughts and faulty thinking patterns, you create a new state of being.

Confidence, then, is an embodied experience that can only occur through repeated thinking, doing, and feeling—when your mind's beliefs and the experience of your body become woven together. I'm proposing that you think of confidence as the embodied experience of a deep belief in your capability and resourcefulness. You emotionally feel a deep sense of confidence because you literally "feel" it in your body—this time in a "good" way. Consider confidence the felt sense of "can-do"-itiveness.

> *Confidence is the felt sense of "can-do"—itiveness.*

Now, we want to take your can-do-itiveness to the next level—to what will help you thrive.

Finding It Easier to Ask Others for Help

More often than not, people tell me that they don't want to lean on anybody or ask for help because they don't want to burden anyone with their troubles or be let down or disappointed if the requested help isn't forthcoming. How often do you feel either way?

Though it may seem paradoxical, the US military, thought of as a symbol of strength, offers a great analogy for dealing with feelings, vulnerability, and asking for help simultaneously. At the outset of any military campaign in a new region, the planners and strategists consider all points of vulnerability and weakness. Once they have identified the areas where they lack readiness to deal with perceived threats, they arrange for assistance to supplement their existing resources and strength. They might bring in engineers, crisis teams, special forces, reconnaissance teams, or infantry for extra support. Interesting, isn't it? The act of identifying deficits and admitting "weakness" is what allows them to become considerably stronger—but only if they take action to address those potential vulnerabilities.

This is also true for you. As you move forward in your growth, it is important to keep in mind the following three truths:

- ◆ Asking for help is not a burden.
- ◆ Asking for help strengthens you and adds to your emotional resources.
- ◆ Asking for help compliments the listener and leads to your friends valuing you and your friendship more highly.

Reverse the roles for a moment. Has anyone ever asked you for advice? What was your emotional reaction when you were asked? Did you like that you were being sought out? Did you feel like your opinion might be important? Did you feel like the person valued you? Did you feel respected?

If you offered your help (e.g., assisted with a move, babysitting, or running an errand) or provided guidance or advice, did you feel closer to that acquaintance, friend, or family member? If your experience of being sought out was generally positive—and most of us do have experience of when others genuinely wanted our opinion or perspective—then it likely felt like a compliment to have been the person or one of the people your friend or family member trusted. Being sought out accords value to you and value to the friendship.

Asking for help is really a compliment to others. Holding this perspective enables you to ask for what you truly need. You are not burdening the other person; in the process of asking, you're acknowledging their importance to you. Additionally, when you ask for help, not only do you feel more resourceful, your connections with others are deepened.

Journal 11: Asking for Help

Are you aware of your needs and limitations? Do you ask for help when you need it? What is it like for you to receive assistance from others? If you do ask, how has it changed the quality of your relationships? What thoughts do you have about not asking for help when you would clearly benefit from receiving it? What will you do differently going forward to get the help you really need?

Asking for help is one way you turn your vulnerability into emotional strength and confidence. Since we've been talking about the more dependent and vulnerable side of our nature, let's take a look at trust and its relationship to emotional strength.

Reframe Trust

Most people think of trust as an experience, or, if you will, connective tissue *among* people. It is often reflected in statements like: "That person is really trustworthy," "I can't trust a thing she says," "I'm not sure I trust him," or "I don't trust him."

There are two distinctions I want you to consider. First, I think of trust as an experience that is *in you* and *has to do with you* rather than being something between you and another person. In other words, it's less about whether you trust the other person and much more about whether you trust yourself to handle a situation if it doesn't turn out well. What it means to trust yourself is that you know that you can handle the resulting feelings—yes, we're back to the eight difficult feelings—of whatever the situation is, if things don't turn out the way you want. In other words, trust has to do with your confidence in yourself and knowing that you are inherently capable and resilient.

Second, notice what happens when you replace the word *trust* with the word *believe*. "I don't *trust* him," becomes "I don't *believe* him." My guess is that simply replacing the word elicits a whole different visceral experi-

> *Emotional Strength =*
> *Capable and Resourceful =*
> *Confidence = Trust.*

ence in you regarding what the word really means. In this case, *trust,* or *trusting yourself,* translates into believing you are capable, resourceful, confident, and resilient.

How, then, do you develop a capacity to truly believe in yourself?

1. **By experiencing encouragement and reinforcement with regard to how you are valued by others.** In the best of circumstances, this starts early and continues throughout life—simply the valuing that you are here, and the joy and pleasure others experience in your "being-ness" helps you value yourself. Clearly, this does not always happen, which leads to the grief we saw in the last chapter.

2. **By mastering a body of knowledge or developing a knowledge-based area of expertise.** Reading or studying helps you build and develop in-depth knowledge and expertise in one or more areas or domains. Increasing competence leads to increasing confidence. It is a self-perpetuating cycle of positive growth.

3. **By being present to as much of your moment-to-moment experience as possible.** This means being aware of, acknowledging, experiencing and trusting the eight difficult feelings. Allowing yourself to move toward pain and deal with the feelings that result from things not turning out the way you want builds emotional strength.

4. **By expressing yourself.** The act of speaking changes you. You develop confidence by freely and authentically giving voice to your thoughts, feelings, beliefs, values, concerns, and dreams and come to know yourself better when you do. Speak your truth from a positive, kind, and well-intentioned place.

5. **By taking action.** You develop confidence by taking action, or taking risks. It is the "doing" itself that helps you build confidence. As many personal development trainers say: It's not always about achieving the dream or getting the goal; it's about who you become in the process.

6. **By embracing and taking in compliments.** The intent is to really absorb and integrate praise and recognition into your being so that your best qualities and attributes fully register as part of your "sense of self."

Rock-solid confidence develops over time, yet experiences that change this perception of yourself can happen more quickly and easily than you might expect. What helps people believe they can handle life more effectively? Trusting that you are emotionally strong is the foundation, followed by speaking, taking action, and absorbing compliments. Last, let's understand the important role compliments have in building and maintaining confidence.

Compliments

Compliments are, in many ways, the flip side of the coin of harsh self-criticism. Harsh self-criticism depletes; compliments replenish. However, harsh self-criticism depletes far more than compliments can supplant, which leaves a gaping deficit. If you are harshly self-critical and don't allow yourself to absorb compliments, this quickly becomes a major problem—a losing strategy that will only nudge you down the path of soulful depression. When you engage in harsh self-criticism, you are metaphorically depleting your own fountain of energy with nothing to replace your resources. It's no wonder that you would feel alone, anxious, vulnerable, or tapped out. Learning to accept genuine compliments plays a central role in developing your confidence, living authentically, and designing a life you love.

Accepting vs. Refusing the Compliments of Others

Are you a person who refuses compliments by immediately devaluing them, dismissing them, explaining them away, or playing them down? Even though you receive sincere compliments, do you ever question why someone would be complimenting you? Do you ever think you aren't deserving of kind words of praise or recognition? Or do you ever question people's sincerity, thinking that they are only complimenting you to be nice or to get something from you? Perhaps you simply don't believe the compliments. Maybe you have thought: "Yeah, but if you knew the real me, you would never say that." For many people, these kinds of responses are second nature—but there's a real downside if you never take in the compliments you receive. Dismissing or refusing compliments holds you to your old life story, where you often relive thoughts, feelings, memories, and patterns that compromise your confidence, resilience, and authenticity.

Why Taking in Compliments Is So Hard

Most people either find it difficult to accept genuine compliments or simply choose not to accept them. There are many possible reasons for this. In the list below, check off the reasons that fit with your experience.

Compliment Blockers™

☐ When you were a child, you were repeatedly told not to take in compliments because you would get "too big for your britches," develop a big ego, or become selfish.

☐ As you grew up, you were told it was better to be humble than proud—and that "pride" was negative and unappealing.

☐ You dismiss compliments because you think accepting them will lead to arrogance, conceit, "a big head," or something similar.

☐ You refuse compliments simply because you don't know what to say or do once you receive them.

☐ Accepting compliments challenges your cultural or ethnic beliefs and what you were taught as a child.

☐ You were taught you were not worthy of compliments.

☐ You don't like being the center of attention or feel embarrassed when others notice you.

☐ You give false compliments and believe others do the same; as a result, others' compliments are not believable to you when you receive them.

☐ You dismiss compliments because you were taught and now believe that all compliments about you are insincere.

☐ You might think you don't deserve such kind words and responses.

☐ You know you are attractive, skilled, or talented and don't want to let on to others that you know, so that it appears you don't care or are less competitive with them.

☐ You dismiss compliments so you can continue to undervalue yourself and not be made to feel vulnerable or exposed to critique, even though this prevents you from reaching your highest potential; you are "playing it safe."

☐ You selectively choose what to believe about yourself and arbitrarily assign higher value to your harsh self-criticism, thus dismissing the compliments you receive.

☐ You believe you have to be perfect; because you think you are "not enough," haven't reached your own standard of perfection, and think that you could be better still, so you brush off or dismiss compliments. Doing so fends off your own feelings of disappointment about your current level of progress or mastery.

☐ The compliment is incongruent with how you see yourself; as a consequence, it's not believable to you (this may be the most common reason for dismissing compliments).

What would it take for you to believe the compliments you receive?

The compliments you hear may, in fact, reflect you or your work genuinely and accurately. The problem is that when you find compliments incongruent with your current self-image, no one can cheerlead you into believing them. If you typically remain quiet, *refuse to speak your truth, and prevent others from knowing your authentic self,* then the absence of genuineness and truth-telling leads to a reaction of: "Yeah, but if you knew the real me, you would never say that." You have created a pattern of hiding your true self from others, which is why you can't accurately gauge how you are viewed by others nor find their responses believable. All this changes when you start speaking up.

Lots of people act as if compliments they receive were just pulled out of thin air, completely arbitrary and apropos of nothing. The fact is, most compliments don't just show up out of nowhere, nor do they occur in a vacuum. Something about *you or your actions* had to spark the thought behind the comment that you are struggling to accept. It's important to change your understanding of the nature of compliments so you can begin to take in and really absorb the energy, experience, connection, and value they bring to your life.

Absorbing positive feedback from others is an essential aspect of the 90 Seconds approach. Taking in new information by way of compliments is like updating your software to the most current and relevant version. When you absorb and integrate the compliments you receive, rather than rejecting them outright, not only will you update your self-image but you'll also live more authentically, which, in turn, solidifies your confidence.

Jillian, 33, now a partner at a graphic design firm, was a bright and dedicated student all through her academic studies, yet she described having to work hard for everything she achieved. She never saw herself as genuinely creative or brilliant and was haunted by imposter syndrome despite her obvious intelligence and unique outlook on the world. When she started designing, her coworkers frequently commented on her creativity and intelligence. As she presented her work professionally, she was repeatedly met with the same responses from peers, clients, and colleagues: *What a smart and unique perspective you offer!*

As we worked together, I helped Jillian realize how extensively she had dismissed the compliments and positive feedback she had received over the years, and how rejecting compliments kept her locked in an outdated perception of herself and her professional value. She was able to recognize how she continued to see herself as if she had just started her career, even though she was actually a distinguished professional in her field. She was also able to describe the pressure she continued to put on herself, as well as the emotional strain that resulted, simply because she hadn't allowed the compliments to land. Based on the consistency of these compliments over time and across

243

several aspects of her life, she was finally willing and able to hear, accept, and incorporate these compliments into how she sees herself. Not only was she able to let go of the notion that she was an imposter, she now understands she is both creative and brilliant. It has allowed her to be more confident in her choices personally and professionally.

Journal 12: Compliments

What compliments have you brushed away over the years? What do people tell you that you play down or dismiss? How might that change your sense of self if you really let yourself experience the reflections of you back to you?

You are an ever-evolving human being who is capable of being more, should you so desire it—especially if you are intentional about defining and pursuing your goals. If you have ever dreamed of being a certain kind of person, understand that absorbing compliments is an essential element in making that happen. Once you take in these compliments and positive feedback, you will begin to believe that you are becoming who you most desire to be, or you may even recognize that you are *already living* as the person you desire to become. That's an awesome moment of awareness and a huge step forward in confidence. It is also a turning point as you get a real sense that you are settling comfortably in your own skin.

> *Once you take in compliments and positive feedback, you will begin to believe that you are becoming who you most desire to be, or even that you are already living as the person you desire to become.*

Absorbing the Positive

1. Find a quiet place to sit. Place your hands together in an open position with your pinky fingers touching alongside each other, extend your arms out away from your body (as if you are holding and reading an open book). In that position, look at both palms.

2. Start by taking a few deep breaths to center yourself. Now, think of the positive words that people have been saying to you. You can draw from things you've been told recently or from any time in the past. It doesn't matter whether these compliments came from family, friends, coworkers, school peers, or even children. With each compliment, pause and think about what each person said—then allow yourself to really feel it. Breathe and fully take in every positive word. Let yourself experience the truth of their words.

3. Imagine yourself stacking each one of those positive statements and memories, one on top of the other, in the palms of your hands. When you have stacked several of them, take a few more slow, deep breaths as you pause, embrace, and enjoy what has been said. When you are ready, place both of your hands over your heart and breathe in the fullness of their words once again.

4. Go through this process several more times right now.

5. Continuously use this process to help yourself really take in and absorb the compliments you receive.

Experiences you thought were beyond you—love, accepting compliments, being nurtured and supported—can now be received openly and warmly. Learn to become comfortable with the experience of and need for both independence and dependence. As you continue using this technique, you'll feel capable (well connected to yourself) and resourceful (well connected to others), with increased emotional strength. You'll feel the joy of knowing you are becoming who you most desire to be.

Taking It to the Next Level

Continued use of the Rosenberg Reset, speaking up, taking action, and accepting compliments helps solidify your sense of confidence. The ability to experience the eight difficult feelings without being swept away by them enables you to feel capable of facing challenges as they present themselves, while empowering you to be vulnerable, take risks, ask for help, and pursue your dreams. This growing sense of capability provides the groundwork for all that follows in your personal growth.

Be open to asking for help and understand that when you do, the benefit is twofold: not only do you feel more resourceful and thus more confident, you also compliment others by asking for their help. The dependent side of our nature is simply an expression of our humanity. When we can allow ourselves to ask for help or reach toward others, it deepens the social connections we have and need throughout adulthood. Caring, supportive, and loving relationships are a protective factor that promotes good health throughout life.

Finally, take in the compliments you receive. As I've emphasized, compliments uplevel your experience of you and help you update your self-image. They also solidify the positive changes you make and confirm and affirm the steps that you are taking to enhance your life. Make the commitment to fully absorbing them instead of brushing them off. What good comes from having your efforts and hard work validated if you choose to disregard the evidence of them?

Not only are capability and resourcefulness key elements of

well-being, they are also at the foundation of resilience. With these aspects of emotional strength in place, you will be better pre-

> *If you have the capacity to think, you have the capacity to change.*

pared to persevere and eventually thrive through setbacks and disappointments. Your resourceful attitudes make all the difference in upleveling your confidence and resilience so that you can thrive.

CHAPTER 10

Committing to Your True Self

So now we've come full circle. You've learned and practiced the Rosenberg Reset—the method designed to help you stay fully present to your feelings and experience. I hope you have been able to incorporate it with ease by making that one choice to stay aware of and experiencing your feelings instead of avoiding them. I hope that you've seen how the eight difficult feelings act as the single thread and hidden driver behind your confidence, resilience, and authenticity. Likewise, I hope those 90 seconds helped you recognize you really are capable of dealing with difficult feelings.

If you can ride one or more 90-second waves of one or more of eight unpleasant feelings, then you can pursue anything you want in life. This is the pathway to a more fully expressed, more alive you. That's where we are now: identifying the few remaining elements that will be the final steps in empowering you to create and live a life you love. This will allow you to achieve that something *more* I mentioned at the beginning of the book.

How do we help you be *more*? Imagine, once again, who you would like to become and the impact you would like to have. Start living that vision of yourself. Become intentional in the choices you make, and you will take inspired action toward your goals and dreams.

Imagined impact. Intentional choices. Inspired action. These three steps lead to a life filled with purpose and meaning.

Be Impactful

Who you *choose to be* on a daily basis leads you right into *who you can be* as your life unfolds over time. Now that we've had an opportunity to confront the mental and emotional obstacles that have held you back, to release the old stories from the past, and to empower you to live from a more centered, peaceful place in the present, what better time to think about the future than now?

Dreaming about your future and manifesting those dreams will only happen with clear intention followed by inspired actions to make them a reality. Daily efforts or daily actions turn into habits. Yes, effort will always be part of the equation. *The way you make anything happen is by translating your ideas into action and by then engaging in those actions.*

Design a Life of Meaning

Most of us would like to live meaningful and purposeful lives, lives of such impact that someone noticed that we were here—that we mattered. However, we often get wrapped up and held to the conditions, circumstances, and situations of our everyday lives. As a consequence, we don't consciously think about what we want our lives to look like, nor do we fully consider what our impact or legacy—what I call our "imprint"—will be.

Journal 13: Designing Your Life

Designing your life starts with your imagination. Imagine your life three years from now. Using pictures, what does your life look like? What do you dream of? What would you love to have or create in your life? (If you did the similar exercise at the beginning of this book, take a look at the notes you jotted down and build on what you first wrote.)

Vision statements are written in the past tense, as if all you dreamed of had already come true. Take the time to write a one- or two-page narrative of what your life would look like *at the end* of this three-year time period. Use specific images and descriptive words that indicate what you saw, heard, felt physically, and felt emotionally.[1] Where are you living? What job do you have? What does your personal life look like? What hobbies or meaningful pursuits are you engaged in? How are you giving back to others? You can also consider what gives you meaning and leaves you feeling gratified and fulfilled. Do you have a mission? Believe in a cause? Have a message to deliver that would change all the lives you touch? How can you serve? What would you like your legacy to be?

Use these images as you dream forward, though be open to having it unfold differently than you imagined—in other words, don't get stuck on the specifics.

We often develop a sense of purpose and meaning through contribution. What goes into finding your contribution? Start by thinking about what you are passionate about—what lights you up, what excites or delights you, what you could get so totally lost in that you would lose all sense of time, an experience known as a "flow" state.[2] Is there more than one area where you experience this sense of flow?

Opportunities abound. You can contribute through volunteerism, activism, or charitable contributions. If you have a group you want to serve or a mission or cause that you support, put your focus there. Do you want to put your efforts into supporting a certain community or population? Or maybe it's some aspect of your environment, like protecting oceans, rain forests, marshlands, rivers, or lakes. Or animal rescue. Or supporting the arts. Or promoting economic development. Consider that you might be the answer to someone else's need.[3]

Prime Your Brain

It's important to keep your desired way of being in the world in the forefront of your conscious awareness and allowing it to guide your day. You need to prime your brain to do so. Build in a minimum of ten minutes at the beginning and end of your day for periods of reflection. Keep a pad of paper and the narrative of your vision next to your bed.

Morning Ritual

1. When you wake up in the morning, grab your notepad.
2. Start each day with gratitude. Write down a minimum of five things you are grateful for.
3. Follow with three values or qualities you intend to embody that day. Who do you want to be and how do you want to show up?[4]
4. Set your intentions—what would you like to see accomplished when your day is complete? Identify three items to complete or achieve.[5]
5. Read the vision you wrote earlier and mentally live it as if it were already complete.[6]

Evening Ritual

1. At the end of the evening, review your day.
2. Were there moments you could have handled better? Think through those situations; identify what you can learn from them and do a mental replay with your desired response.
3. Take time to read your vision again, immersing yourself once more in what you wrote.
4. Write down your wins.[7]
5. Take a moment to reflect on any recognition or compliments you received. Stack the positive. Absorb them. Ask yourself: Am I becoming who I most want to be?
6. End with gratitude.
7. Remember to set aside time weekly, monthly, quarterly, and yearly to review and change your goals and dreams and to see what you have accomplished and how you have developed.

Companion worksheets, guided exercises, and more resources can be found at www.DrJoanRosenberg.com/resources90/

Be Intentional

Of the ways to develop confidence, here are the top few I've talked about:

- ◆ **Experience.** Be aware of and in touch with as much of your moment-to-moment experience as possible. This idea has been otherwise described as "knowing what you know" and has to do with your capacity to move toward pain and tolerate the eight difficult feelings. It will help you handle the ambiguities and uncertainties of life. Your ability to experience and move through the eight feelings is the unifying thread throughout the book; it also supports resilience and perseverance. Accepting the truth of your experience is your starting point.

♦ **Express.** To express is to speak your truth. Speaking your truth not only helps you know yourself better, it enables you to experience the greatest single gain in your self-confidence. It catapults you onto an upward recursive spiral; with that boost you speak more, and with speaking more you foster more confidence, resilience, and authenticity. Speaking your truth aligns your thoughts, feelings, and words and moves you into the right relationship with yourself and with others; it's the linchpin for living more authentically. When you live more authentically, love for yourself naturally emerges.

♦ **Engage.** Taking action is the third major way to build confidence. Most of us understand we have to do something in order to achieve our goals, yet many of us are reluctant to go after what we want. Similar to speaking, engaging is not a situation where you have confidence and then take risks or act. Instead, it is *through* taking action that you develop confidence. Your efforts result in a sense of progress and completion, and over time they can result in increasing levels of competence and, eventually, mastery. As you take risks, your capacity to comfortably negotiate difficult feelings cushions the effect of things not turning out the way you want and helps you develop the emotional agility to be resilient.

You'll see the first shifts in your sense of emotional strength and confidence when you start to embrace all of you, especially the eight difficult feelings. You will notice more significant shifts when you use your voice to speak your truth. Speaking up is essential for creating these changes, and they lead to increasing confidence and authenticity—followed, of course, by taking action.

How to Develop Confidence

1. Be **encouraged**:

   Through encouragement and reinforcement, you are valued because you are you.

2. Develop **expertise**:

   You master a body of knowledge through study in one or more areas or domains.

3. **Experience** fully:

   You notice, accept, and trust the eight difficult feelings, enabling you to more comfortably experience your whole range of feelings and feel more fully yourself.

4. **Express** yourself:

   You speak your truth from a positive, kind, and well-intentioned place.

5. **Engage** boldly:

   You take action and take risks to pursue what you want and to grow.

6. Embrace **esteem**:

   You absorb and integrate compliments, recognizing they reflect you back to you; fully accepting compliments helps you update your view of yourself.

Be Inspired

Be "In-Sync" with Yourself

Change and growth aren't casual. They demand effort. When you consistently practice acknowledging the truth of what you think, feel, need, or perceive, and when you do the same by speaking your truth, then you naturally start to move into living your truth. As I described in chapter 7, *congruence* is when your actions match your words, and your words and actions consistently match your thoughts, feelings, beliefs, and values. It leads to an experience of being comfortable in your own skin. It's both an aspirational ideal and something you may need to work on daily to live as fully present and genuinely as you can. Being congruent is the base of confidence, emotional strength, and authenticity.

People who are congruent are spontaneous, flexible, and open to experience the fluidity of life. They are centered and grounded, which leads to them living substantive lives. Being congruent doesn't mean that you won't ever have to face hard times. It's just that you'll be able to handle uncomfortable situations more quickly and effectively. You'll be able to face these challenging life obstacles and the eight unpleasant feelings without ever again experiencing yourself as a flawed human being, nor as undeserving or unworthy. Of course, you'll still experience unpleasant feelings as reactions to life events, but you'll be able to say goodbye to the equation that "bad feelings = bad self." The natural result of congruence is to love yourself, which grows into a desire to create a life you love.

Stay the Course: Growth Is Not Linear

Our natural tendency as humans is to move toward growth, to be something more than we are right now. Yet growth is not linear. You can learn something new or have a profound insight or experience that, in just a moment, completely changes how you view your past, how you live in the present, or how you want to live in the future. The smallest instant and simple insights can lead to massive changes in how and what you think, feel, or do. That's what happened for Liana.

Liana, a college-educated woman in her late 30s, recently had a chance to practice the Rosenberg Reset and proceeded to fill me in on what happened. Her husband had asked her to attend a professional networking event, something, as she put it, she was dreading. She said one of her "superpowers" was social awkwardness, so she was reluctant to go. Since she had just learned the Rosenberg Reset, she decided to experiment with the concept and apply it to the networking event. Figuring she could hang out with anyone and with any feeling for 90 seconds, she imagined attending the event and moved toward the dread, by way of the eight feelings, to understand what was driving her reluctance. What was it about groups of strangers and small talk that she hated and that made her feel so uncomfortable? What was she doing to psych herself out before such events?

She realized she generally felt vulnerable, feared embarrassment, and was concerned that others would see her as an imposter. As a consequence, she thought she wasn't worthy of attending this type of gathering. Previously, she would typically find herself engaged in small talk or synopsizing her résumé to prove her worth to others in attendance. Using the Reset, she let her vulnerability and embarrassment wash over her and simply rode the waves of them — in this case, in her imagination. It took the edge off the emotions that would usually stop her. Turning toward those emotions before the event helped her realize they weren't so bad after all. She recognized that if those feelings were to come up during the event, she could handle them, because she had already allowed herself to experience them ahead of time. She described it as feeling "as if the ice had already been broken."

Using the Rosenberg Reset during the event appears to have worked just as well as it had before the event. Liana described feeling like she was worthy of being in the room when she got there—she was no longer consumed by the fear that she had to prove her worth to the other attendees. By acknowledging her vulnerability, Liana was calmer, which not only enabled her to engage in meaningful conversations but also allowed her to feel more confident because she had something to offer the individuals she met. Her husband even complimented her after the event, saying that he had never seen her being so social before. Liana now realizes she can go into similar situations and actually look forward to them instead of having intense dread. She also recognizes that she can apply this approach to a variety of other life situations as they come up. The best part? She told me she had shed her old identity and carries herself differently as a result. She said: "I felt like I was able to be the person I always wanted to be." What's even more exciting is that she had only learned the Reset two days before!

Liana essentially experienced the arc of this book in this one situation. I am aware of many others who have used the Reset and made significant changes in a very short time. It can happen for you, too.

Not all changes come so quickly, however, and you may need to exert more effort over a longer period of time to achieve the changes you desire. This might involve concentrating on a particular issue, thought, feeling, sensation, or action. Through repeated use of the strategies I've described, over time, you'll make the changes you seek. They may need time so that new connections in the brain can be stimulated and new neural paths developed. Your perseverance is key here.

Perhaps you worry about changing some aspect of yourself that you really want to keep. Know that you have control over the changes you make. What do you want to change? What do you want to keep? What goals would you like to achieve?

It may, at times, feel like you spiral back to some aspect or attribute you already worked on. That is quite common. If it happens for you, you'll likely be tackling the same issue from a different angle and often at a deeper level. Stay aware. Notice these patterns in your life. One change in a pattern can lead to many other desired changes. When you allow yourself to face painful issues or concerns, you move toward growth and an experience of wholeness within yourself.

Live by a Code of High Values

By choosing to live congruently, you are cultivating the skills needed to experience emotional strength and sustain a high level of confidence. Establishing deep connections with others and contributing to your community or society completes the circle, sharing what you know. A life filled with purpose and meaning is the outcome.

But, really, how do you get there? You start by getting clear about the values you hold and the values or standards by which you want to live. You can use these as measures for every aspect of your life: career, health, relationships, business, finances, and more. What are those standards for you? How do you want to interact with others and how do you want them to treat you? How do you want to show up in the world? Who do you want to be?

Journal 14: Your Code of High Values

Think of three to five values, qualities, or attributes that you want to define you and/or define how you want others to experience you in various contexts (e.g., family, professional, social). Choose qualities that fall into what I call a "code of high values"— qualities that are limitless by their very nature, such as gentleness, kindness, warmth, respectfulness, compassion, acceptance, or generosity. Embody those daily.

Values are aspirational and dynamic. We may hold firm to a value, but in order to "have" it, at times, we must exhibit and embody the value through effort and practice—that is how we bring that value into being. For instance, to see yourself as a generous person, you must "be" generous (e.g., with your time, money, service) to embody the value.

Many people believe others "make them feel" a certain way—pushed into reacting with angry, defensive, or blaming words or behavior. Beyond riding the 90-second waves, there is another centered and centering way you can experience and move through your intense feelings and reactions. You can use your values or desired qualities to guide how you respond in upsetting or stressful situations. In other words, how you want to see yourself and how you want to treat others becomes a barometer for your behavior.

Values become self-regulating; they invite and lead us to be the *more* we desire to be. An example: Let's say you described yourself as a cynical and pessimistic person, yet you realized that you no longer liked how that felt and you noticed the effect your attitude and remarks had on others; people were not spending time with you as they had in the past. Once you made your decision to change, early on you had to "catch yourself" being cynical and pessimistic and consciously shift your attitude into an open-minded, optimistic one. The more you practiced, the more it "became you"; subsequent experiences you faced were filtered through this new mindset.

One of my highest values is kindness. Several years ago, I was driving in Los Angeles and was stopped in heavy traffic. While stopped, I felt the car behind me hit my rear bumper with some force. You can imagine my reaction. Anger, irritation, and frustration were among my first feelings.

Yet in those first moments, I had just enough time to think about how I could respond once I got out of the car. In those seconds, I thought about who I wanted to be in the world and how I preferred to handle myself. Given how I value kindness, I decided to experience my reactions calmly and internally, rather than conveying them harshly through unkind words to the driver. She hadn't meant to hit my car; she couldn't do anything to fix what had already occurred. Reflecting on this gave me a chance to realize there was no need for hostility. When I got out of the car, I went back to inspect the damage to the bumper, quietly and methodically exchanged the proper insurance information with the other driver, and then continued on with the rest of my day. I was left to handle the remaining irritation on my own, without it negatively impacting anyone else or coloring how I saw the day; one event equaled one event so it didn't "ruin" my day. What I had chosen to do was to filter my response through the value of kindness. It takes awareness, deliberate decision-making, and daily conscious action to live our highest selves.

> *What if you responded to others, events, and situations from your core values instead of your immediate reactions?*

Going forward, make the decision to have all your words and actions reflect your values. It's about being congruent. Let no argument or situation elicit a reaction from you that is not filtered through these values or qualities first. This approach provides you total freedom in your behavior and in your responses to others. There is no need to get defensive, to go "tit for tat" and "even the score," to cast one of you as bad and the other good, or any other kind of response that traps you in the situation rather than allowing you to move beyond it.

As with any new skill, you must consistently practice it in order for it to become second nature to you. Practice living these values until you embody them with less effort and thinking—almost automatically. If you want, choose one at a time and concentrate on mastering it in the span of a week or a month before moving on to what you want to embody next. When you are totally clear on these values/qualities, nothing can pull you off center. Quick, harsh reactivity disappears. Centered, rock-solid intentional responses appear in its place.

Code of High Values Grid™

In the grid below, choose three qualities that reflect the values you wish to hold, or add your own. For the next 14 days, act in ways that embody those values every day.

	WHO I AM NOW	WHO I INTEND TO BE	WHAT I MUST DO TO EMBODY THE VALUE
COMPASSIONATE			
ENGAGED			
EXPRESSIVE			
FORGIVING			
GENEROUS			
GRATEFUL			
HUMBLE			
JOYFUL			
KIND			
LOVING			

(Continued)

	WHO I AM NOW	WHO I INTEND TO BE	WHAT I MUST DO TO EMBODY THE VALUE
OPTIMISTIC			
PATIENT			
PLAYFUL			
FULLY PRESENT			
RESPECTFUL			
RESPONSIVE			
THOUGHTFUL			
UNDERSTANDING			

Companion worksheets, guided exercises, and more resources can be found at www.DrJoanRosenberg.com/resources90/

How to Create a Confident, Resilient, and Authentic Life of Your Design

Encapsulated below are the ten essential keys for developing emotional mastery and creating a confident, resilient, and authentic life of your design.

1. Check your attitudes.

- Resolve to be curious, open, and flexible in the face of change and adversity.
- Exhibit a willingness to learn from every life experience.
- Commit to having an optimistic attitude, perseverance, and the mindset to become a lifelong learner.

2. Choose awareness, not avoidance.

- Be aware of and in touch with as much of your moment-to-moment experience as possible.
- Master the eight difficult feelings using the Rosenberg Reset—this is the essence of feeling capable in the world.

- Lean into and choose vulnerability—make it your greatest strength.

3. Diminish distractions.
- Do what you can to live fully present and aware.
- Identify your distractions, notice what they help you avoid, and move toward the unpleasant feelings.
- Relieve anxiety by identifying, experiencing and expressing the difficult feelings underneath.

4. End faulty thinking and harsh self-criticism.
- Break free from pessimism, cynicism, cognitive distortions and use of "Bad Emotional Math"—redirect to more constructive, expansive, open, and optimistic thinking.
- Notice your harsh self-criticism and use it as a signal that something hard to bear is making itself known to you.
- Ask yourself, "What is difficult for me to know, feel, or bear right now?" and bring it more fully into consciousness. Then use the Reset if painful feelings surface.

5. Speak. Take Action.
- Approach others and speak from a positive, kind, and well-intended place.
- Speak your truth so that you can live your most authentic self.
- Decide what you want to pursue or achieve, identify the first small step, and take it.
- Identify the next step, and take that one, too. Keep taking action and persevere until you reach your goal.

6. Release your old story.
- Make sense of your life stories.
- Let go of grief and disguised grief.
- Forgive. Embrace a new story. Access joy and deepen connections.

7. Ask for help.

- ◆ Know that asking is the essence of resourcefulness and a key aspect of emotional strength and resilience.
- ◆ Create a social safety net. Develop closer relationships with family and friends.
- ◆ Draw from the experiences of prior successes.

8. Accept and absorb compliments.

- ◆ Understand that compliments are a reflection of you and update your self-image.
- ◆ Absorb them…over and over and over again.

9. Live by a code of high values.

- ◆ Be congruent. Make sure your words and actions match your thoughts, feelings, beliefs, and values.
- ◆ Generate the values you want to embody. Live who you want to become.
- ◆ Be intentional: think, speak, and act *only* in the direction you want your life to go.

10. Design your life.

- ◆ Create your future. Imagine what you would love. Write down what you have envisioned. Who and what do you want to become? What will give you purpose and meaning?
- ◆ Engage in daily practices of gratitude, setting intentions, and reviewing your vision and wins to establish the momentum you need to achieve your goals and dreams.

People often go searching for confidence outside themselves, yet the type of growth and change that results in confidence is an inside job. It's up to each of us, individually, to make the decision to be more than we are today—and to make the

> *"If an egg is broken by outside force, Life ends. If broken by inside force, Life begins. Great things always begin from inside."—Jim Kwik*

choices and engage in the actions every day that help us become who we most want to be.

That initial decision, and each big or small one that follows it, is the key to any transformation. Choose to grow and keep making that same choice with every obstacle, every leap forward, every setback, and every success.

It's important to understand that life is dynamic, creative, and changeable—almost as if life has a life of itself. As you demand more of yourself, you'll demand more from life—and that's how you will influence life's unfolding.

Just as change is the constant in life, you, too, are also ever-evolving. Understand that the wounds you have experienced along the way might be your awakening moments, a portal into growth that is either inviting or demanding that you be something more than you are now. And when you feel frustrated that you haven't reached your goal or doubt your ability to keep pressing forward, just be aware: that is life testing your commitment for what you really want.

Release those distractions. Release the harsh self-criticism, and release your old story. The difficult feelings that you avoided or that used to hold you back are no longer barriers to taking risks. The Rosenberg Reset handles that. It's eight feelings between you and your success.

Feel, express, and live the truth of who you are. Commit to your true self.

Know that you really do have the capacity to develop into the person you imagine. You have a strong hand in creating a life you love—one that enables you to be authentic, confident, emotionally strong, enthusiastic, purpose-driven, and resilient. Choose this growth.

You are capable of experiencing far more than your circumstances and conditions. Pursue those dreams. Do so with confidence. How far do you want to stretch?

Living who you want to be is one choice away...it starts with making the one choice to be well connected to your moment-to-moment experience, and riding one or more 90-second waves of one or more of eight difficult feelings. When you commit to this, you are committing to every goal, every dream, and every possibility you can imagine for yourself.

You are committing to something *more*.

Simple, huh?

Welcome home.

Acknowledgments

This book is a reflection of a lifelong personal and professional journey and there are a number of people who have been instrumental in supporting me along the way. I offer my deepest gratitude to each one of them for their mentoring and friendship and for their extended hands, invitations, and opportunities. To each mentioned below, I thank you for your support, encouragement, belief in me and my message, and for opening doors leading beyond Thoreau's invisible boundary.

Dr. Dan Siegel: You advanced and redefined psychotherapy as you developed the field of interpersonal neurobiology. Your mentoring and knowledge opened up a world to me. The opportunity to study with you across those years left an indelible print on me personally and professionally—the information I first learned with and from you serves as the grounding base for my 90 Seconds approach. You continue to inspire me.

Brendon Burchard: You challenged us to get our messages out there so others could benefit from hearing our voices. Thank you for modeling the same, for your strategic thinking, risk-taking, and for your focus on providing high quality content. Not only were you the first to encourage me to publish this material, you created a place for me to deliver it onstage.

Pam Hendrickson: Your first reading of my material and your response to it instilled in me so much hope. Your brilliance with content reigns supreme. Thank you for your mind and heart. I love both and am so grateful for your friendship. And to your co-traveler, *Mike Koenigs*—for your marketing brilliance and encouragement. With you, ideas and everything else comes more alive.

Bo and Dawn Eason: I first followed you across the stage several years ago and then never stopped. It is your presence, commitment to practice, the effort it takes to be the best, and the invitation into authenticity through one's own story that remains so compelling. Thank you for your friendship and the opportunity to be co-travelers with you.

John Assaraf: I connected with you immediately over our love of neuroscience. Thank you for your ongoing generosity and friendship. Being part of your training faculty was pure joy for me.

JJ Virgin: Chance meetings are never chance meetings. I am grateful we met and for your vision for health professionals... and that it included psychologists. Your friendship, support, demand for more, risk-taking, and the community you have created is meaningful to me in ways that words will never capture. *Karl,* the same holds true for you. Connections and opportunities have unfolded in ways I could have never dreamed of.

Naomi Whittel: Your vulnerability, drive, and exquisite professionalism in one elegant mix is simply inspiring. Your support of my efforts is invaluable. Your friendship and guidance is cherished. Thank you will never be enough.

Zemira Jones: Simpatico. Thank you for helping me get my voice out there, and for working to make this my day. Thank you for your unconditional support and friendship.

Mary Morrissey: Your wisdom, mentoring, guidance, and friendship mean more than words can say. My gratitude knows no bounds for what you've brought into my life—a way of seeing the invisible, a way of hearing the limits, a way of feeling that is grounded in love and compassion, and a way of being, personally and professionally, that will serve as a model for me to emulate for years to come. With you comes a village.... *Joe Dickey* for your friendship, encouragement, way with words and laughter; John, Rich, Jennifer, Mat, Blaine and Bridges for your ongoing support and your unique set of strengths and gifts; and Hiedi, Tami, Scott and crew. In ways too many to enumerate, this has been a place to call home. All I can say is feel the love and gratitude. Endless.

Tracy Behar: Feel my deepest respect and appreciation for your wise mind, clear vision, discerning eyes, and guiding hand. As my editor at Little, Brown, you challenged me to make everything better. Thank you for believing in me and my work; with you, this will make a difference and change people's lives. Thank you for saying yes and thank you for upleveling everything I did. I will always be grateful.

Cassie Hanjian: I extend my deepest appreciation to you, my literary agent, though I'm thinking you might really be an undercover talent scout. You not only reached out, you understood the importance of the overall message. I thank you for your dedication to bringing important ideas into the world and for your unwavering support and encouragement across this process, regardless of the form it took. Thanks for finding me, thanks for watching over me, and thank you also for your friendship.

Tiffany Yecke Brooks: I offer my most sincere thanks to you for your insightful perspective and generous editing support in the preparation of this manuscript. Your willingness to step in at such a critical juncture helped make this book a reality.

Erin Santos: My sincere thanks go to you for so graciously providing an extra set of eyes and hands at key points throughout this writing process. Your efforts were invaluable.

Jay and Susan: Spoken or unspoken, I hold your love and support in my heart. Young or older, individually or collectively, you have challenged me to grow in ways I could have never predicted. I love you more than you know.

Chele and Ruben Marmet: You redefined family for me and

provided the safe haven, love, encouragement, and support that allowed this book to be written. Your generosity is unparalleled and simply underscores my belief that no one succeeds alone. My gratitude and heart knows no limits for what you have done.

Rene Ragan: Your friendship and mentoring over all these decades started it all. I cherish you and the depth of our connection like no other. Time and distance really know no bounds.

Susanne Bennett, Nalini Chilkov, Hyla Cass, and Grace Suh: Your collective creativity, support, love, and encouragement has been an anchor point for me across these past several years.

And who doesn't make it in this world without a group of special friends—you are all amazing! Pamela Bowen, Teri Cochrane, Ann Shippy, Robyn Benson, Felicia Searcy, Debora Wayne, Sandra Joseph, Joe Tatta, Mary Kincaid, Debra Atkinson, Katie Augustine, Carla Amthor, Barbara Tintori, Gina Eubank, and Damon Darnell. This includes my exceptional friends and mastermind partners across the globe and across the Burchard, Eason, Morrissey, Virgin/Mindshare, and ATL communities. Your friendship and your support of me touches my heart more deeply than you can ever imagine. You inspire me on a daily basis.

And to my dear colleagues, clients, and students, I am awed by our connection and grateful for all that you have given, all that you've risked, and all that we share.

And to everyone else I may have forgotten to give thanks and praise. I love supporting and serving you. You are my big why and it's a profoundly moving experience to share in your personal and business unfolding, growth, and transformation.

Thank you for the opportunity and even more, for the blessing.

Appendix I
THE ROSENBERG RESET™

Make the

ONE CHOICE TO BE AWARE OF AND IN TOUCH WITH

YOUR MOMENT-TO-MOMENT EXPERIENCE

and

RIDE ONE OR MORE 90 SECOND WAVES OF

ONE OR MORE OF 8 DIFFICULT FEELINGS

so you can

PURSUE ANYTHING YOU WANT IN LIFE.

Appendix II
90 Seconds to a Life You Love

Emotional Mastery Training

> Cut through the overwhelm and self-doubt holding you back.
> Create radical and sustained change in your life.
> Deepen your emotional mastery using the 90 Seconds approach.
> Learn at your own pace.
> Get the course at DrJoanRosenberg.com/ emotionalmasterycourse/

Emotional Mastery Corporate Culture Program

> Enhance team engagement and the quality of connections in your company.
> Uplevel leadership effectiveness by changing the emotional reactivity from your customers to sales to CEO.
> Keynote speaking, executive coaching, or custom-designed trainings.
> Schedule your consultation at DrJoanRosenberg.com/culture/

Emotional Mastery Train the Trainer

> Training for mental health professionals, health or life coaches, and related service professionals.
> Facilitate sales and marketing teams, managers, and executive leadership.
> Learn more at DrJoanRosenberg.com/trainer/

This book is just the start of our conversation together.
Keep in touch and tell me how things are unfolding for you.

Please connect with me at:
    Facebook: https://www.facebook.com/drjrosenberg/
    Instagram: https://www.instagram.com/drjoanrosenberg/
    LinkedIn: https://www.linkedin.com/in/joanirosenbergphd/
    Twitter: https://twitter.com/DrJoanRosenberg

Notes

Introduction

1. Jeff Spencer, personal communication, October 2015.

Chapter 1: Living a Life by Design

1. Mary Morrissey, "Transformation and Thoreau" (keynote, Experts Industry Association Annual Meeting, Santa Clara, CA, November 6–9, 2012).
2. Mary Morrissey, "Concord Conversations 2013" (training session, Concord Experience: Understanding Transcendentalism, Concord, MA, September 2013).
3. Morrissey, "Concord Conversations 2013."
4. Steven Hayes and others, "Experiential Avoidance and Behavioral Disorders: A Functional Dimensional Approach to Diagnosis and Treatment," *Journal of Consulting and Clinical Psychology* 64, no. 6 (1996): 1152–68. doi:10.1037//0022-006x.64.6.1152.
5. I've observed a type of depression that I call *"soulful depression*™*"* that occurs when people are cut off from their feelings, especially unpleasant ones—no matter what strategies they use to distract themselves or avoid these feelings. It is a result of avoidance through disconnection or distraction (or *"trying not to know what you know"*) that, over time, results first in feeling increased anxiety, vulnerability, and bodily symptoms, or feeling less control, no control, or being out of control. If these later experiences continue for a long period, I find people feel even more cut off from themselves, and in this instance, the aspect of ourselves that can observe our thoughts and feelings is disconnected from our experiencing self (e.g., knowing you are sad and being unable to

275

feel the sadness). Here, people describe feeling numb, empty, or dead inside—this is the point of soulful depression. It can morph further into feeling alienated, isolated, and then suicidal, all of which are linked to unbearable and intolerable pain.

Chapter 2: The Rosenberg Reset

1. Daniel J. Siegel, *Mindsight: The New Science of Personal Transformation* (New York: Bantam Books, 2010).
2. Daniel J. Siegel, *The Mindful Therapist: A Clinician's Guide to Mindsight and Neural Integration* (New York: W.W. Norton & Company, 2010).
3. Daniel J. Siegel, *The Developing Mind: How Relationships and the Brain Interact to Shape Who We Are* (New York: Guilford, 1999).
4. Jon Kabat-Zinn, *Wherever You Go, There You Are: Mindfulness Meditation In Everyday Life* (New York: Hyperion, 2005).
5. Kabat-Zinn, *Wherever You Go.*
6. Kabat-Zinn, *Wherever You Go.*
7. Marsha Linehan, *DBT® Skills Training Manual,* 2nd ed. (New York: Guilford Press, 2014).
8. Steven Hayes and Kirk Strosahl, eds., *A Practical Guide to Acceptance and Commitment Therapy* (New York: Springer, 2004).
9. Siegel, *The Mindful Therapist.*
   Daniel J. Siegel and Tina Payne Bryson, *The Whole-Brain Child: 12 Revolutionary Strategies to Nurture Your Child's Developing Mind* (New York: Delacorte Press, 2011).
   Daniel J. Siegel and Debra Pearce McCall, "Mindsight at Work: An Interpersonal Neurobiology Lens on Leadership," *Neuroleadership Journal*, no. 2 (2009): 1–12V.
10. Siegel, *Mindsight.*
    Daniel J. Siegel, "Science Says: Listen to Your Gut," *Inspire to Wire,* January 23, 2016. http://www.drdansiegel.com/blog/2016/01/23/science-says-listen-to-your-gut/ (accessed February 9, 2018).
11. Daniel J. Siegel, *Mind: A Journey to the Heart of Being Human* (New York: W.W. Norton & Company, 2017).
12. Pat Ogden and others, *Trauma and the Body: A Sensorimotor Approach to Psychotherapy* (New York: W.W. Norton, 2006).

13. Daniel J. Siegel, *The Developing Mind: How Relationships and the Brain Interact to Shape Who We Are,* 2nd ed. (New York: Guilford, 2012).

14. Joseph LeDoux, *The Emotional Brain: The Mysterious Underpinnings of Emotional Life* (New York: Simon & Shuster, 1996).
    While most people can experience and express feelings, there are some individuals who are described as alexythymic; these individuals have difficulty identifying and describing feelings.

15. Siegel, *The Mindful Therapist.*
    Siegel, *Mindsight.*
    Siegel, *The Developing Mind.*

16. Siegel, *Mind.*

17. Antonio Damasio, *Descartes' Error: Emotion, Reason, and the Human Brain* (New York: Penguin, 2005).

18. Lauri Nummenmaa and others, "Bodily Maps of Emotions," *Proceedings of the National Academy of Sciences* 111, no. 2 (2014): 646–51, doi:10.1073/pnas.1321664111.

19. Jill Bolte Taylor, *My Stroke of Insight: A Brain Scientist's Personal Journey* (New York: Viking, 2008).

20. Candace Pert, *Molecules of Emotion: The Science Behind Mind-Body Medicine* (New York: Scribner, 1997).

21. Bolte Taylor, *My Stroke of Insight.*

22. Bolte Taylor, *My Stroke of Insight.*

23. Lou Cozolino, *The Neuroscience of Psychotherapy: Healing the Social Brain,* 3rd ed. (New York: W.W. Norton & Company, 2017).

24. Philippe Verduyn and Saskia Lavrijsen, "Which Emotions Last Longest and Why: The Role of Event Importance and Rumination," *Motivation and Emotion* 39, no. 1 (2014): 119-27, doi:10.1007/s11031-014-9445-y.

25. Richard A. Dienstbier, "Arousal and Physiological Toughness: Implications for Mental and Physical Health," *Psychological Review* 96, no. 1 (1989): 84-100, doi:10.1037//0033-295x.96.1.84.
    Verduyn and Lavrijsen, "Which Emotions Last Longest."

26. Bolte Taylor, *My Stroke of Insight.*

27. Siegel, *Mindsight.*

28. Daniel Wegner and others, "Chronic Thought Suppression," *Journal of Personality* 62, no. 4 (1994): 615-40.

Daniel Wegner and others, "Paradoxical Effects of Thought Suppression," *Journal of Personality and Social Psychology* 53, no. 1 (1987): 5–13.

29. Wegner and others, "Paradoxical Effects of Thought Suppression."

30. Eric Rassin and others, "Paradoxical and Less Paradoxical Effects of Thought Suppression: A Critical Review," *Clinical Psychology Review* 20, no. 8 (2000): 973–95.
Richard Wenzlaff and David Luxton, "The Role of Thought Suppression in Depressive Rumination," *Cognitive Therapy and Research* 27, no. 3 (2003): 293–308.

31. Lou Cozolino, *The Neuroscience of Psychotherapy: Healing the Social Brain,* 3rd ed. (New York: W.W. Norton & Company, 2017).
Verduyn and Lavrijsen, "Which Emotions Last Longest."

32. Daniel J. Siegel and Mary Hartzell, *Parenting from the Inside Out: How a Deeper Self-Understanding Can Help You Raise Children Who Thrive,* 10th ed. (New York: TarcherPerigee, 2013).

Chapter 3: Understanding the Eight Unpleasant Feelings

1. Rick Hanson, *Hardwiring Happiness: The New Brain Science of Contentment, Calm and Confidence* (New York: Harmony Books, 2013).
Pert, *Molecules of Emotion.*

2. Ira Roseman and others, "Appraisal Determinants of Emotions: Constructing a More Accurate and Comprehensive Theory." *Cognition and Emotion* 10, no. 3 (1996): 241–77.
Wilco van Dijk and Marcel Zeelenberg, "Investigating the Appraisal Patterns of Regret and Disappointment," *Motivation and Emotion* 26, no. 4 (2002): 321–31.

3. Helen Mayberg and others, "Reciprocal Limbic-Cortical Function and Negative Mood: Converging PET Findings in Depression and Normal Sadness," *American Journal of Psychiatry* 156 (1999): 675–82.

4. Jonathan Rottenberg and others, "Sadness and Amusement Reactivity Differentially Predict Concurrent and Prospective Functioning in Major Depressive Disorder," *Emotion* 2, no. 2 (2002): 135–46.

5. Mayberg and others, "Reciprocal Limbic-Cortical Function."

6. Gordon H. Bower, "Mood and Memory," *American Psychologist* 36, no. 2 (1981): 129–48.

7. Cozolino, *The Neuroscience of Psychotherapy.*

8. Paul Gilbert and Sue Procter, "Compassionate Mind Training for People with High Shame and Self-Criticism: Overview and Pilot Study of a Group Therapy Approach," *Clinical Psychology and Psychotherapy* 13 (2006): 353–79.
   Siegel, *The Developing Mind*, 2nd ed.
9. Lou Cozolino, *Attachment-Based Teaching: Creating a Tribal Classroom* (New York: W.W. Norton & Company, 2014).
10. Sally Dickerson and others, "When the Social Self Is Threatened: Shame, Physiology, and Health," *Journal of Personality* 72, no. 6 (2004): 1191–1216.
11. Dickerson and others, "When the Social Self."
12. Dickerson and others, "When the Social Self."
13. Ilona de Hooge and others, "Not So Ugly After All: When Shame Acts as a Commitment Device," *Journal of Personality and Social Psychology* 95, no. 4 (2008): 933–43.
14. Dickerson and others, "When the Social Self."
15. Dickerson and others, "When the Social Self."
16. de Hooge and others, "Not So Ugly After All."
17. Mária Kopp and Jaános Réthelyi, "Where Psychology Meets Physiology: Chronic Stress and Premature Mortality—the Central–Eastern European Health Paradox," *Brain Research Bulletin* 62 (2004): 351–67.
18. Kopp and Réthelyi, "Where Psychology Meets Physiology."
19. Kopp and Réthelyi, "Where Psychology Meets Physiology."
20. Kopp and Réthelyi, "Where Psychology Meets Physiology."
21. Kopp and Réthelyi, "Where Psychology Meets Physiology."
22. van Dijk and Zeelenberg, "Investigating the Appraisal Patterns."
23. Janne van Doorn, *On Anger and Prosocial Behavior* (Ridderkerk: Ridderprint, 2014).
24. James Gross and others, "Emotion and Aging: Experience, Expression, and Control," *Psychology and Aging* 12, no. 4 (1998): 590–99.
25. Rottenberg and others, "Sadness and Amusement Reactivity."
26. World Health Organization, *Violence Prevention: The Evidence: Changing Cultural and Social Norms that Support Violence* (Geneva, Switzerland, WHO Press, 2009).
27. Peter Drummond and Saw Han Quah, "The Effect of Expressing Anger on Cardiovascular Reactivity and Facial Blood Flow in Chinese and Caucasians," *Psychophysiology* 28 (2001): 190–96.

28. Joan Rosenberg, "Emotional Mastery and Neuroleadership: Bringing Neuroscience to Life in Organizations and Work" (Special presentation, Orange County Neuroleadership Local Interest Group, Irvine, CA, May 31, 2012).

29. Robert Edelmann and others, "Self-Reported Expression of Embarrassment in Five European Cultures," *Journal of Cross-Cultural Psychology* 20, no. 4 (1989): 357–71.

30. Dacher Keltner and Ann Kring, "Emotion, Social Function, and Psychopathology," *Review of General Psychology* 2, no. 3 (1998): 320–42.

31. van Dijk and Zeelenberg, "Investigating the Appraisal Patterns."
Marcel Zeelenberg and others, "The Experience of Regret and Disappointment," *Cognition and Emotion* 12, no. 2 (1998): 221–30.

32. Wilco van Dijk and Marcel Zeelenberg, "What Do We Talk about When We Talk about Disappointment? Distinguishing Outcome-Related Disappointment from Person-Related Disappointment," *Cognition and Emotion* 16, no. 6 (2002): 787–807.

33. van Dijk and Zeelenberg, "What Do We Talk."

34. Gerben Van Kleef and Carsten De Dreu, "Supplication and Appeasement in Conflict and Negotiation: The Interpersonal Effects of Disappointment, Worry, Guilt, and Regret," *Journal of Personality and Social Psychology* 91, no. 1 (2006): 124–42.

35. Marcel Zeelenberg and others, "On Bad Decisions and Disconfirmed Expectancies: The Psychology of Regret and Disappointment," *Cognition and Emotion* 14, no. 4 (2000): 521–41.

36. Marcel Zeelenberg and Rik Pieters, "A Theory of Regret Regulation 1.0," *Consumer Psychology* 17, no. 1 (2007): 3–18.
Zeelenberg and others, "The Experience of Regret."

37. M. Sazzad Hussain and others, "Affect Detection from Multichannel Physiology During Learning Sessions with AutoTutor," In *Artificial Intelligence in Education,* edited by Gautam Biswas, Susan Bull, Judy Kay, and Antonija Mitrovic (Berlin: Springer, 2011).

38. Hussain and others, "Affect Detection from Multichannel."

39. Susan Calkins and others, "Frustration in Infancy: Implications for Emotion Regulation, Physiological Processes, and Temperament," *Infancy* 3 (2002): 175–98.

40. Calkins and others, "Frustration in Infancy."

41. Stephen Porges, "Neuroception: A Subconscious System for Detecting Threats and Safety," *Zero to Three* 24, no. 5 (2004): 19–24.

42. Joan Rosenberg, "Therapy Is Choreography" (annual psychotherapy training, Pepperdine University, Graduate School of Education and Psychology, Los Angeles, CA, September 2017).
43. Rosenberg, "Therapy Is Choreography."
44. Siegel, *The Developing Mind.*
45. Ogden and others, *Trauma and the Body.*
    Siegel, *The Developing Mind.*
46. Ogden and others, *Trauma and the Body.*
47. Ogden and others, *Trauma and the Body.*
48. Siegel, *The Developing Mind.*
49. Siegel, *The Developing Mind.*
50. Siegel, *The Developing Mind.*
51. Siegel, *The Developing Mind.*
52. Siegel, *The Developing Mind.*
53. Siegel, *The Developing Mind.*
54. Siegel, *The Developing Mind.*
55. Ogden and others, *Trauma and the Body.*
    Siegel, *The Developing Mind.*
56. Elaine Aron, *The Highly Sensitive Person: How to Thrive When the World Overwhelms You* (New York: Kensington Publishing Corp, 2013).
57. Matthew Lieberman and others, "Putting Feelings into Words: Affect Labeling Disrupts Amygdala Activity in Response to Affective Stimuli," *Psychological Science* 18, no. 5 (2007): 421–28.
58. Katharina Kircanski and others, "Feelings into Words: Contributions of Language to Exposure Therapy," *Psychological Science* 23, no. 10 (2012): 1–6.
    Matthew Lieberman and others, "Subjective Responses to Emotional Stimuli during Labeling, Reappraisal, and Distraction," *Emotion* 3 (2011): 468–80.
59. James Pennebaker, "Writing about Emotional Experiences as a Therapeutic Process," *Psychological Science* 8, no. 3 (1997): 162–66.

Chapter 4: Identifying and Overcoming Distractions

1. Ogden and others, *Trauma and the Body.*
   Siegel, *The Developing Mind,* 2nd ed.
2. Hayes and Strosahl, eds., *A Practical Guide.*

Chapter 5: Releasing Anxiety

1. Thomas Borkovec and others, "Worry: A Cognitive Phenomenon Intimately Linked to Affective, Physiological, and Interpersonal Behavioral Processes," *Cognitive Therapy and Research* 22, no. 6 (1998): 561–76.

2. Thomas Borkovec, "Worry: A Potentially Valuable Concept," *Behaviour Research and Therapy* 23, no. 4 (1985): 481–82.
   Borkovec and others, "Worry: A Cognitive Phenomenon."

3. Barbara Zebb and J. Gayle Beck, "Worry Versus Anxiety: Is There Really a Difference?" *Behavior Modification* 22, no. 1 (1998): 45–61.

4. Zebb and Beck, "Worry Versus Anxiety."

5. David Barlow, *Anxiety and Its Disorders: The Nature and Treatment of Anxiety and Panic,* 2nd ed. (New York: Guilford Publications Inc., 2002).
   David Barlow and Kristen Ellard, "Anxiety and Related Disorders," In *Noba Textbook Series: Psychology,* edited by R. Biswas-Diener & E. Diener (Champaign: DEF Publishers, 2018).

6. American Psychiatric Association, *Diagnostic and Statistical Manual of Mental Disorders: DSM-5* (Arlington: American Psychiatric Publishing, 2013).

7. David Barlow, "Unraveling the Mysteries of Anxiety and Its Disorders from the Perspective of Emotion Theory," *American Psychologist* 55 (2000): 1247–1263. doi:10.1037/0003-066X.55.11.1247.
   Clair Cassiello-Robbins and David Barlow, "Anger: The Unrecognized Emotion in Emotional Disorders," *Clinical Psychology: Science and Practice* 23, no. 1 (2016): 66–85.

8. Thomas Borkovec, "Life in the Future Versus Life in the Present," *Clinical Psychology Science and Practice* 9, no. 1 (2002): 76–80.
   Thomas Borkovec and Lizabeth Roemer, "Perceived Functions of Worry Among Generalized Anxiety Disorder Subjects: Distraction from More Emotionally Distressing Topics?" *Journal of Behavior Therapy and Experimental Psychiatry* 26, no. 1 (1995): 25–30.
   Michelle Newman and Sandra Llera, "A Novel Theory of Experiential Avoidance in Generalized Anxiety Disorder: A Review and Synthesis of Research Supporting a Contrast Avoidance Model of Worry," *Clinical Psychology Review* 31, no. 3 (2011): 371–82.

9. Clayton Critcher and others, "When Self-Affirmations Reduce Defensiveness: Timing Is Key," *Personality and Social Psychology Bulletin* 36, no. 7 (2010): 947–59.
Clayton Critcher and David Dunning, "Self-Affirmations Provide a Broader Perspective on Self-Threat," *Personality and Social Psychology Bulletin* 41, no. 1 (2015): 3–18.
10. Critcher and others, "When Self-Affirmations Reduce."
11. Ethan Kross and others, "Self Talk as a Regulatory Mechanism: How You Do It Matters," *Journal of Personality and Social Psychology* 106, no. 2 (2014): 304–24.
12. Kross and others, "Self Talk as a Regulatory."
13. Bruce Lipton, *The Biology of Belief: Unleashing the Power of Consciousness, Matter, and Miracles* (Carlsbad: Hay House, 2008).
14. Lipton, *The Biology of Belief.*
15. Lipton, *The Biology of Belief.*
16. Joan Rosenberg, *Ease Your Anxiety: How to Gain Confidence, Emotional Strength, and Inner Peace* (Toronto: Brightflame Books, 2016).

Chapter 6: Resolving Faulty Thinking

1. Lipton, *The Biology of Belief.*
2. Bruce McEwen and Elizabeth Lasley, *The End of Stress as We Know It* (Washington, DC: Joseph Henry Press, 2002).
Robert Sapolsky, *Why Zebras Don't Get Ulcers: The Acclaimed Guide to Stress, Stress-Related Diseases, and Coping*, 3rd ed. (New York: Holt Paperbacks, 2004).
3. Pert, *Molecules of Emotion.*
4. Alberto Chiesa and Alessandro Serretti. "Mindfulness Based Cognitive Therapy for Psychiatric Disorders: A Systematic Review and Meta-analysis," *Psychiatry Research* 187, no. 3 (2011): 441–53.
Alberto Chiesa and Alessandro Serretti. "Mindfulness Based Stress Reduction for Stress Management in Healthy People: A Review and Meta-analysis," *Journal of Alternative and Complementary Medicine* 15, no. 5 (2009): 593–600.
Stefan Hofmann and others, "The Effect of Mindfulness-Based Therapy on Anxiety and Depression: A Meta-analytic Review," *Journal of Consulting and Clinical Psychology* 78, no. 2 (2010): 169–83.

Julie Irving and others, "Cultivating Mindfulness in Health Care Professionals: A Review of Empirical Studies of Mindfulness-Based Stress Reduction (MBSR)," *Complementary Therapies in Clinical Practice* 15 (2009): 61–66.

Jon Kabat-Zinn, *Full Catastrophe Living: Using the Wisdom of Your Mind and Body to Face Stress, Pain, and Illness* (New York: Delacorte, 1990).

5. Ruth Baer and others, "Weekly Change in Mindfulness and Perceived Stress in a Mindfulness-Based Stress Reduction Program," *Journal of Clinical Psychology* 68, no. 7 (2012): 755–65.

James Carmody and Ruth Baer, "Relationships Between Mindfulness Practice and Levels of Mindfulness, Medical, and Psychological Symptoms and Well-Being in a Mindfulness-Based Stress Reduction Program," *Journal of Behavioral Medicine* 31 (2008): 23–33.

6. Helen Achat and others, "Optimism and Depression as Predictors of Physical and Mental Health Functioning: The Normative Aging Study," *Annals of Behavioral Medicine* 22 (2000): 127–30.

Edward Chang and Angela Farrehi, "Optimism/Pessimism and Information-Processing Styles: Can Their Influences Be Distinguished in Predicting Psychological Adjustment," *Personality and Individual Differences* 31 (2001): 555–62.

Sonja Lyubomirsky and others, "The Benefits of Frequent Positive Affect: Does Happiness Lead to Success," *Psychological Bulletin* 131, no. 6 (2005): 803–55. doi:10.1037/0033-2909.131.6.803.

7. Barbara Fredrickson, "What Good Are Positive Emotions?" *Review of General Psychology* 2, no. 3 (1998): 300–19.

8. Michael Cohn and others, "Happiness Unpacked: Positive Emotions Increase Life Satisfaction by Building Resilience," *Emotion* 9, no. 3 (2009): 361–68.

Barbara Fredrickson, "The Role of Positive Emotions in Positive Psychology: The Broaden-and-Build Theory of Positive Emotions," *American Psychologist* 56, no. 3 (2001): 218–26.

9. Aaron Beck and others, *Cognitive Therapy of Depression* (New York: Guilford Press, 1979).

10. Beck and others, *Cognitive Therapy of Depression.*

11. Siegel, *The Developing Mind,* 2nd ed.

12. Beck and others, *Cognitive Therapy of Depression.*

13. David Burns, *The Feeling Good Handbook,* revised edition (New York: Plume, 1999).

14. Beck and others, *Cognitive Therapy of Depression*.
    Burns, *The Feeling Good Handbook*.
    Albert Ellis and Russell Grieger, *Handbook of Rational-Emotive Therapy* (New York: Springer, 1977).
15. Burns, *The Feeling Good Handbook*.
16. Porges, "Neuroception."
17. McEwen and Lasley, *The End of Stress*.
18. Gilbert and Procter, "Compassionate Mind Training."
19. Gilbert and Procter, "Compassionate Mind Training."
20. Kristin Neff, *Self-Compassion: The Proven Power of Being Kind to Yourself* (New York: HarperCollins Publishers, 2012).

Chapter 7: Speaking Your Truth

1. Siegel, *The Developing Mind*, 2nd ed.
2. Siegel, *The Developing Mind*, 2nd ed.
3. Pauline Rose Clance, *The Impostor Phenomenon: Overcoming the Fear that Haunts Your Success* (Atlanta: Peachtree Publishers, Ltd., 1985).
4. Siegel, *The Developing Mind*, 2nd ed.
    Siegel and Bryson, *The Whole-Brain Child*.
    Siegel and Hartzell, *Parenting from the Inside Out*.
5. Allen Ivey, and others, *Essentials of Intentional Interviewing: Counseling in a Multicultural World*, 3rd ed. (Boston: Brooks-Cole/Cengage Learning, 2015).

Chapter 8: Moving Through Grief

1. Mary Morrissey, "Developing Persistence" (presentation, Pinnacle Training Event, Los Angeles, CA, January 2016).
2. Siegel, *The Developing Mind*.

Chapter 9: Upleveling Confidence and Resilience

1. "Resilient," Dictionary.com Unabridged, Random House, Inc., accessed March 12, 2018, http://www.dictionary.com/browse/resilient.
2. Barbara Frederickson, "The Value of Positive Emotions: The Emerging Science of Positive Psychology Is Coming to Understand Why It's Good to Feel Good," *American Scientist* 91 (2003): 330–35.

3. Deborah Khoshaba and Salvatore Maddi, *Resilience at Work: How to Succeed No Matter What Life Throws at You* (New York: Amacom, 2005).
4. Carol Dweck, *Mindset: The New Psychology of Success,* updated edition (New York: Penguin Random House, 2007).
5. Angela Duckworth, *Grit: The Power of Passion and Perseverance* (New York: Scribner, 2016).
6. Barbara Frederickson, "The Role of Positive Emotions in Positive Psychology: The Broaden-and-Build Theory of Positive Emotions," *American Psychologist* 56 (2001): 218–26.
7. Frederickson, "The Value of Positive Emotions."
8. Barbara Fredrickson, "Cultivating Positive Emotions to Optimize Health and Well-Being," *Prevention & Treatment* 3 (2000): 1–25. Khoshaba and Maddi, *Resilience at Work.*
9. Lisa Firestone, "Are You Hardy Enough? How Being Your Real Self Helps You Deal with Stress," *Psychology Today Blog,* August 27, 2012, https://www.psychologytoday.com/us/blog/compassion-matters/201208/are-you-hardy-enough. Frederickson, "The Role of Positive Emotions."
10. Dweck, *Mindset.*
11. Duckworth, *Grit.*
12. George Bonanno, "Loss, Trauma, and Human Resilience: Have We Underestimated the Human Capacity to Thrive After Extremely Adverse Events?" *American Psychologist* 59 (2004): 20–28. George Bonanno and others, "Resilience to Loss and Potential Trauma," *Annual Review Clinical Psychology* 7 (2011): 511–35.
13. Morrissey, "Developing Persistence."
14. Joe Dispenza, "Transformational Possibilities" (keynote, Association of Transformational Leaders Annual Meeting, Ojai, CA, March 2018).
15. Dispenza, "Transformational Possibilities."

Chapter 10: Committing to Your True Self

1. Mary Morrissey, "DreamBuilder Live with Mary Morrissey" (training, Mary Morrissey, LifeSOULutions That Work, LLC., Los Angeles, CA, January 2014).
2. Mihaly Csikszentmihalyi, *Flow: The Psychology of Optimal Experience* (New York: Harper Perennial Modern Classic, 2008).

3. Mary Morrissey, "Life Mastery Consultant Certification" (training, Morrissey Life Mastery Institute Training, Los Angeles, CA, March 2017).
4. Brendon Burchard, *High Performance Habits: How Extraordinary People Become That Way* (San Diego: Hay House, 2017).
5. J.J. Virgin, "The Miracle Mindset" (keynote, Mindshare Summit Annual Meeting, San Diego, CA, 2016).
6. Morrissey, "DreamBuilder Live with Mary Morrissey."
7. Dan Sullivan, "Addressing the Gap" (Presentation, Mindshare Summit Annual Meeting, San Diego, CA, 2016).

Index

action, 74, 129–31, 239, 246, 249, 253–54, 263
adversities, 222, 224, 232, 262
affect labeling, 84–86
aggressiveness, 64, 66–68, 105, 207
alcohol use and abuse, 24, 46, 89
amygdala, 63, 84
anger: and affect labeling, 85–86; and anxiety, 118, 130; bodily sensations associated with, 43, 45–47, 48–49, 66; and frustration, 72; and grief, 199–201, 204; and loss, 128; and parental influence, 56–57; and self-criticism, 154; and "should" statements, 142; and speaking up, 173, 181–82; as unpleasant feeling, 10, 26, 30, 35, 55, 60, 65–69
anxiety: and action, 129–31; anxiety and worry words, 118–19; and avoidance of unpleasant feelings, 46, 61, 97, 111; and Bad Emotional Math, 152; bodily sensations associated with, 38, 111, 114, 117; and "Can I? Do I? Will I? Am I?" questions, 120–22; and decision-making, 125–28; and disappointment, 116–17, 130, 220; and the Doubter's Reset, 121–22; and emotional strength, 122–23; and fear, 112–14; and meditation, 133; and misconceptions about emotional strength, 24, 26, 38;

and painful life experiences, 208–9; and perseverance, 227–29; and resilience, 231; Resourcefulness Reset, 129–30; and riding waves of emotion, 54; Rosenberg Anxiety Reset, 119–20; and speaking up, 185; strategies to diminish, 112–25; and talking to yourself by name, 124–25; as unexperienced and unexpressed feelings, 115–19, 263; and vulnerability, 115–16, 219–20; and worry, 109–12, 129–30
arousal levels, 80–83
attitude, 223–27, 262
authenticity: and anxiety, 117; and compliments, 240, 242–43; and congruence, 255; and designing your life, 262–65; and distractions, 98, 100; and self-criticism, 154; and speaking up, 167, 171–72, 176, 184, 195–96, 239, 253–54; and unpleasant feelings, 12–13, 26, 35–36, 58, 61, 86, 248; and worry over other's opinion of you, 148
Awareness Exercise, 44–45, 62

Bad Emotional Math, 132, 143, 150–53, 160, 231, 263
Barlow, David, 110–11
Beck, Aaron, 135, 138

About the Author

Joan I. Rosenberg, PhD, is a cutting-edge psychologist who is known as an innovative thinker, speaker, and trainer. A two-time TEDx speaker and a member of the Association of Transformational Leaders, she has been recognized for her leadership and influence in personal development. She is a professor at Pepperdine University and a United States Air Force veteran.